AF304803

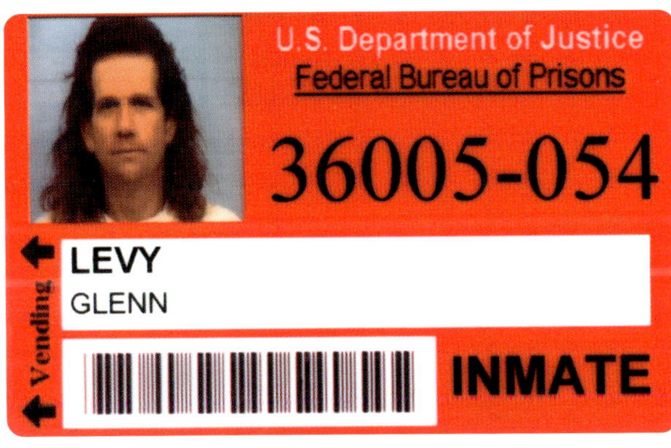
U.S. Department of Justice
Federal Bureau of Prisons
36005-054
Vending
LEVY
GLENN
INMATE

51 MONTHS CARRIE LEVY

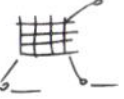

Last Name
LEVY
First Name
GLENN
Middle Name
REG #: 36005-054
ALW
Date of Photo
DECEMBER 8, 1997
36005-054
DECEMBER 8, 1997
Last Name
LEVY
First Name
GLENN
Middle Name
REG #: 36005-054
ALW
Date of Photo
DECEMBER 8, 1997
TENNECO PACKAGING
PITTSBURGH, PA
#58

My father went to jail on my 15th birthday, on January 16th, 1996. I have never asked what happened, and to this day I still don't want to know. Nevertheless, a prison sentence for a family man is a sentence for his family. We were an average Long Island family and we equally, or so we felt, endured the 51 months my father was imprisoned. All we could do was wait. During that time, my mother, my two brothers and I wondered about his return. At the end of the 51 months we were different people.

In my father's absence my mother undertook the roles of both parents for myself and for my two younger brothers. She had three jobs and cared for three children, always loyal to my father. Every weekend she would drive the ten-hour round-trip to Allenwood Federal Prison Camp. Sometimes we all went with her.

My mother kept the family together, and she still does. Taylor, my youngest brother, was too small when my father went to jail to comprehend the transition in his life. At first he thought the visiting room at Allenwood was my father's new office. As he matured Taylor began to understand the reality of his father's life, but made no accusations. He was as he is today, quiet and accepting. Even as the youngest child Taylor made it a priority to make sure everyone else was happy, but always looked to his older brother to lean on.

My brother Grant, who rarely appears in this book, is two years younger than me, and several years' wiser. Grant watched over me and was the calming force in our family. There is no one I admire more.

I recorded the 51 months behind my camera. Making photographs is what I knew, and I felt safe with the distance. This is my diary of his absence. Nine years later each image makes me want to remember. The photographs that have stuck with me are those of detail. These images are what filled the void my father left behind, and oddly represent a nostalgia for a life I no longer live.

I can feel the green-blue carpeting pressed against my feet, the changing seasons through my basement window, and the sound of my brother's video games overtaken by the rattle of the Long Island railroad. I can still feel the touch of my mother's beautiful bony hands after she applied her moisturizer, or see the three lines around her neck. I can recall the speed at which Taylor turned from a child into a teen, and Grant from a boy into a man. I remember my father's initials around my mother's neck and the mail that continued to come after he had gone. Alongside these brief details exist memories of prison visiting rooms, my father lifeless and scared, and my family. They are still there.

Carrie Levy, 2005.

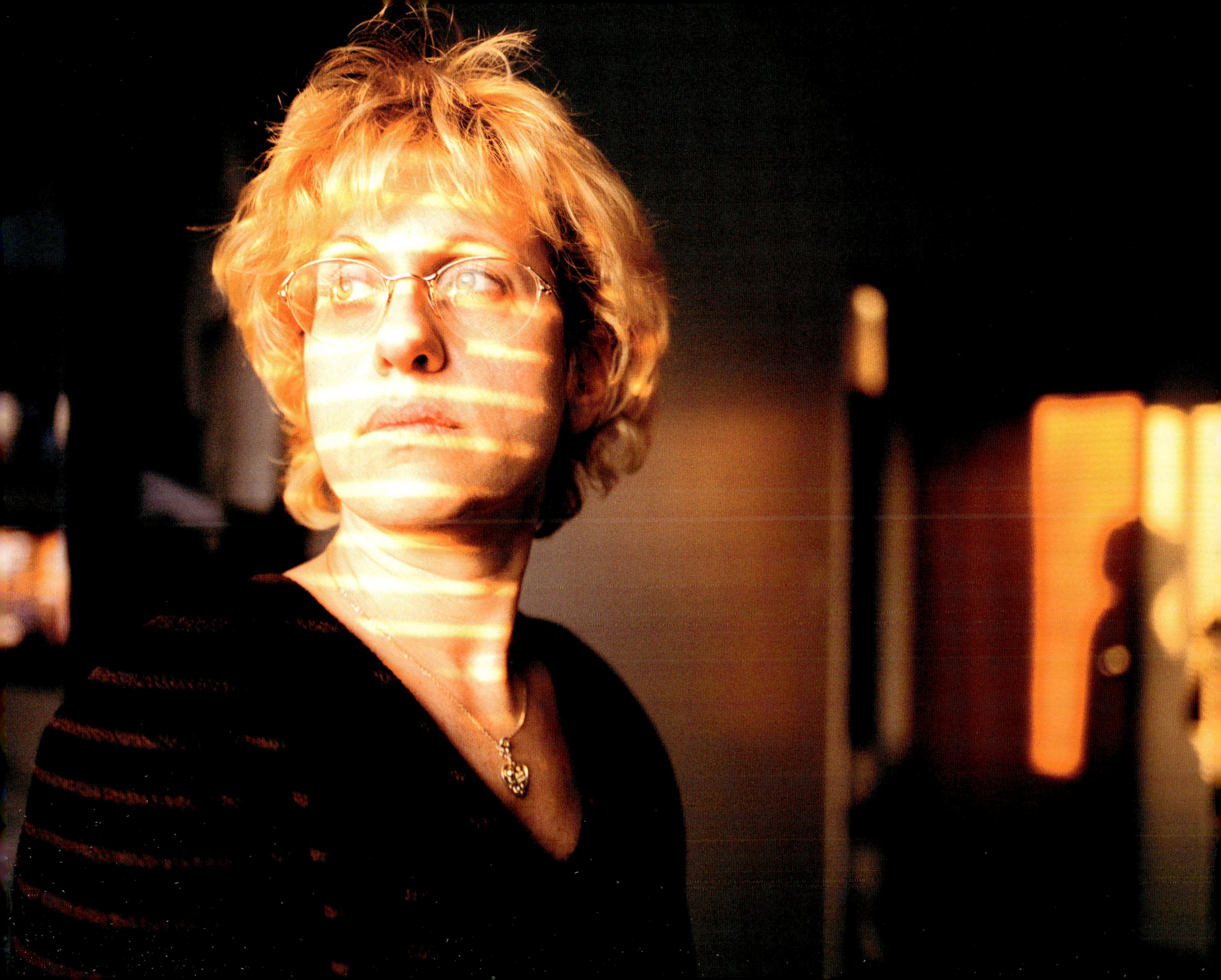

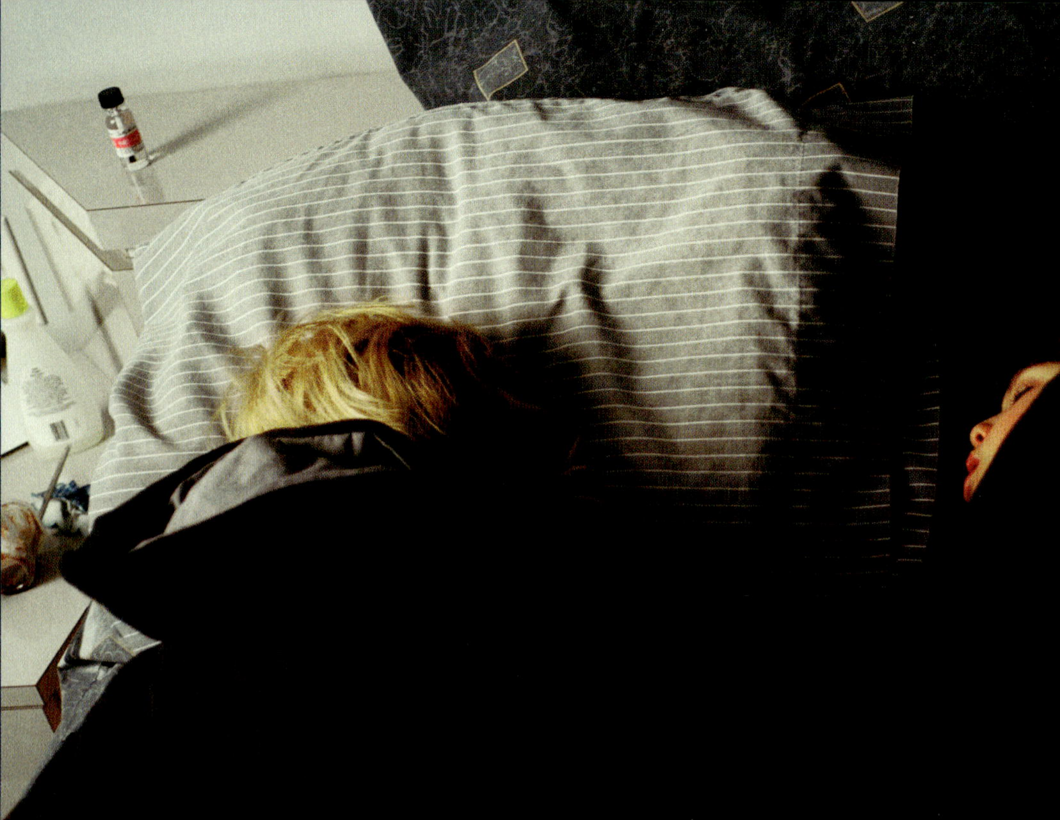

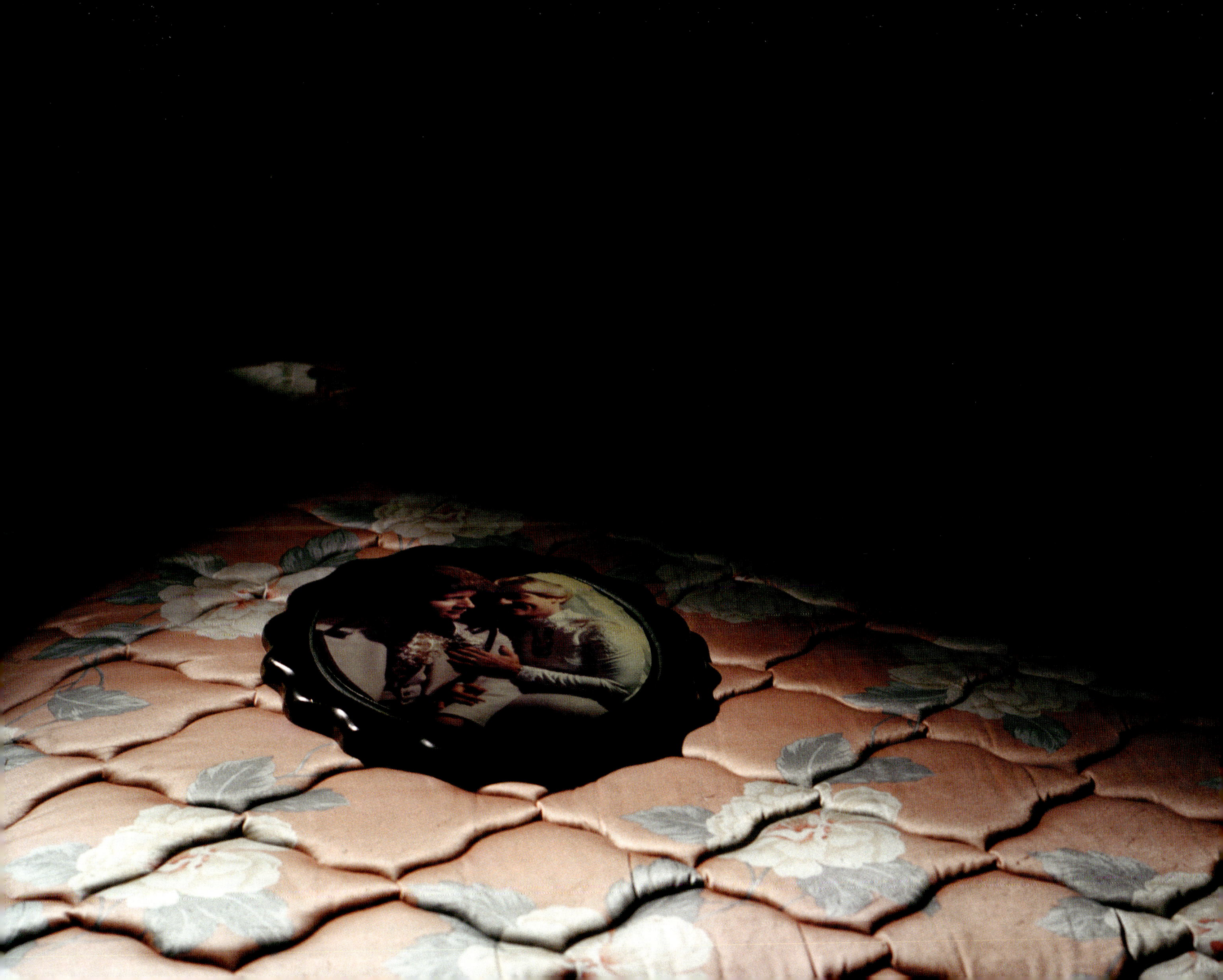

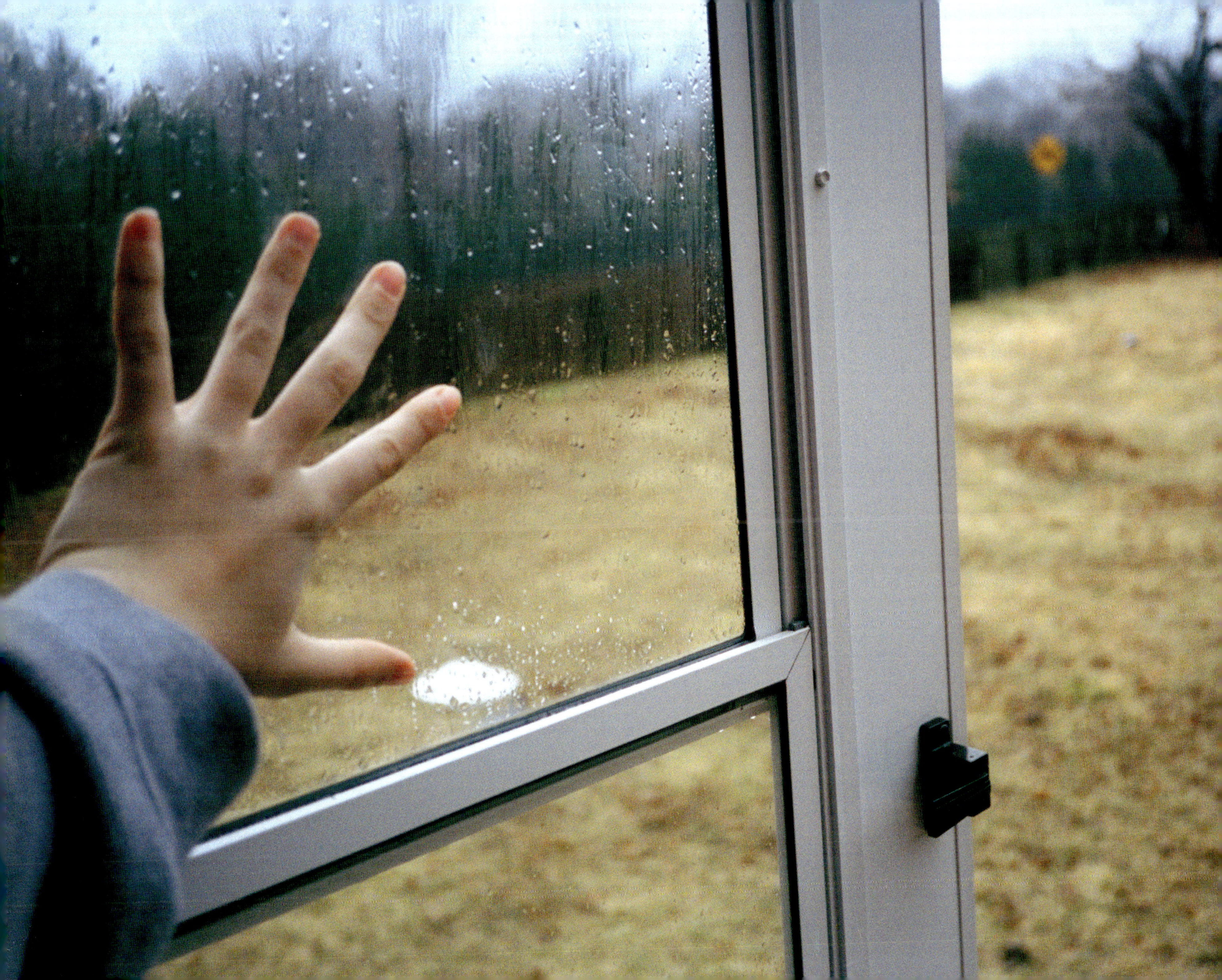

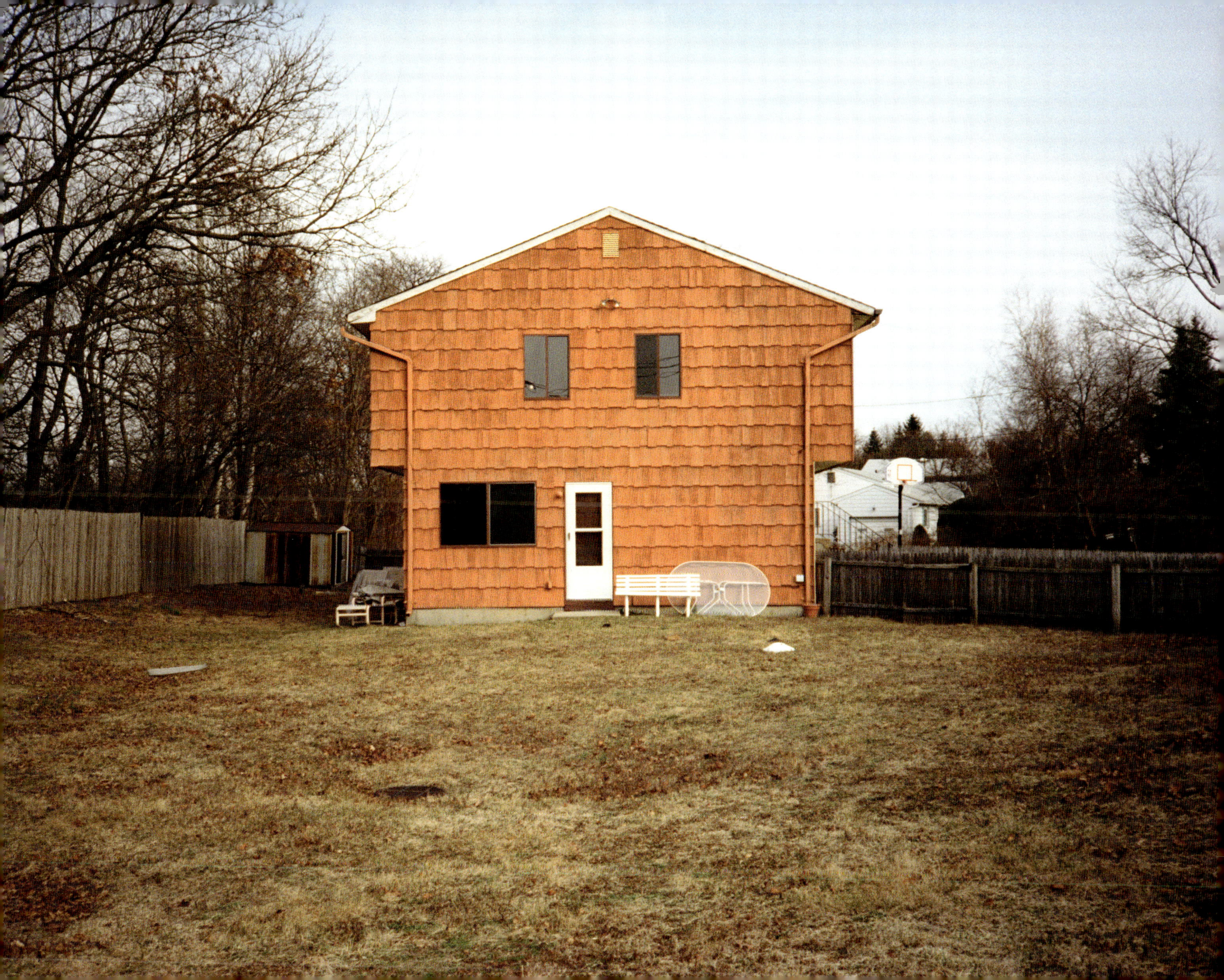

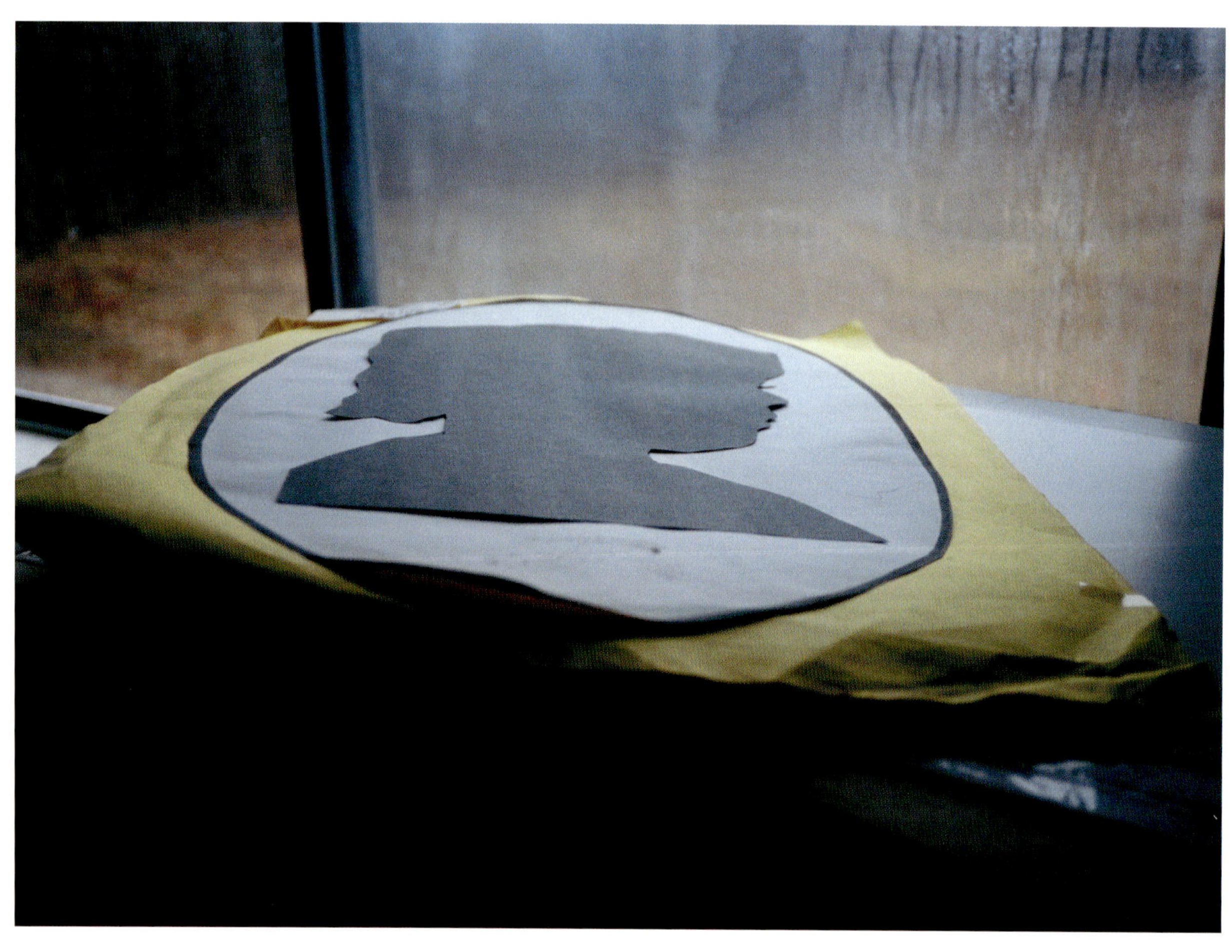

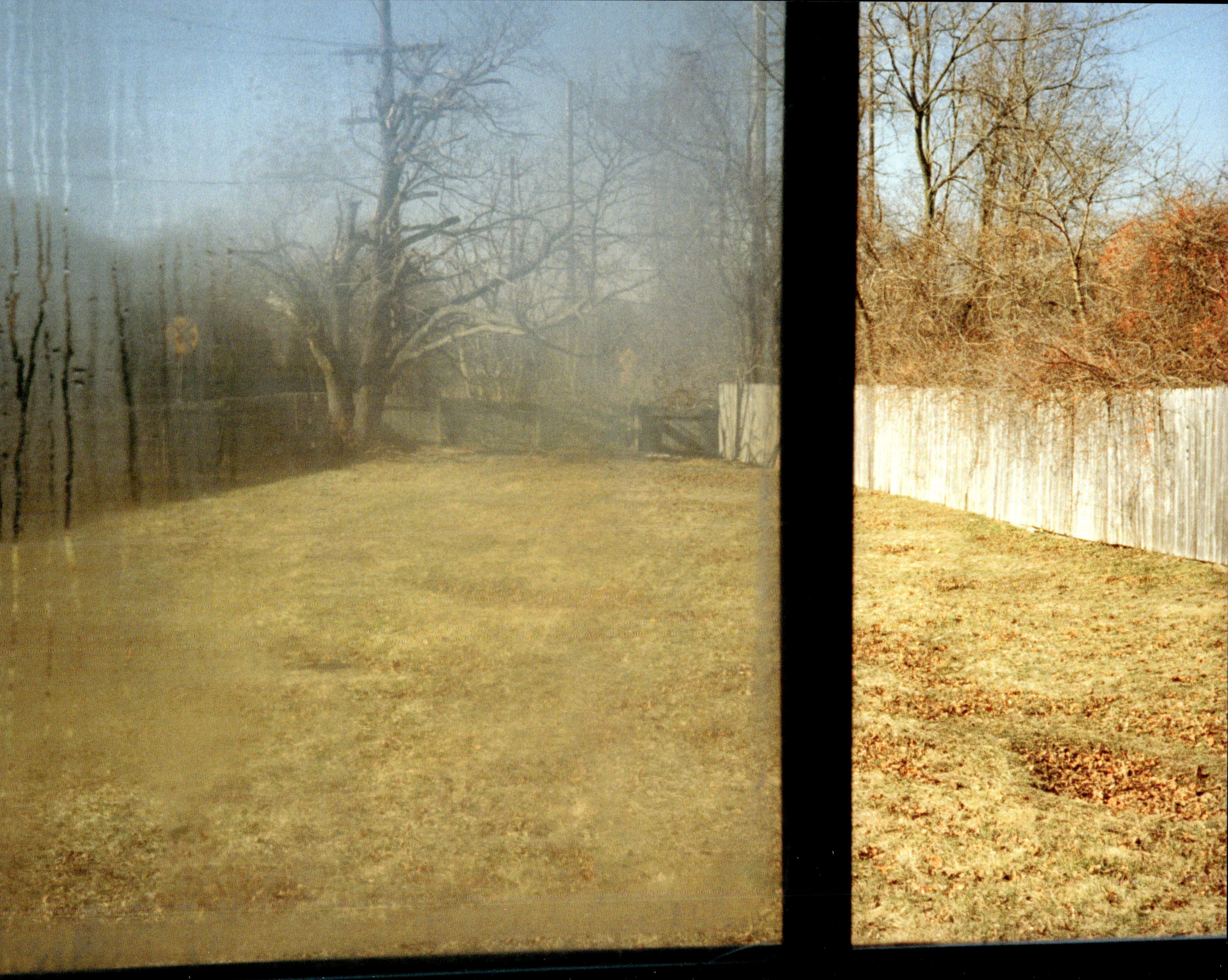

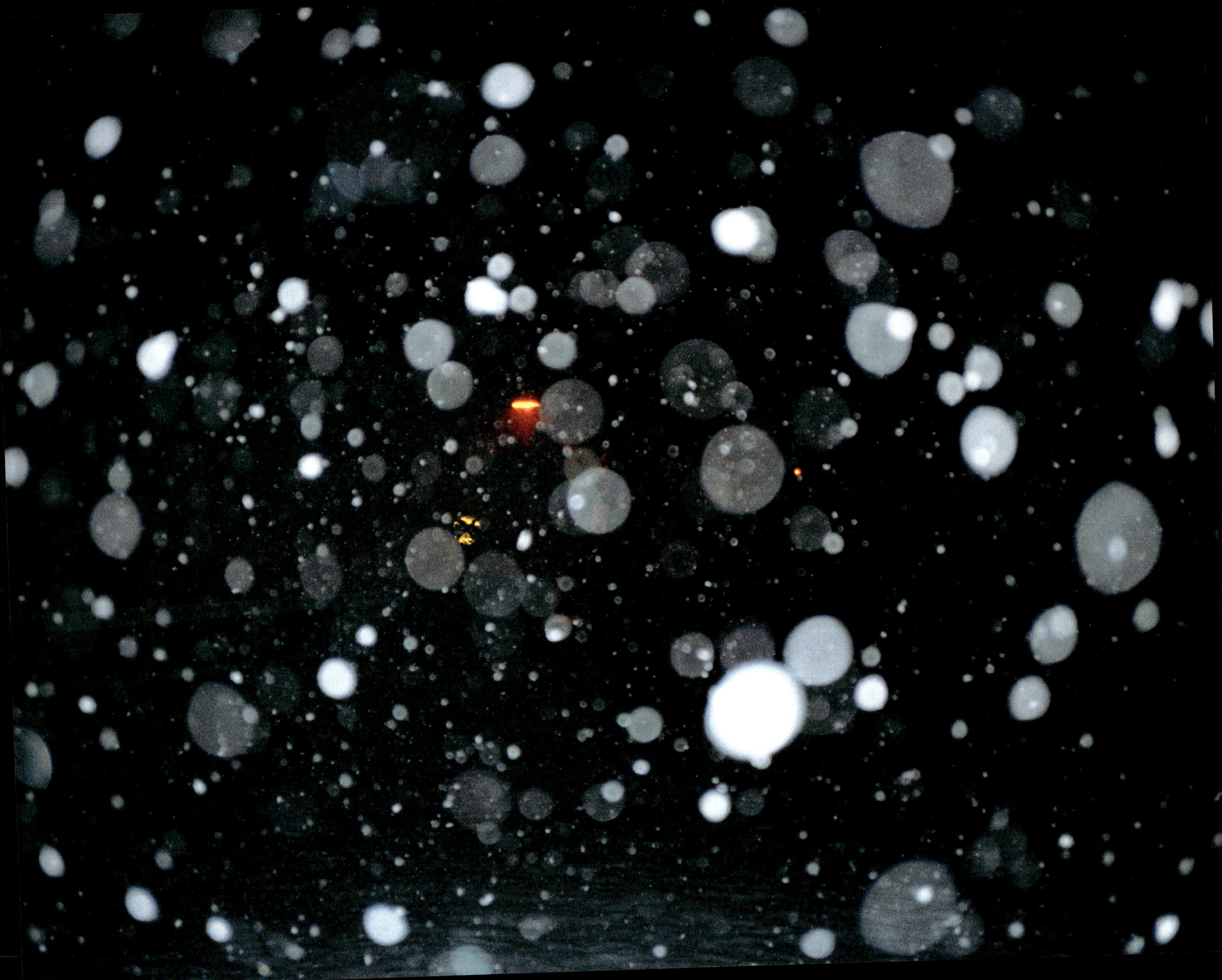

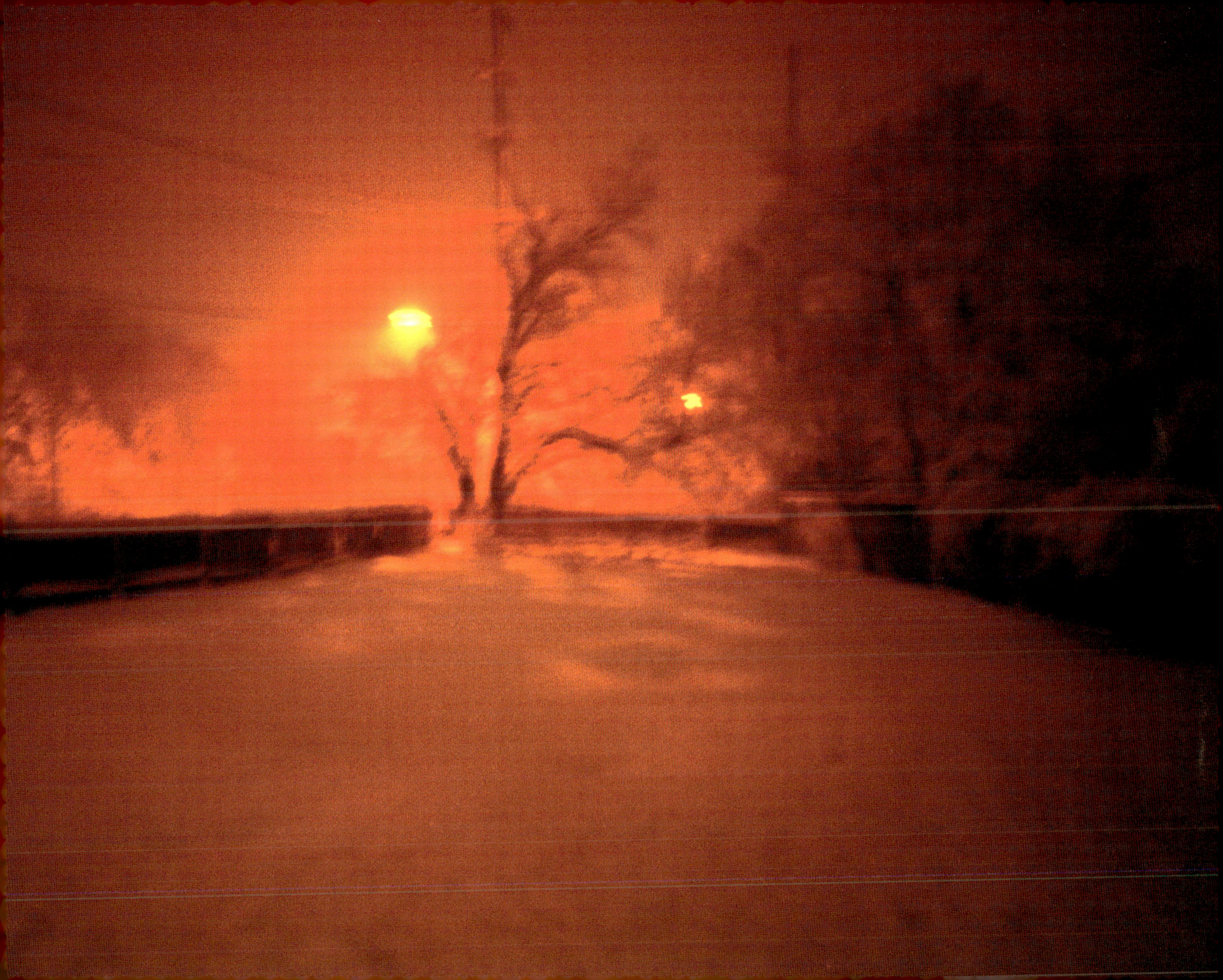

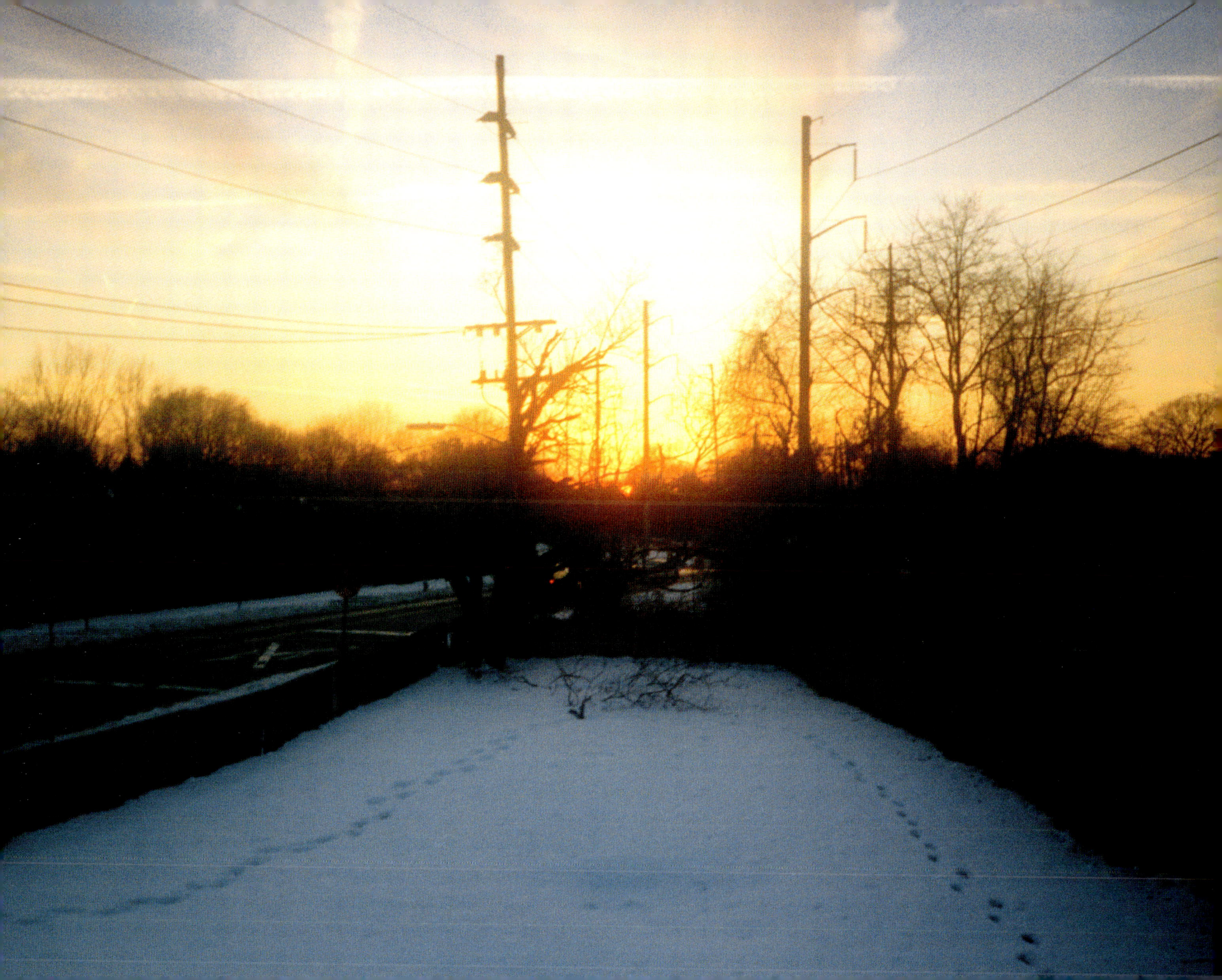

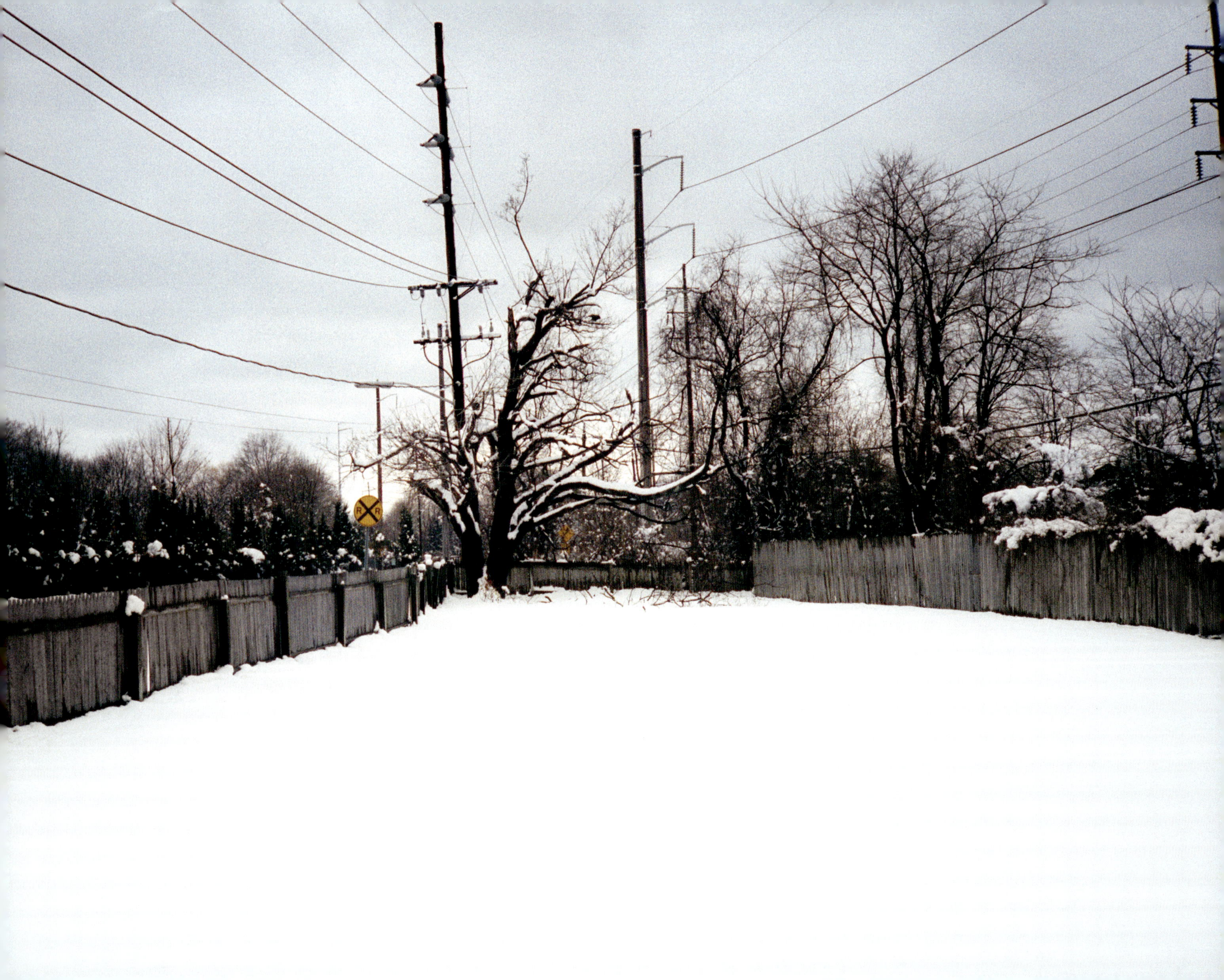

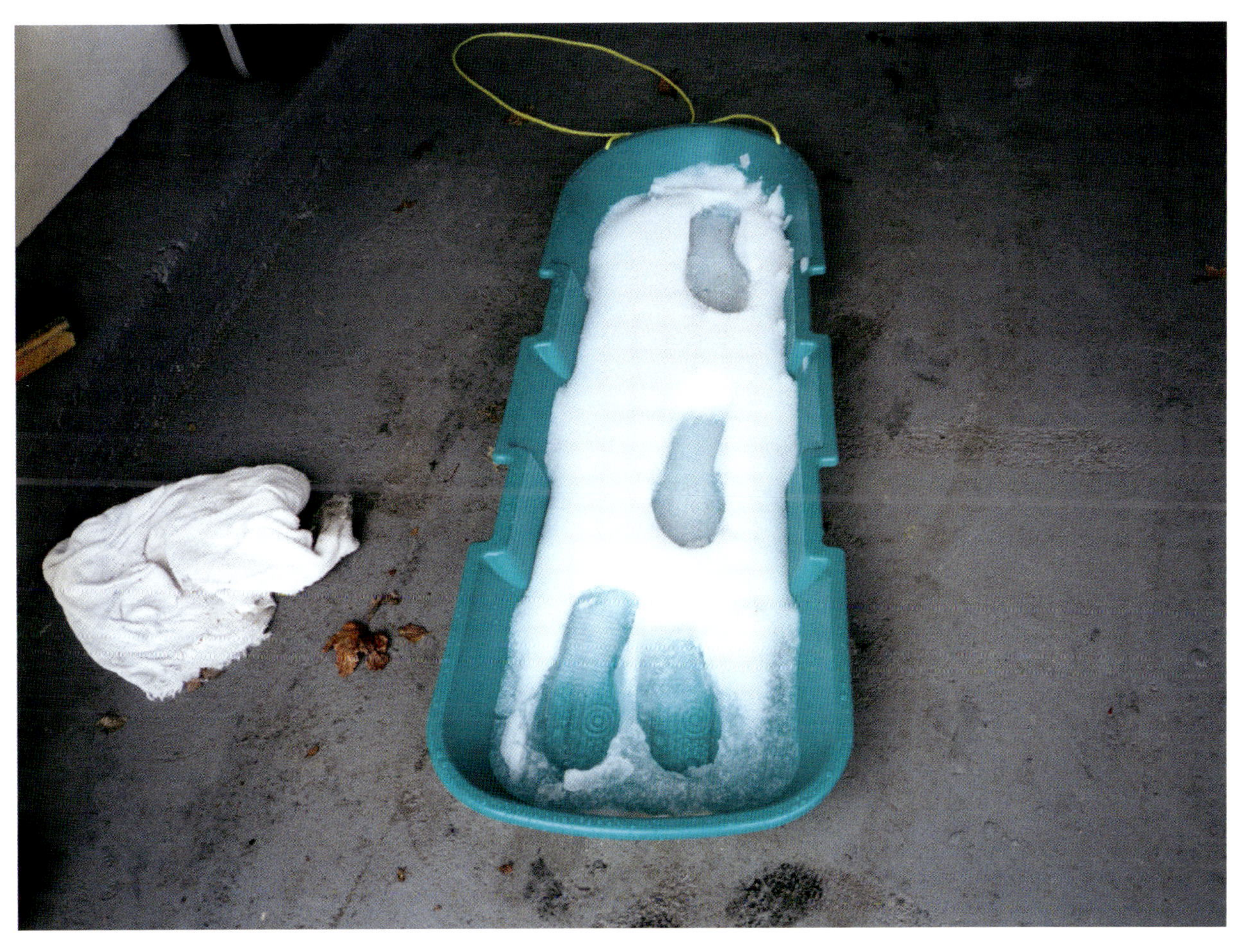

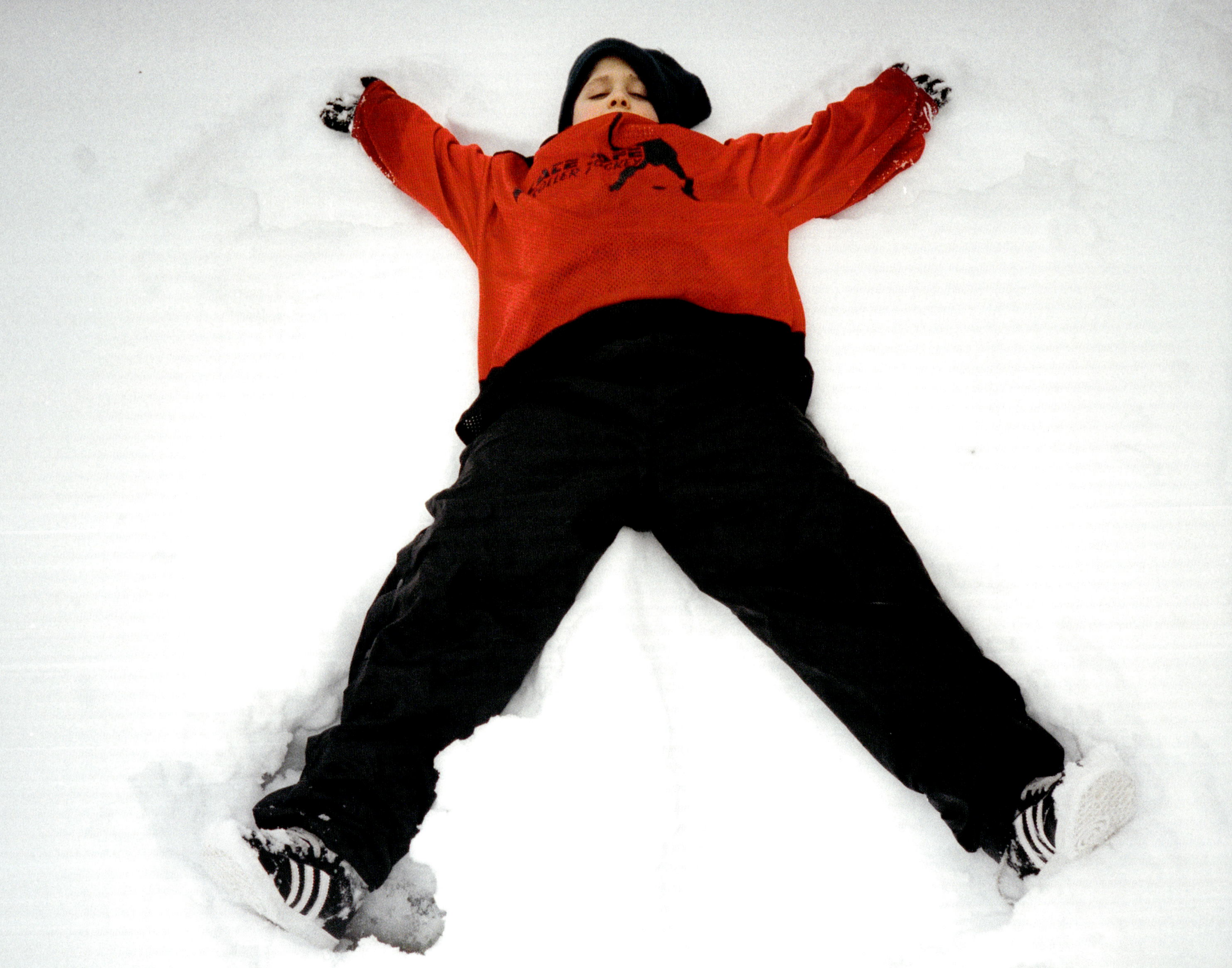

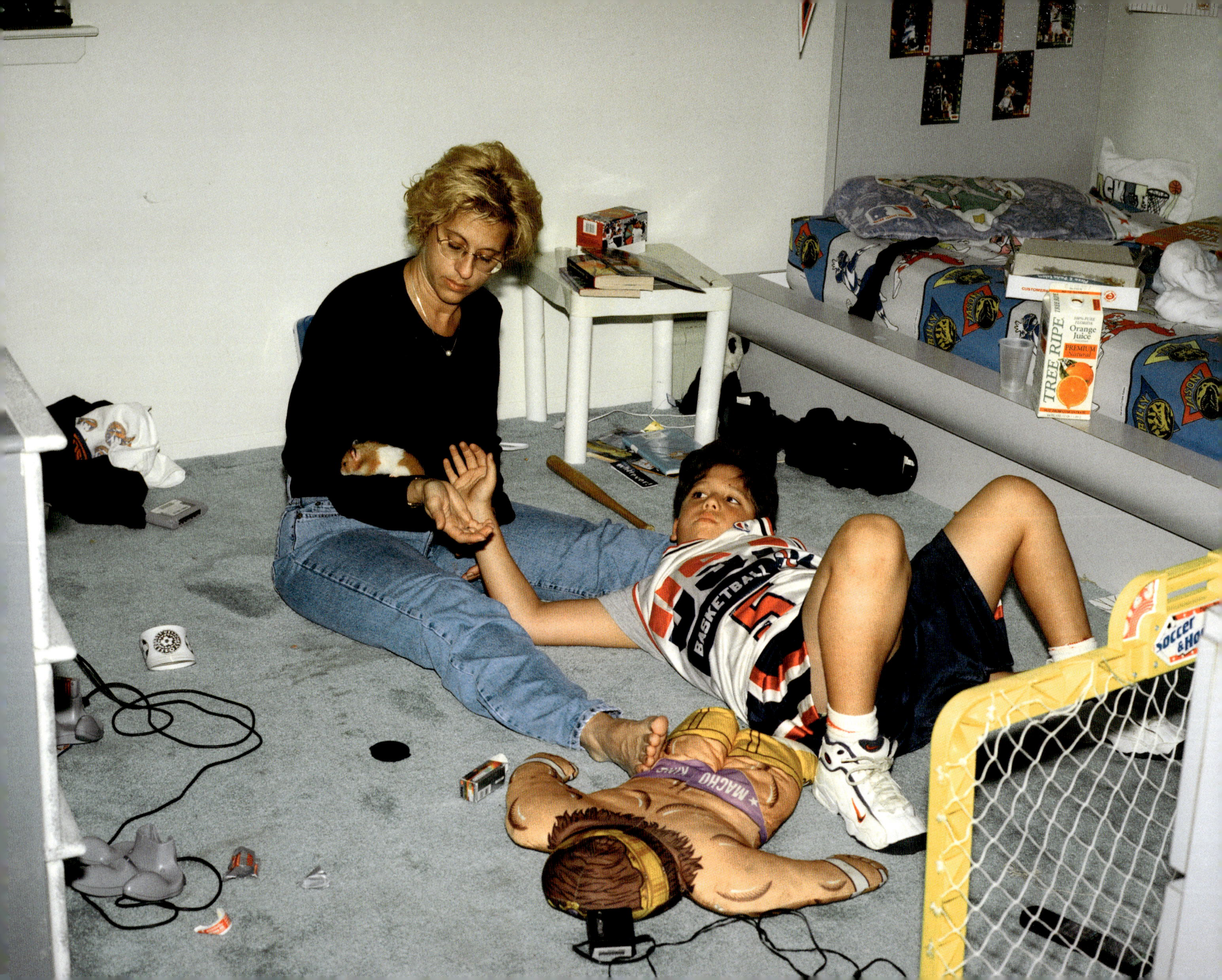

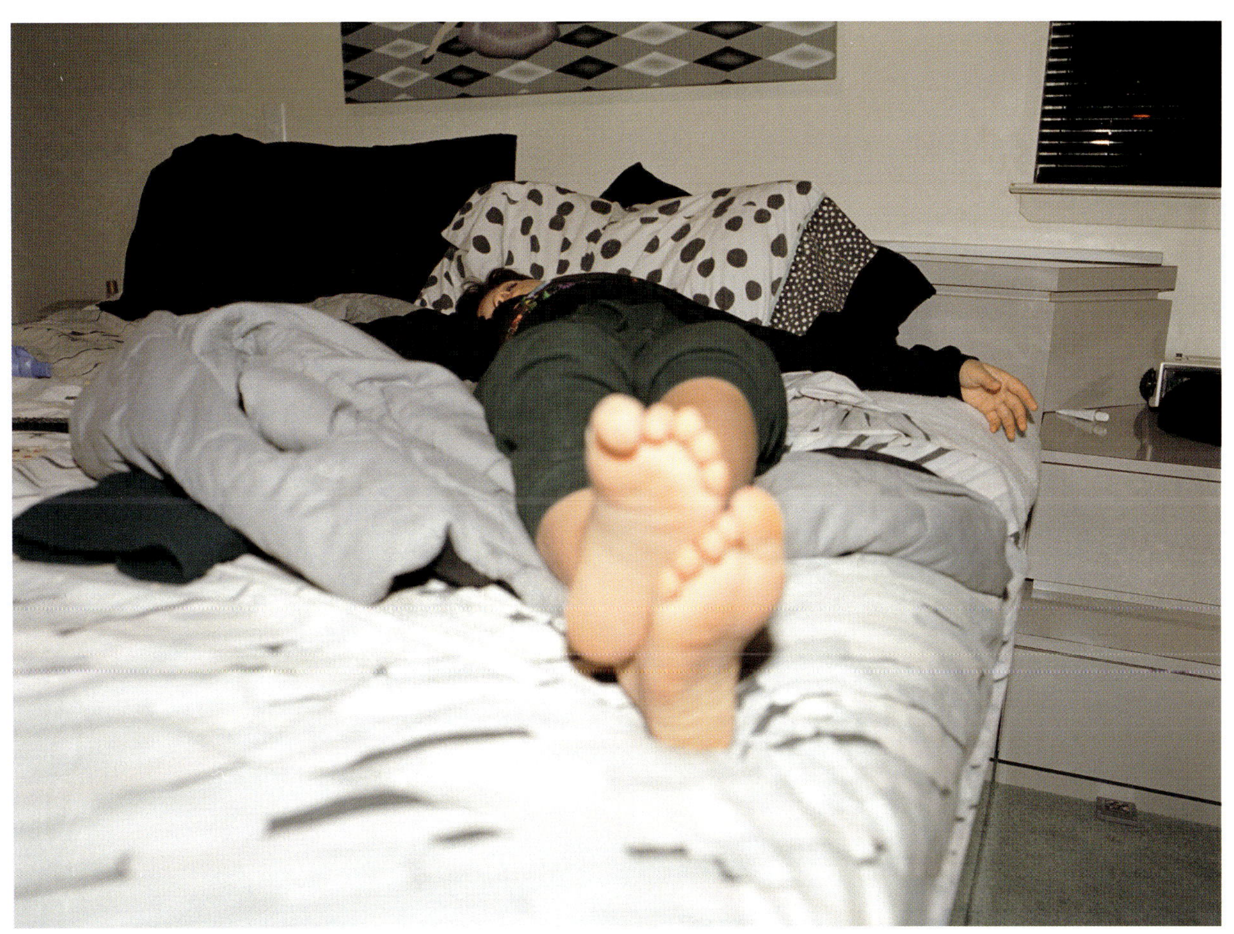

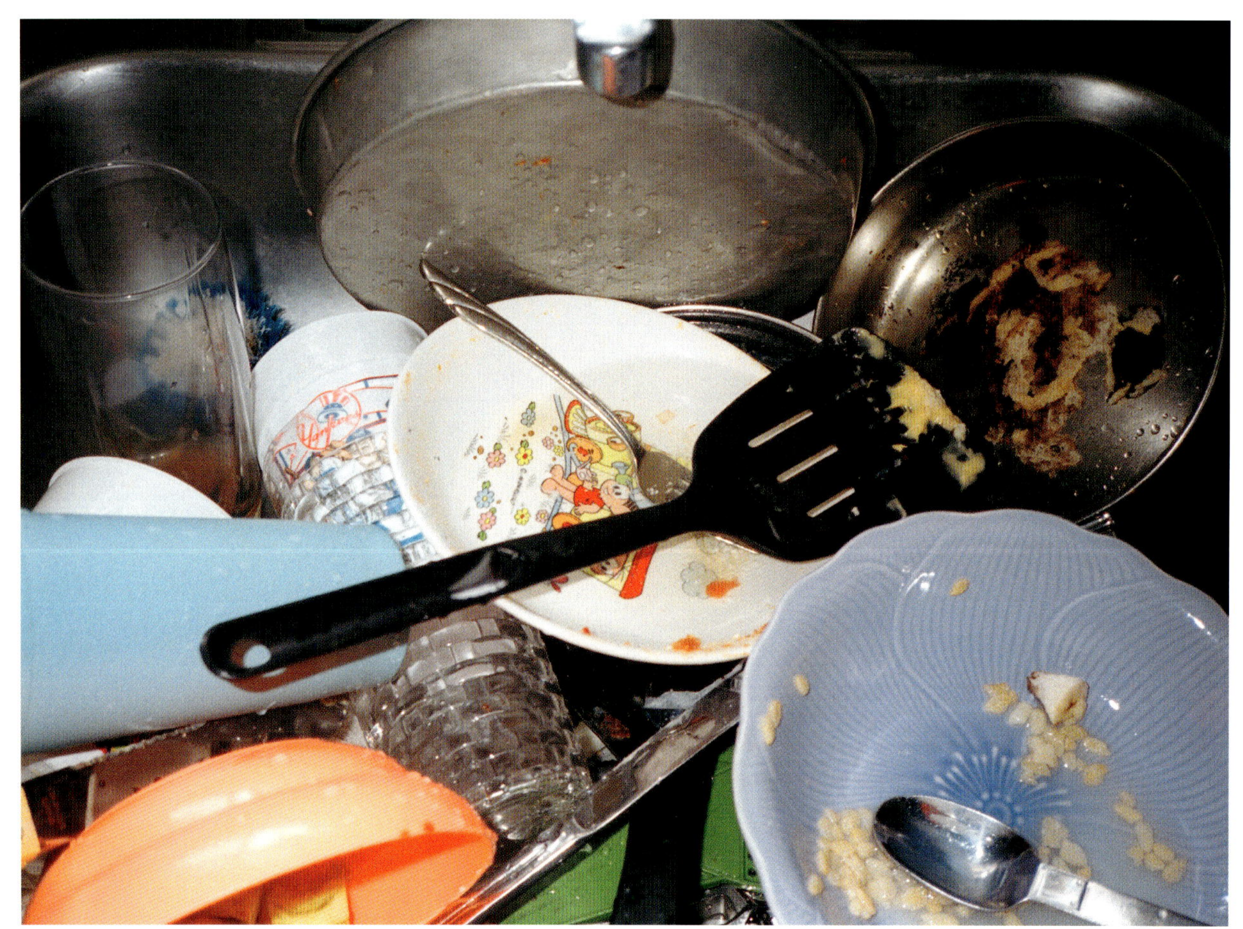

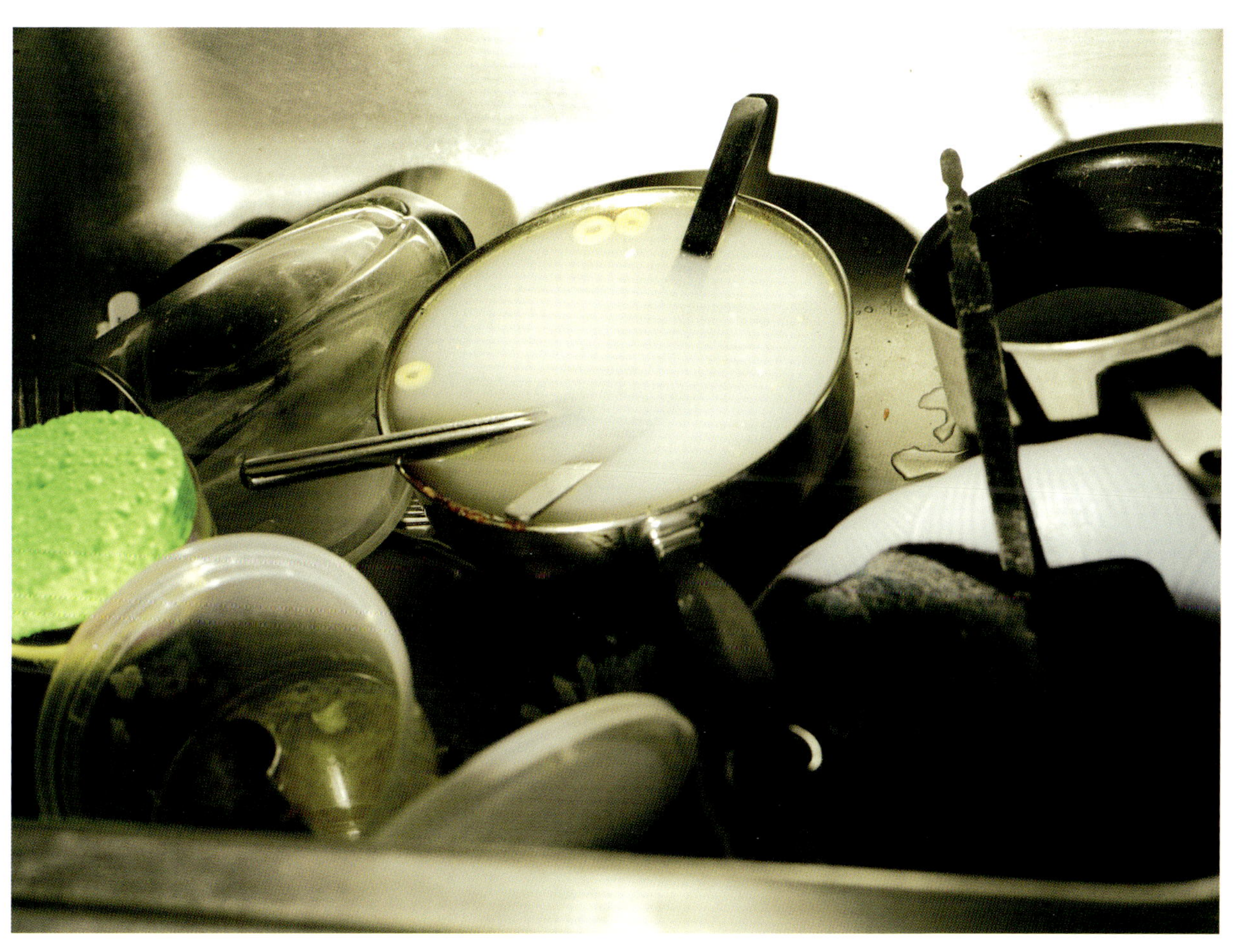

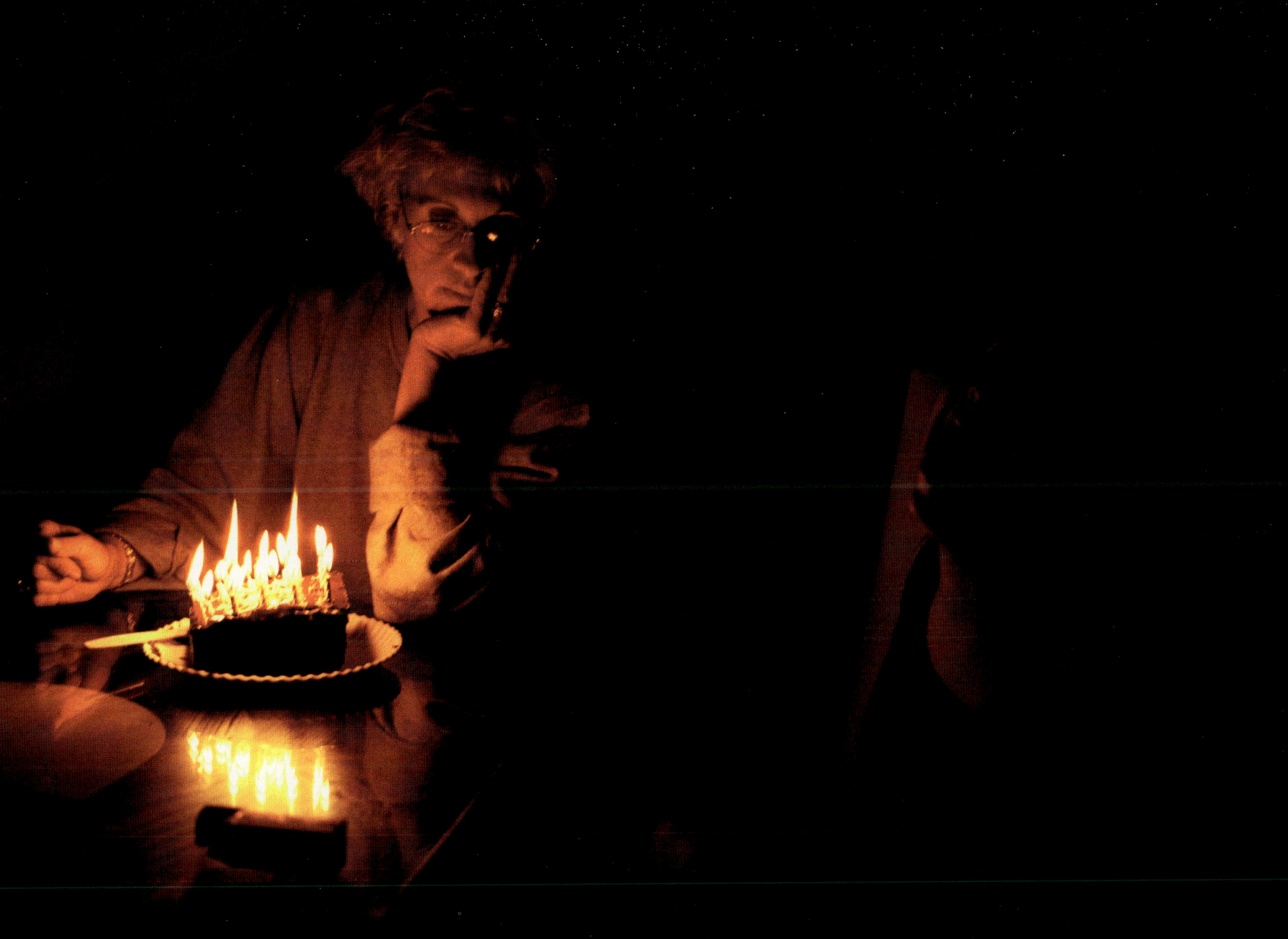

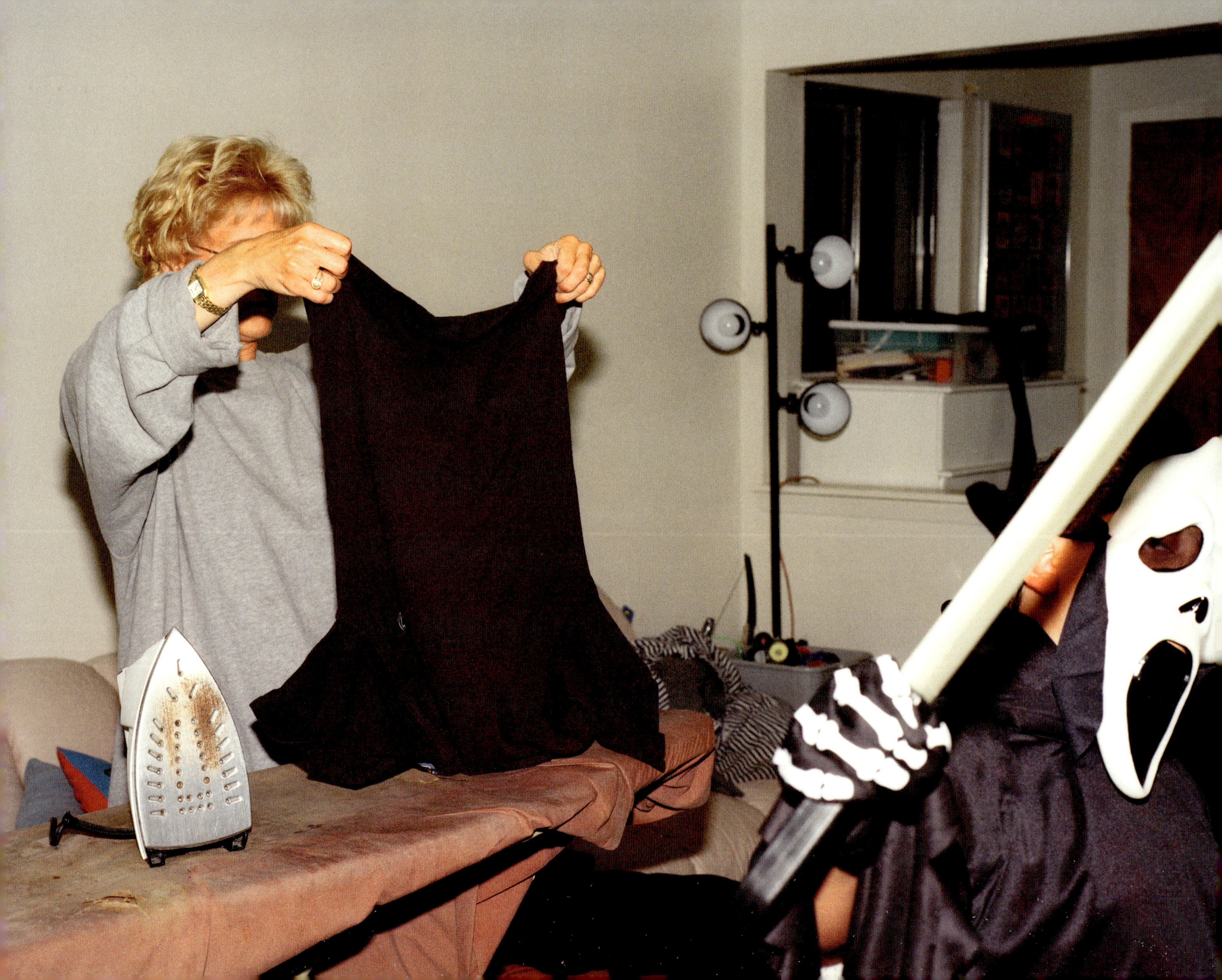

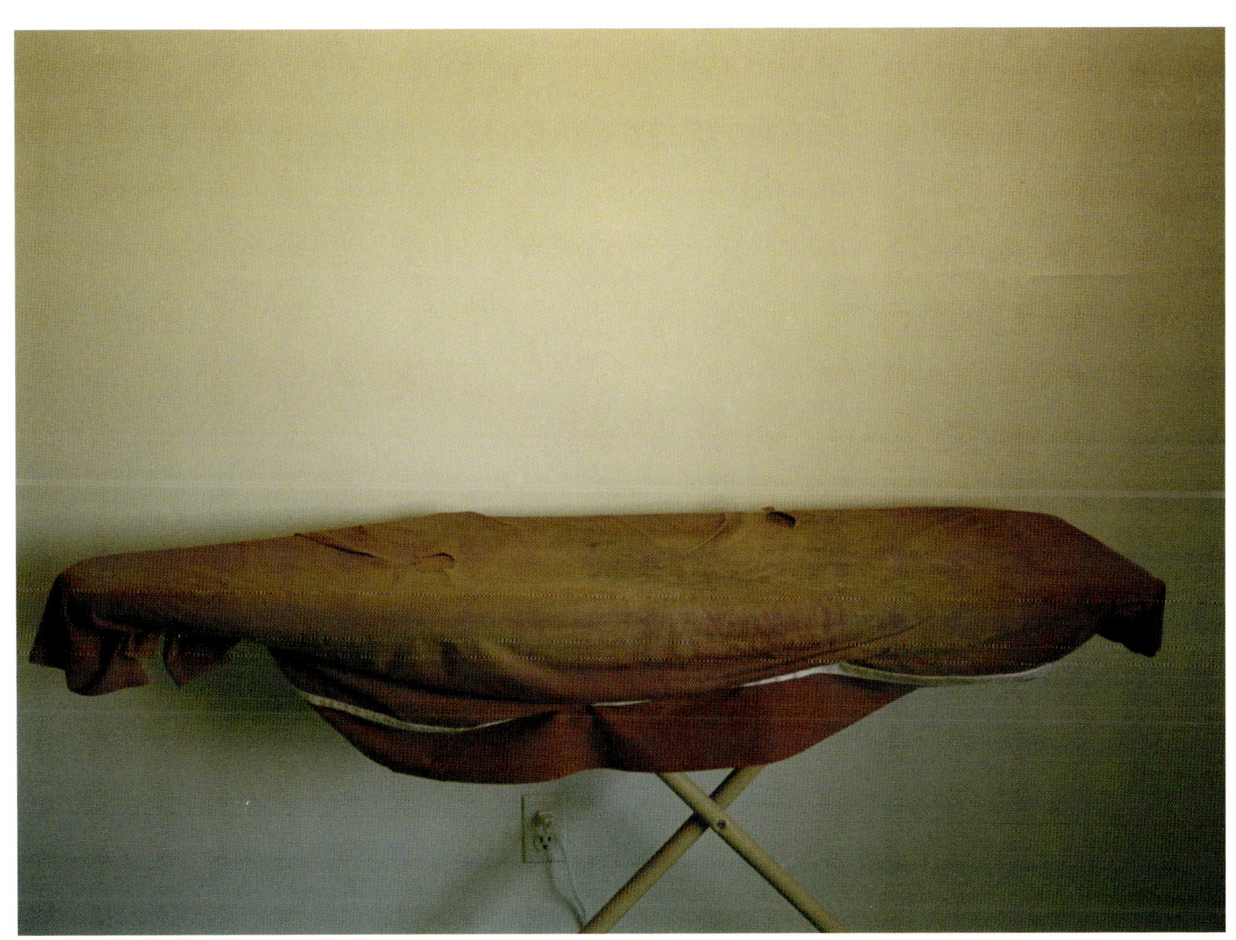

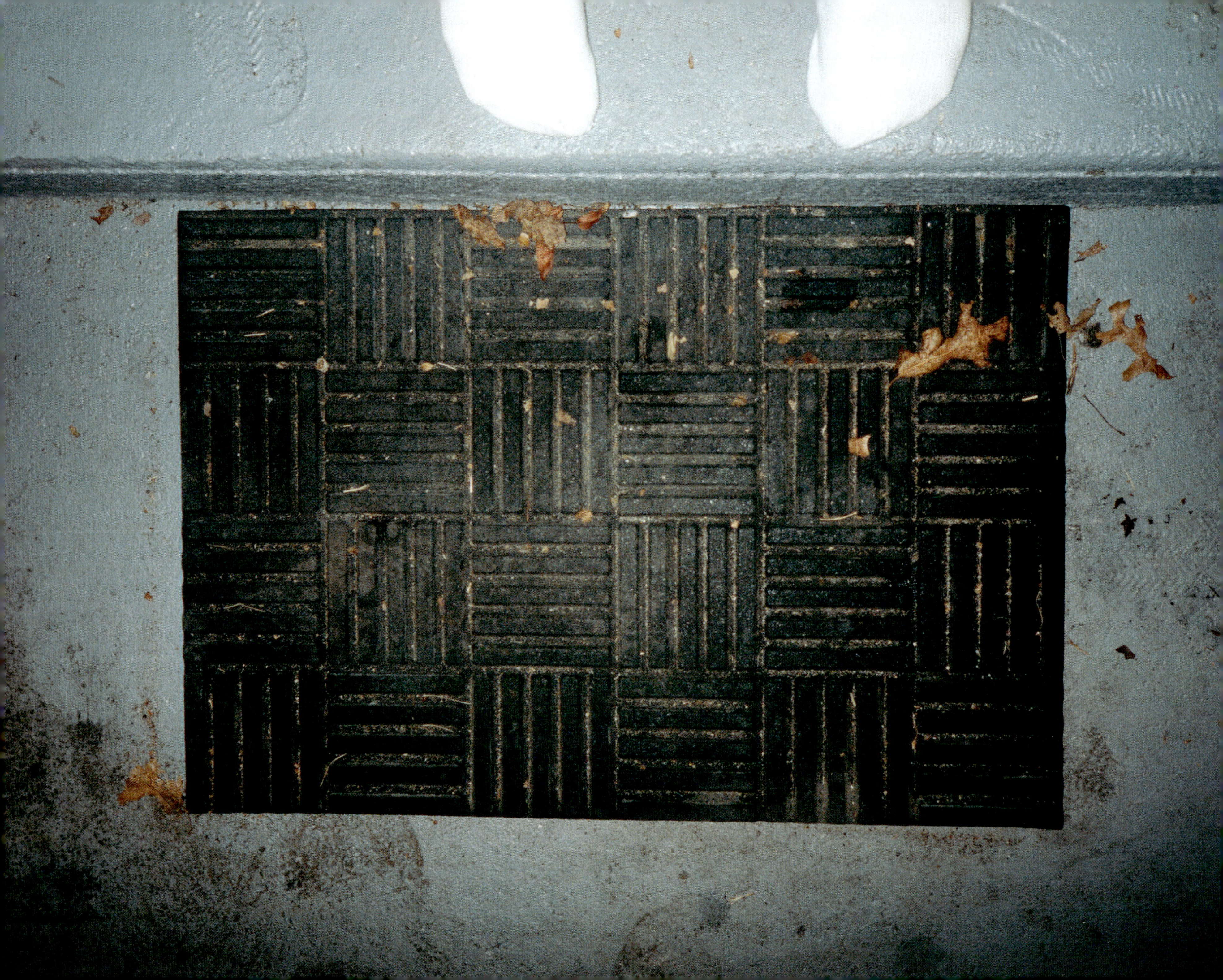

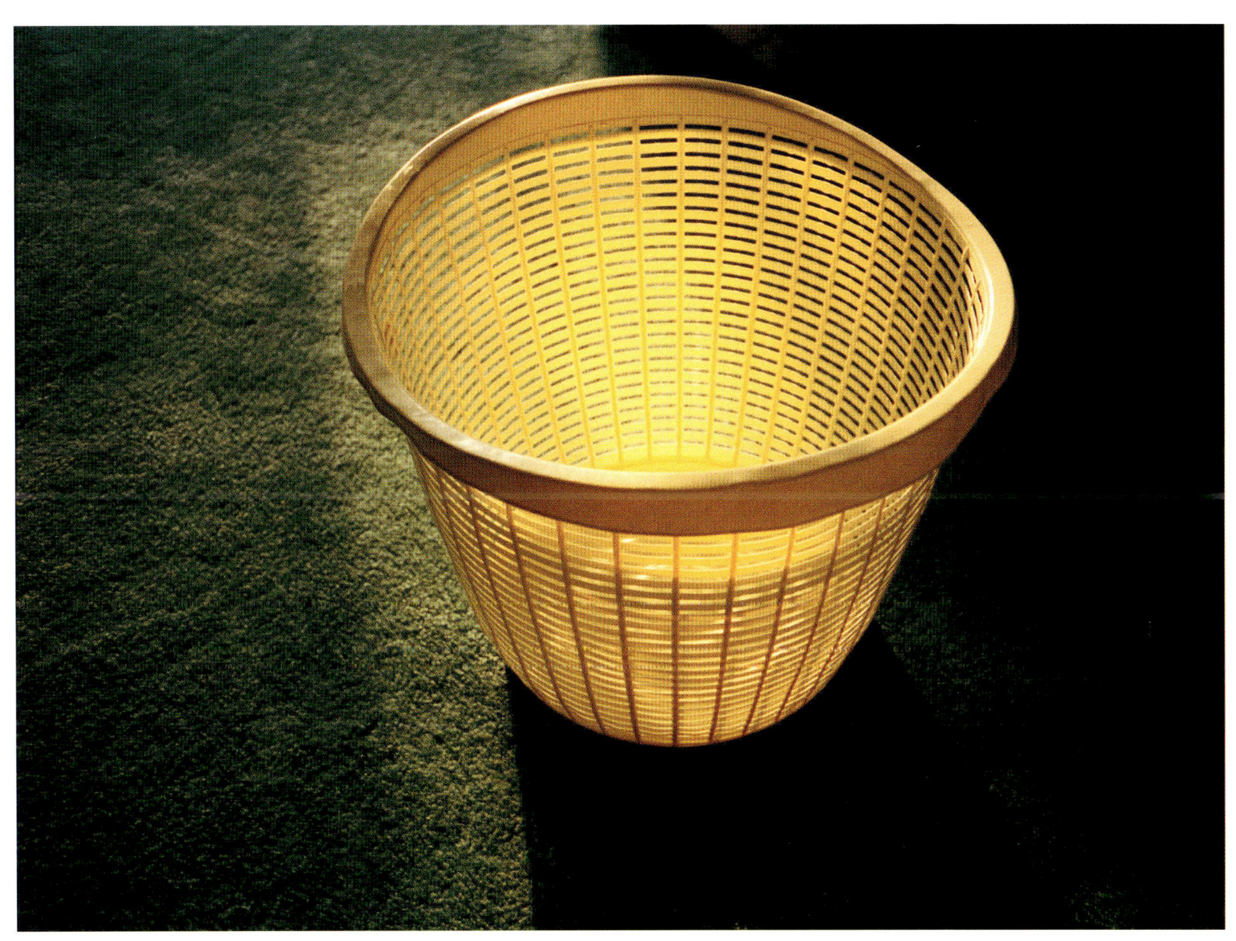

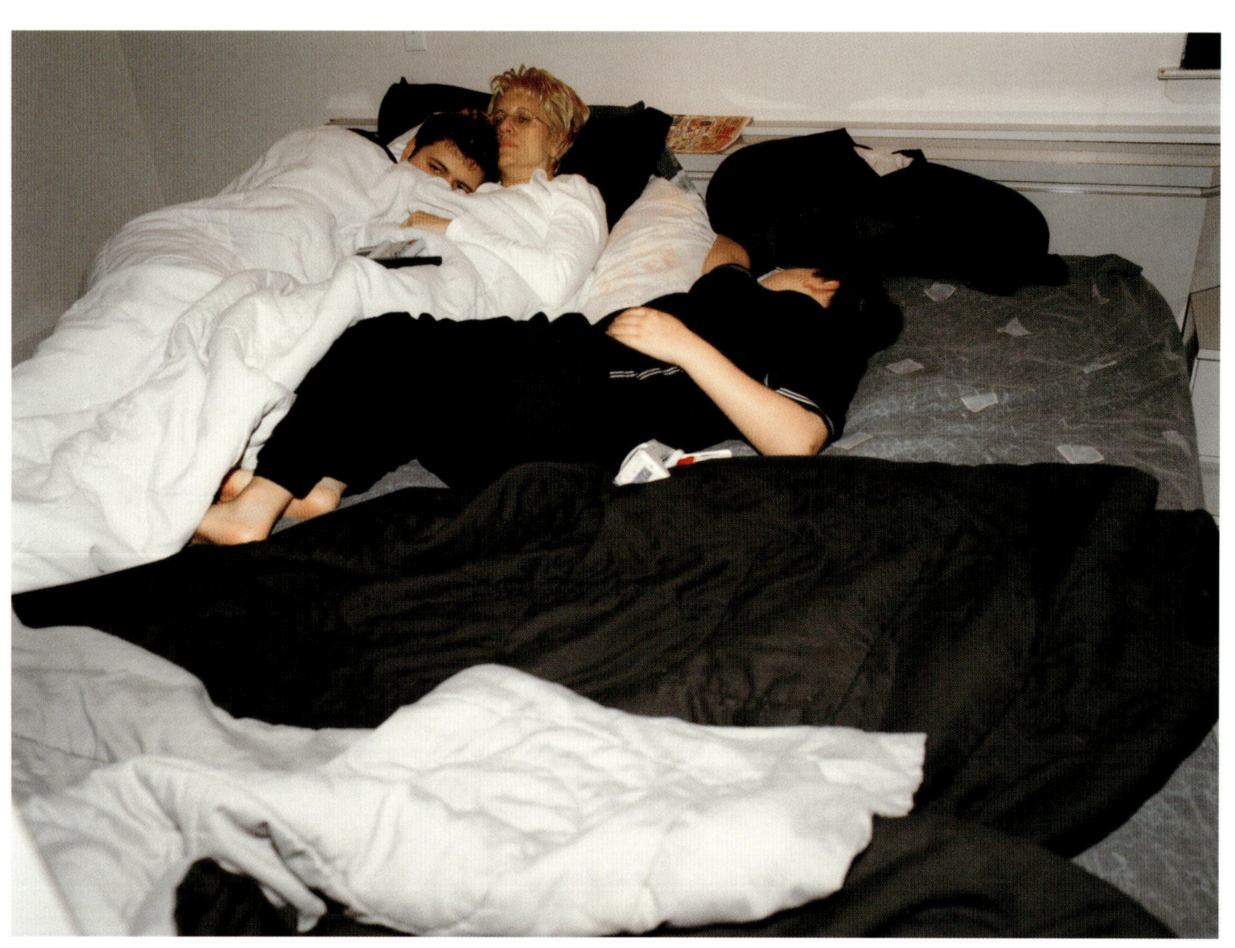

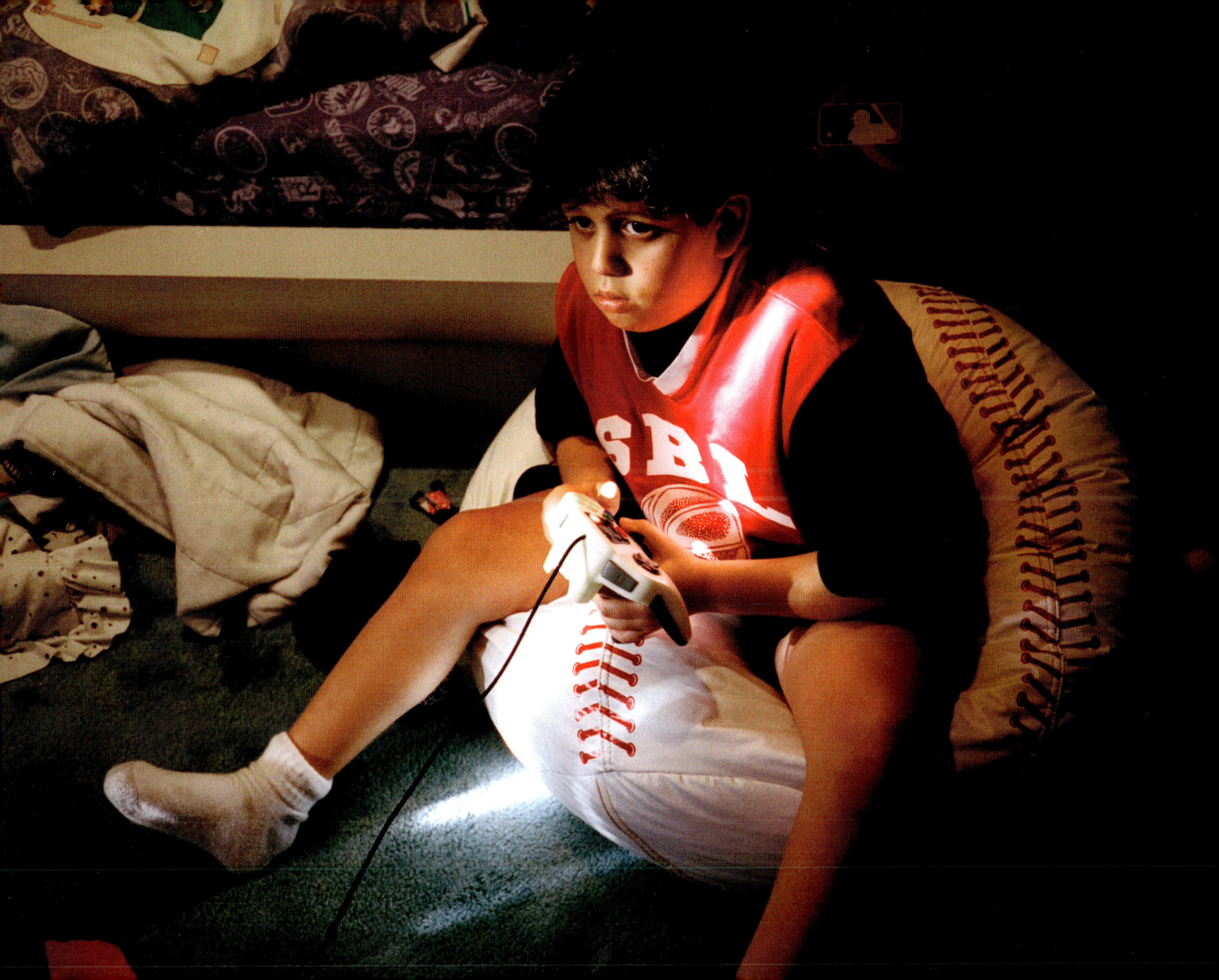

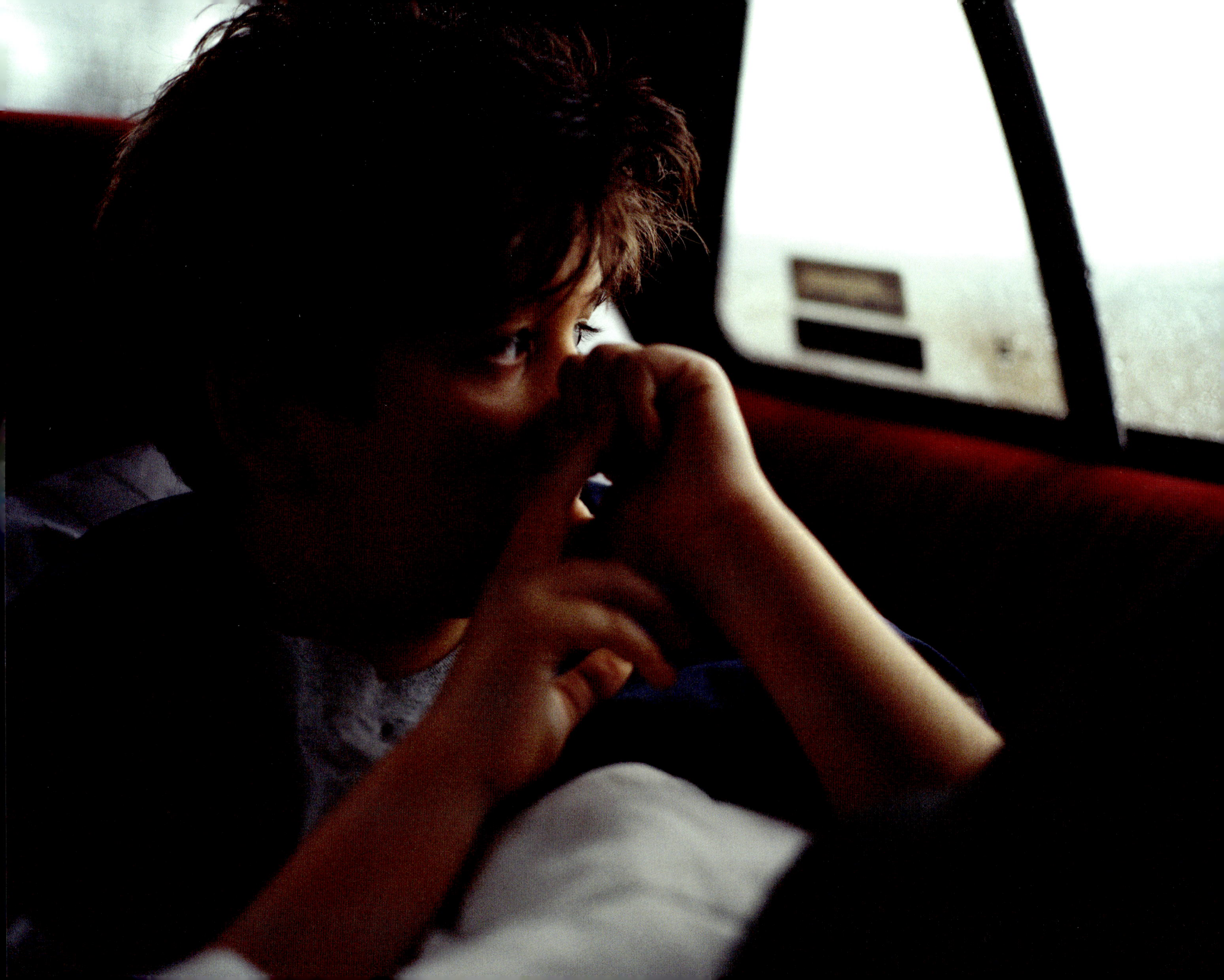

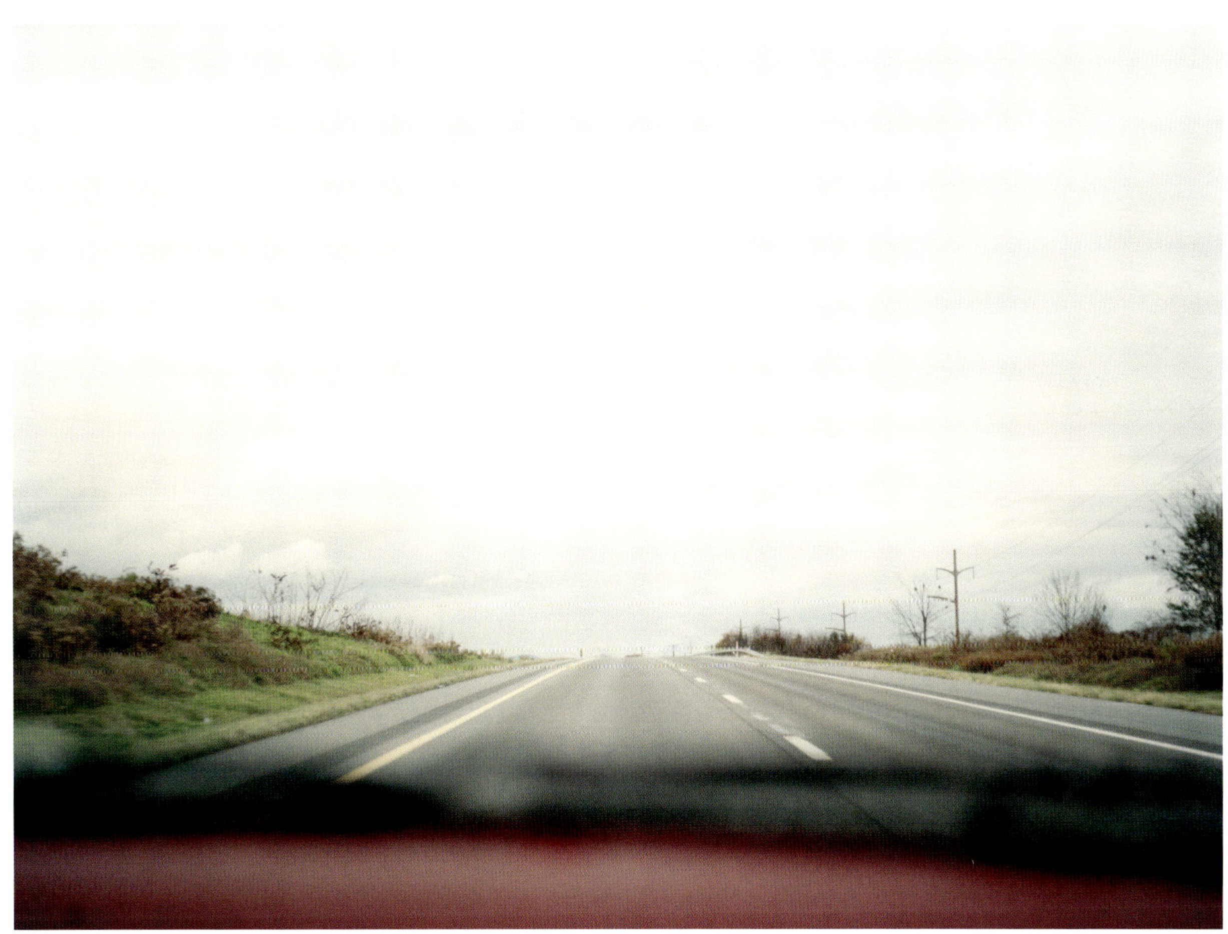

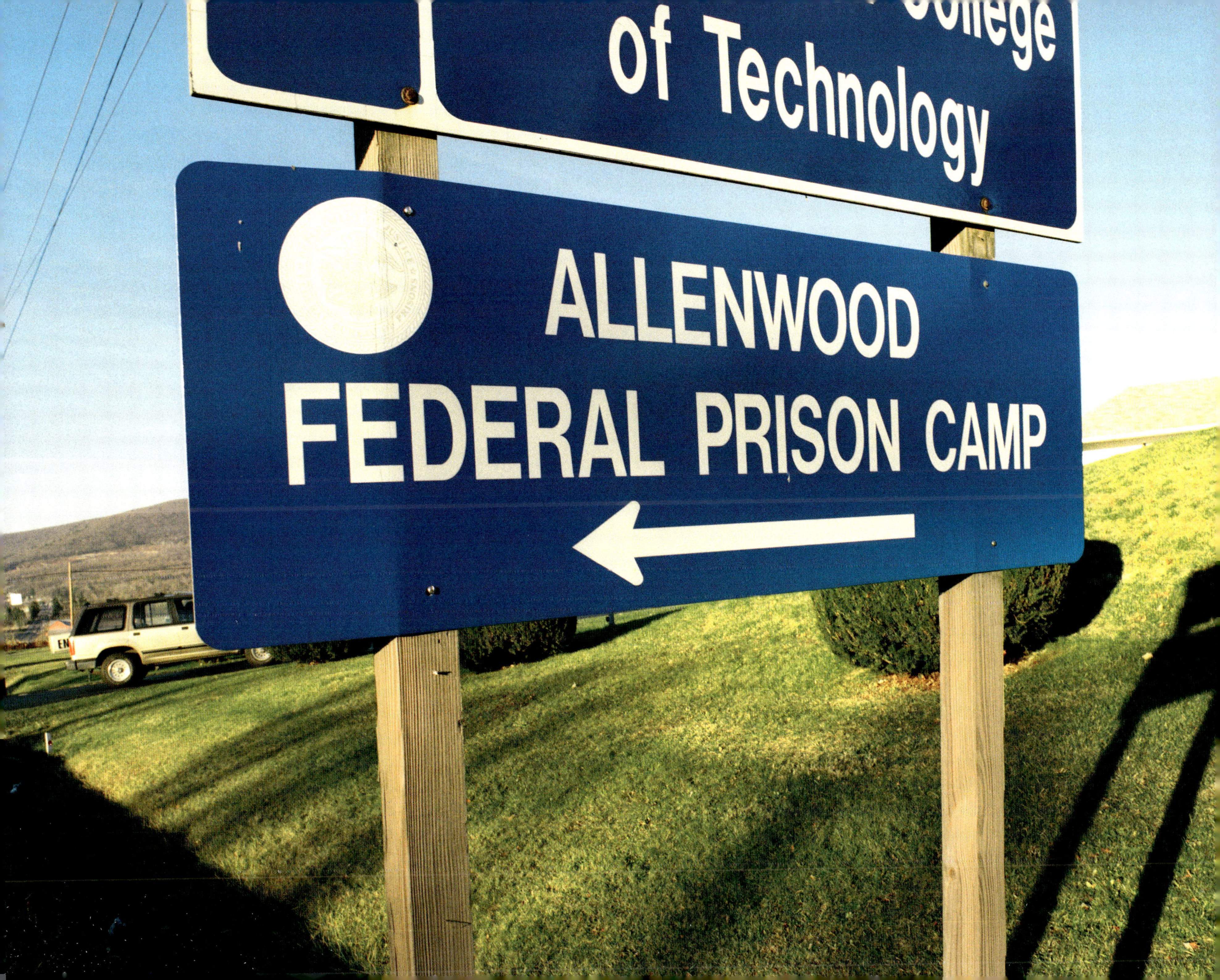
ollege
of Technology
ALLENWOOD
FEDERAL PRISON CAMP

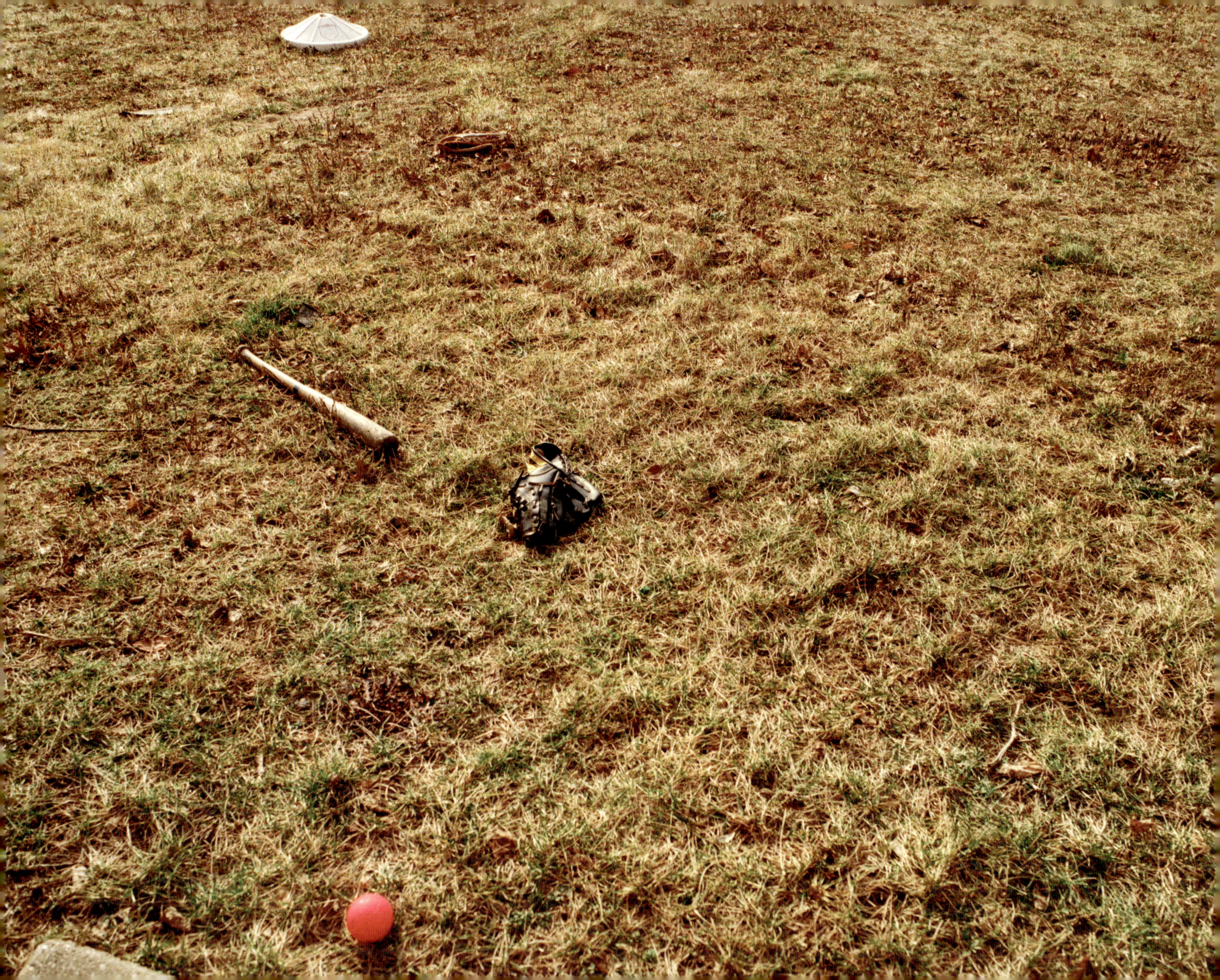

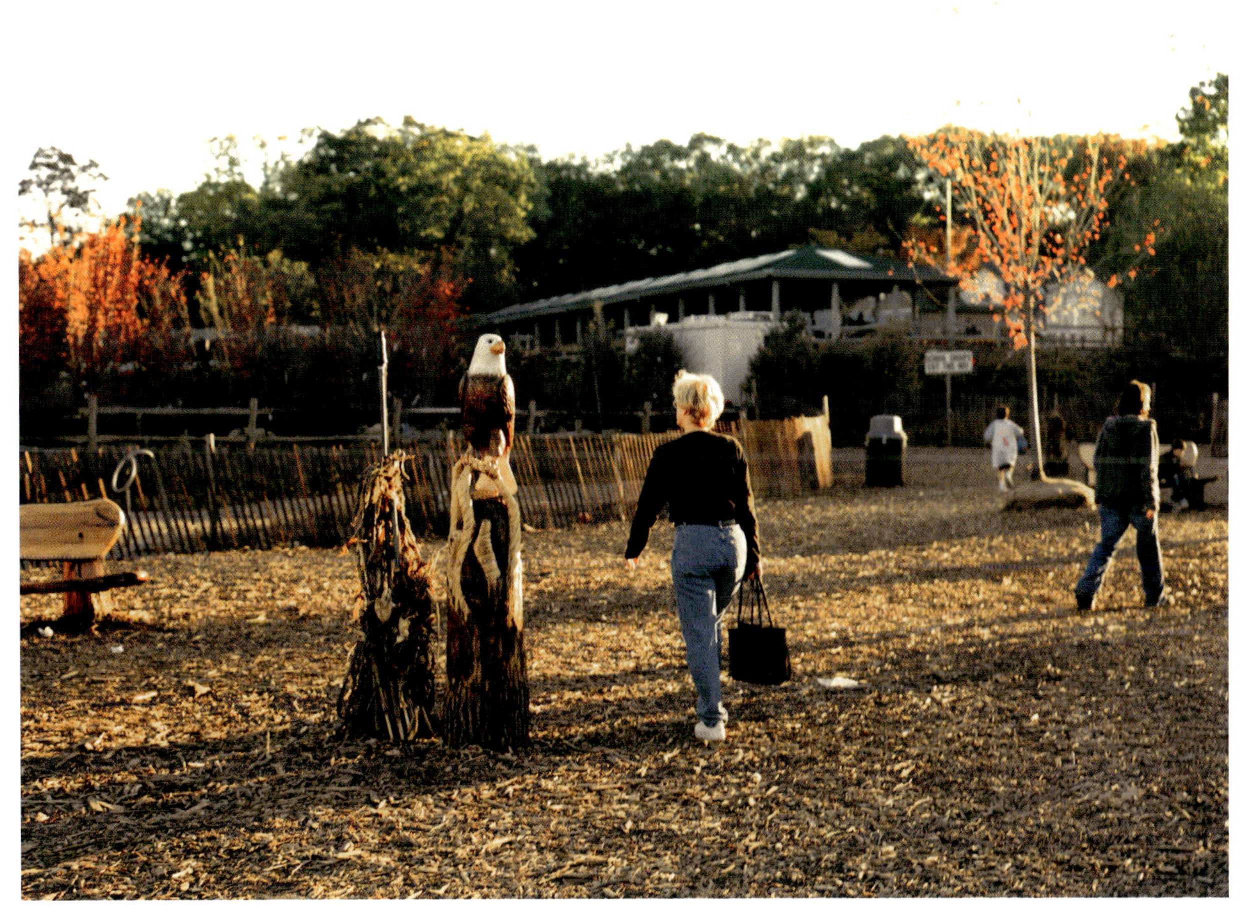

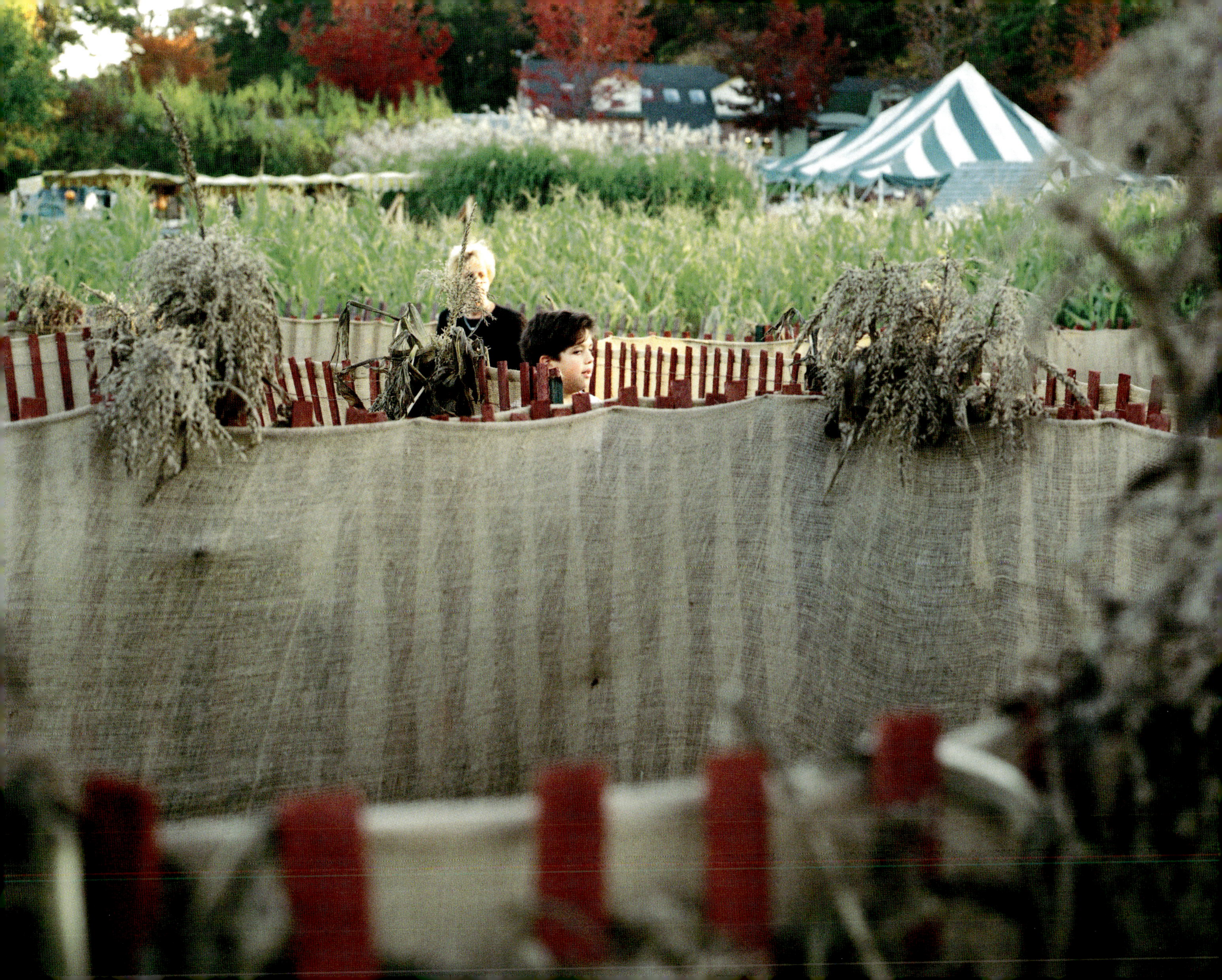

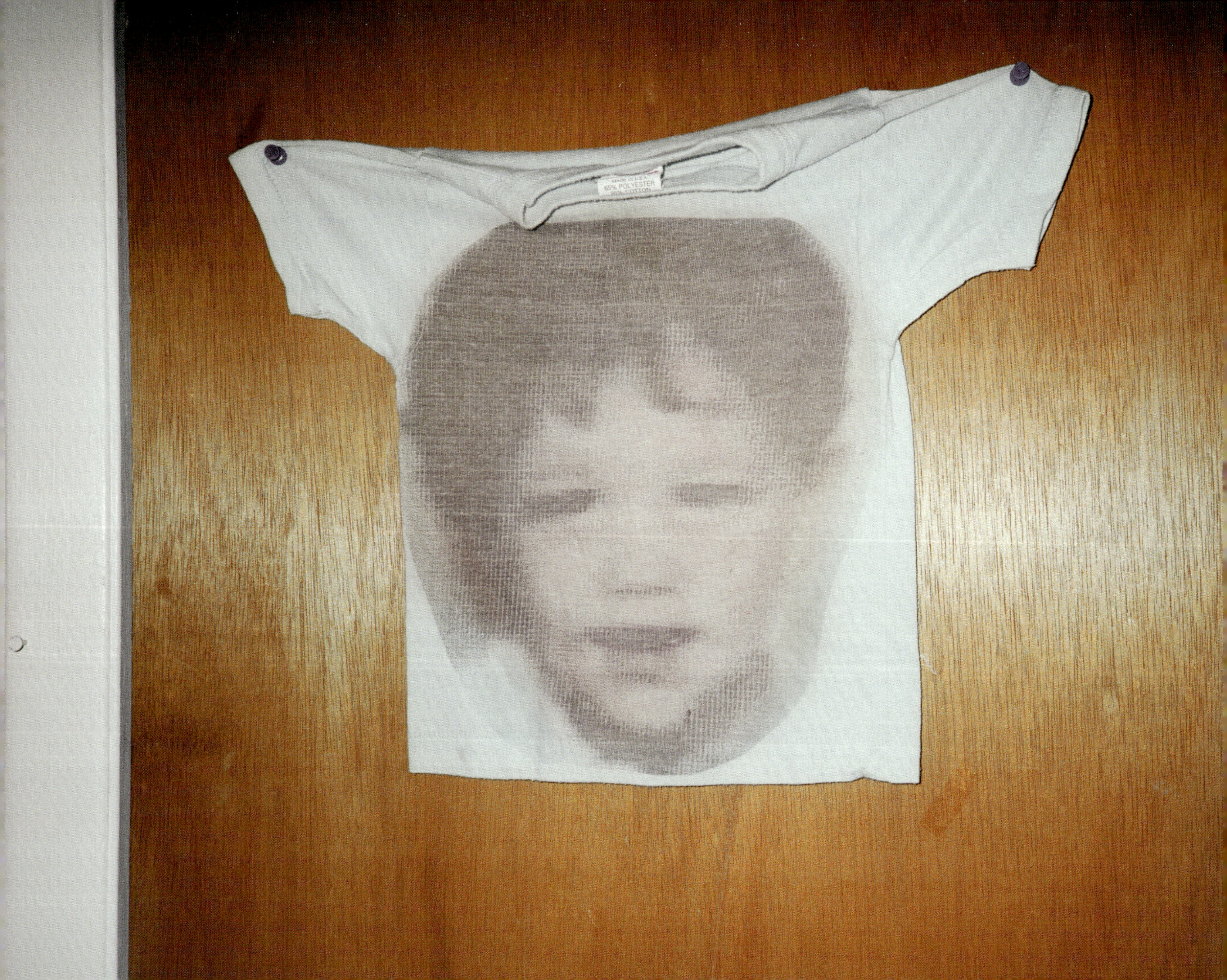

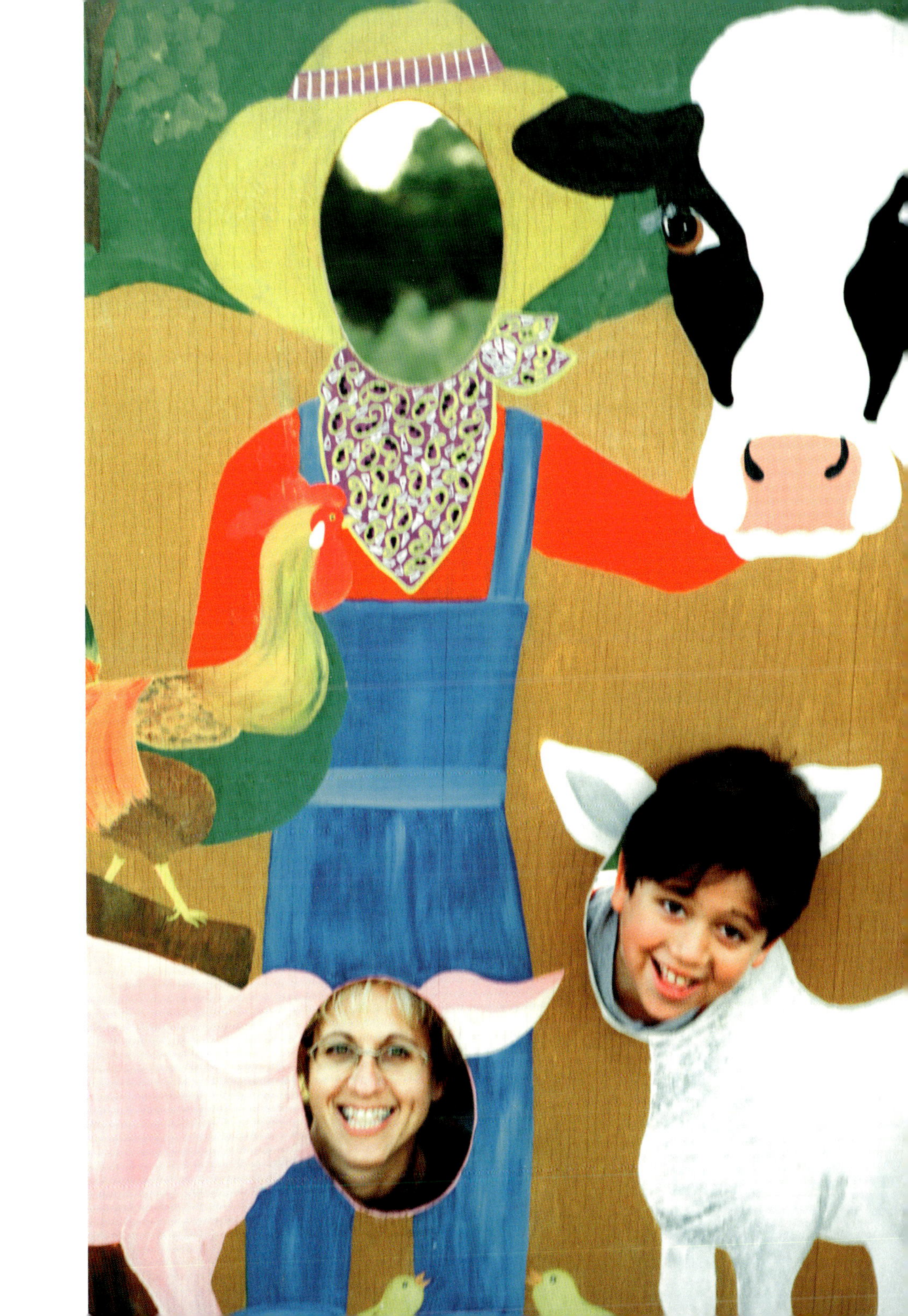

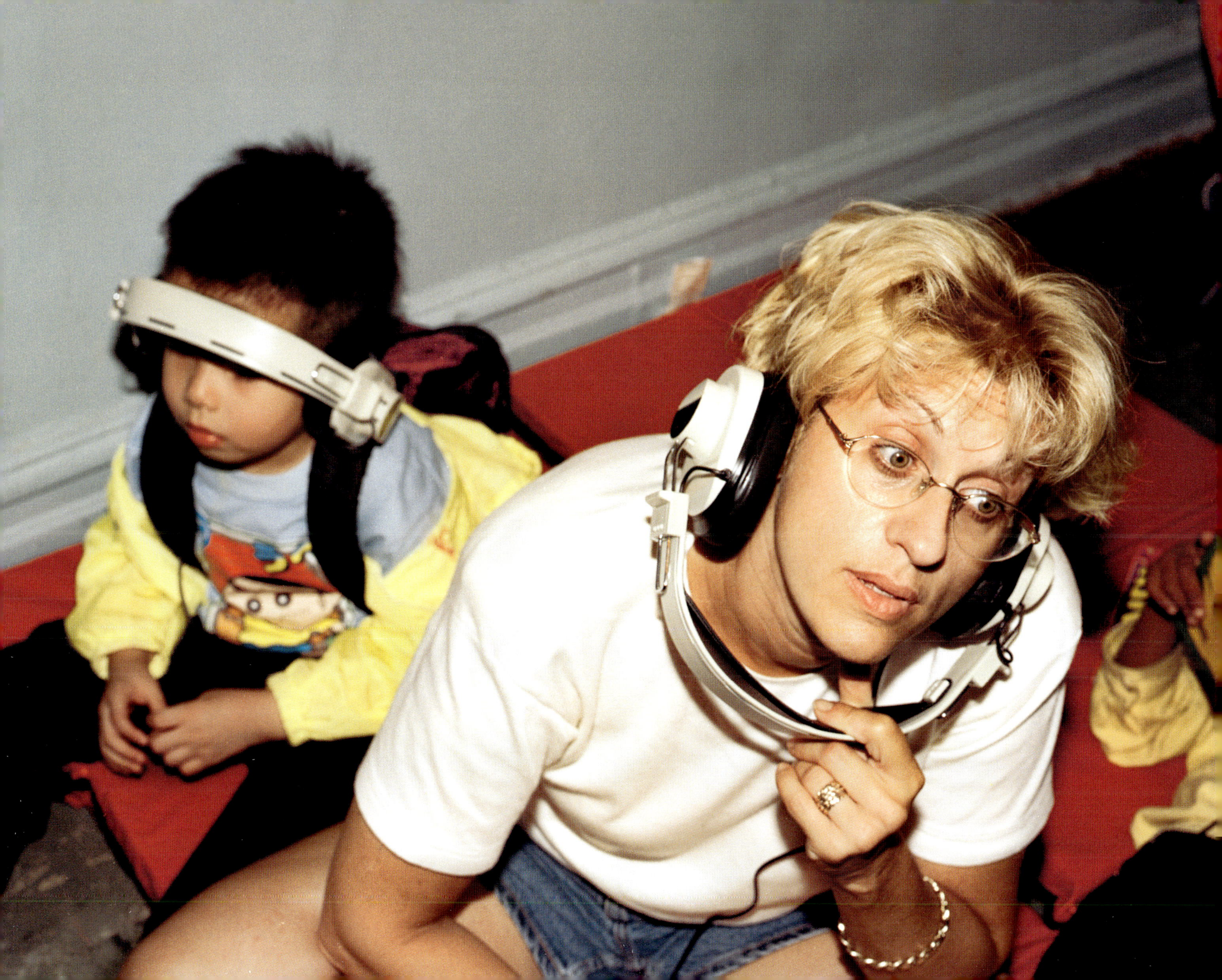

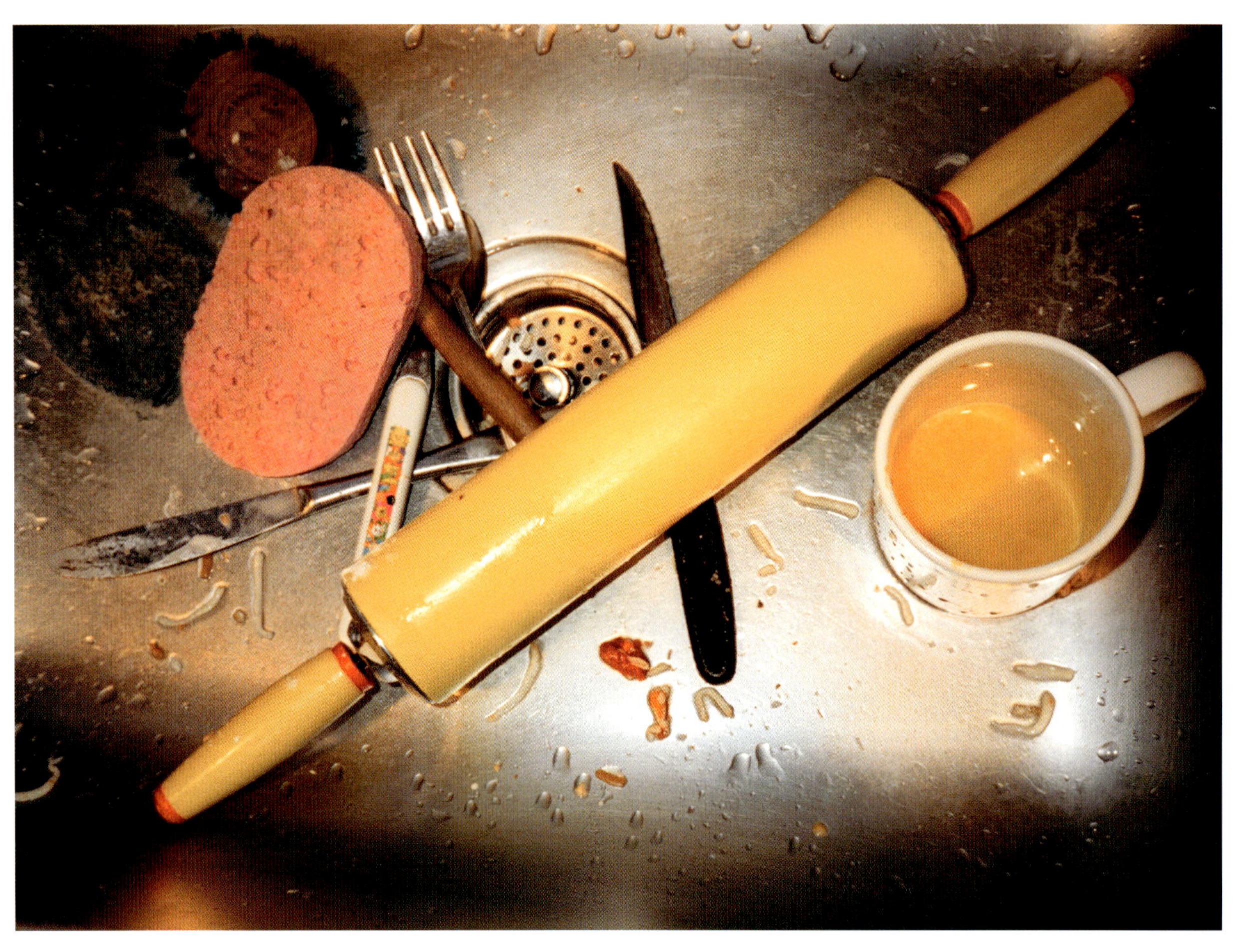

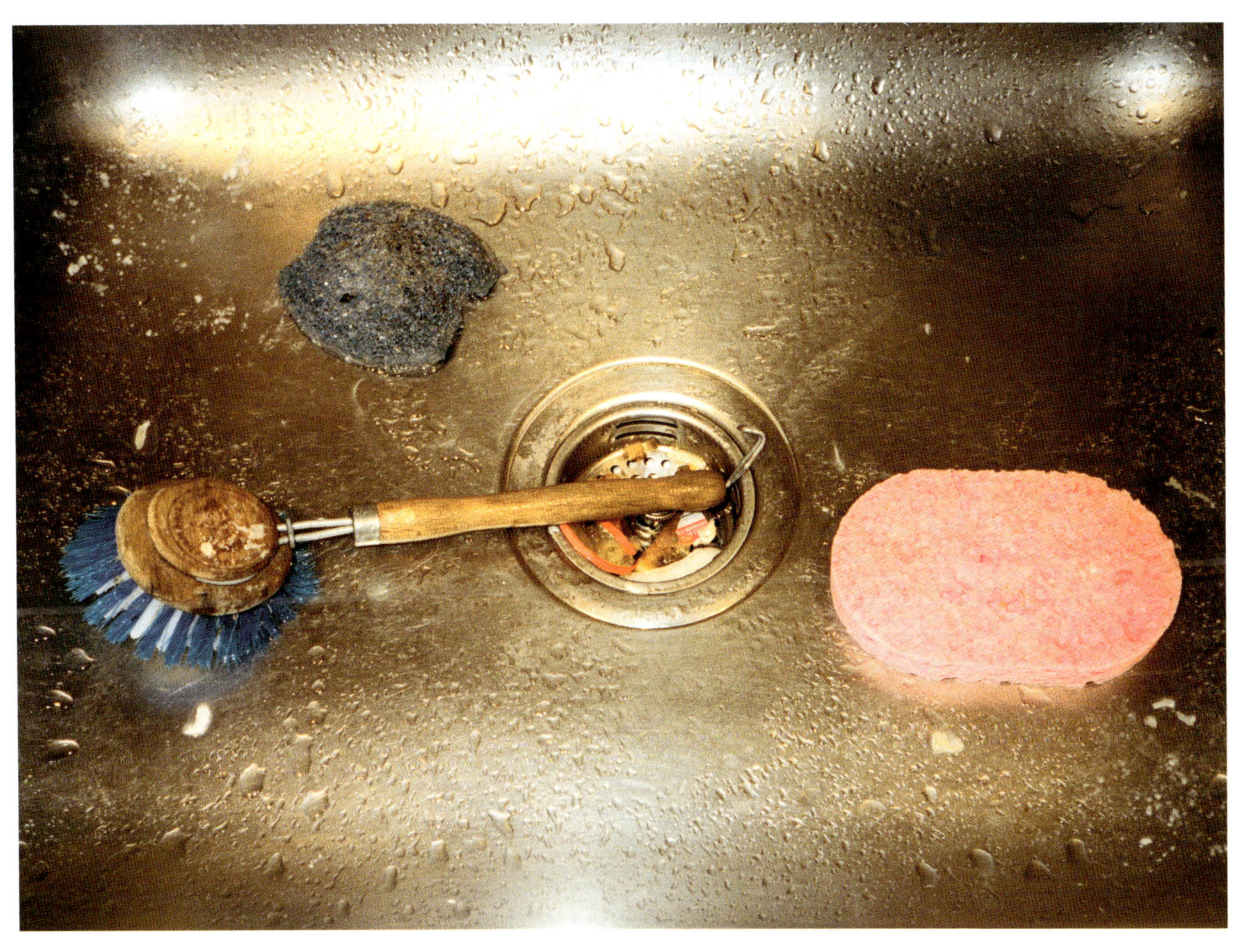

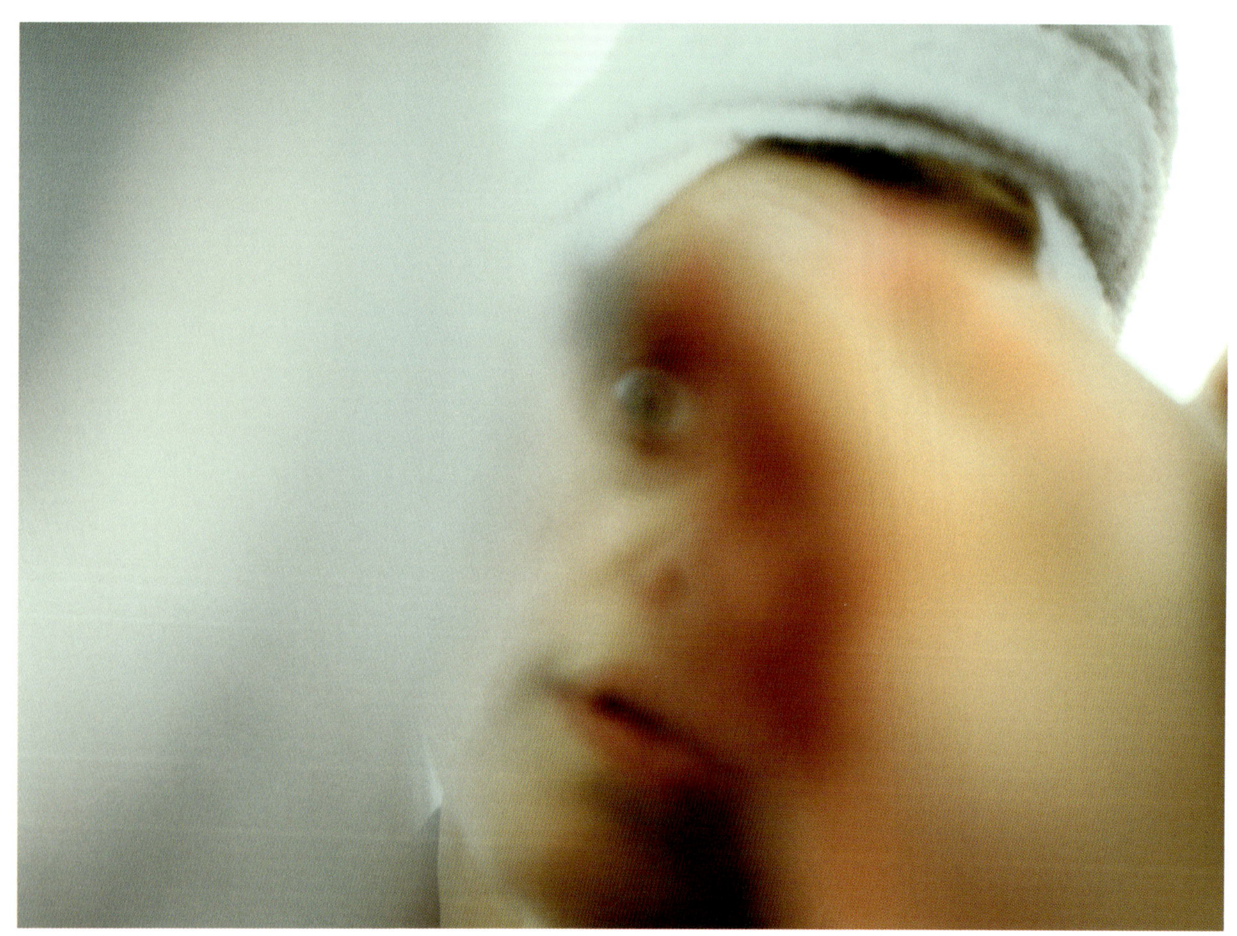

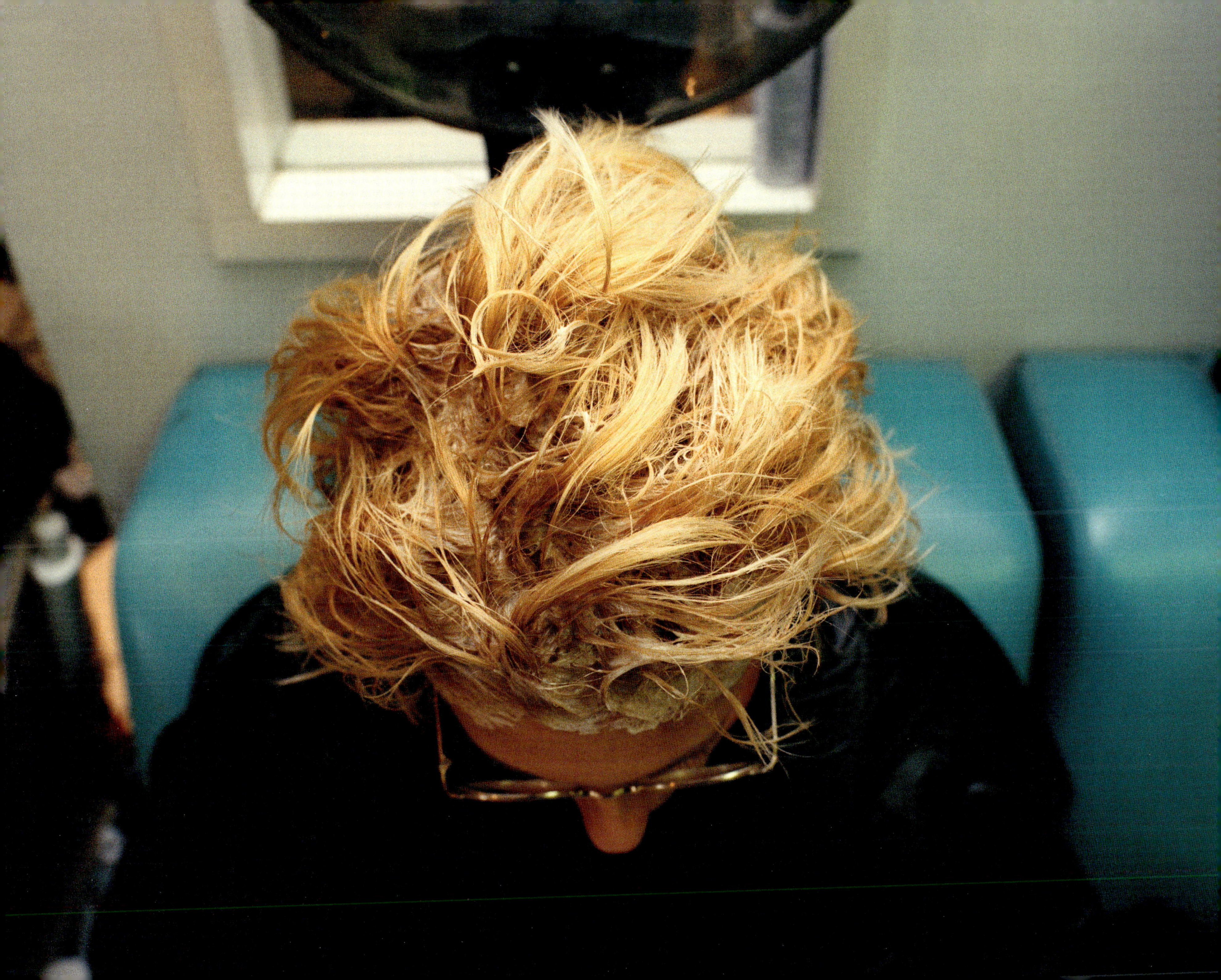

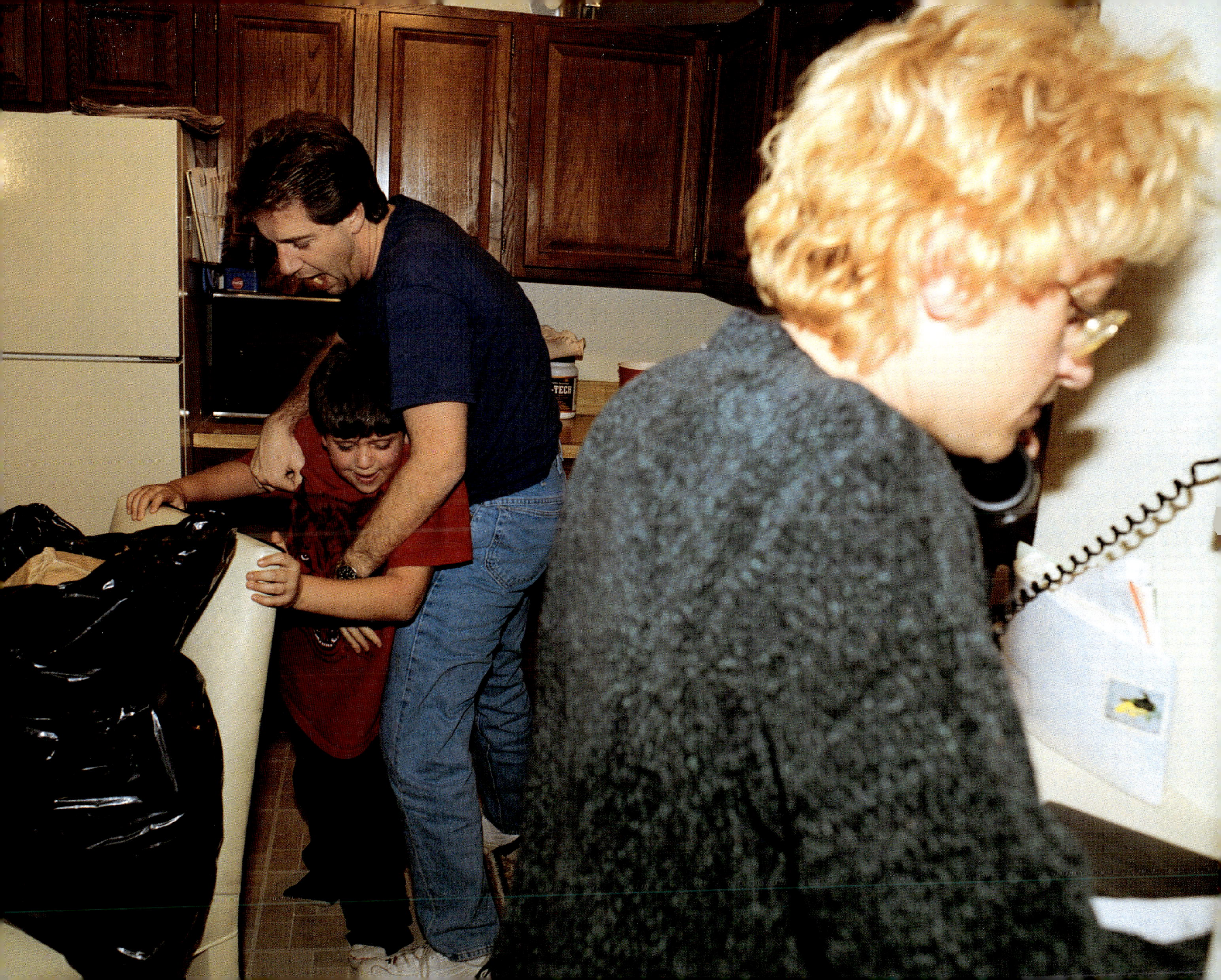

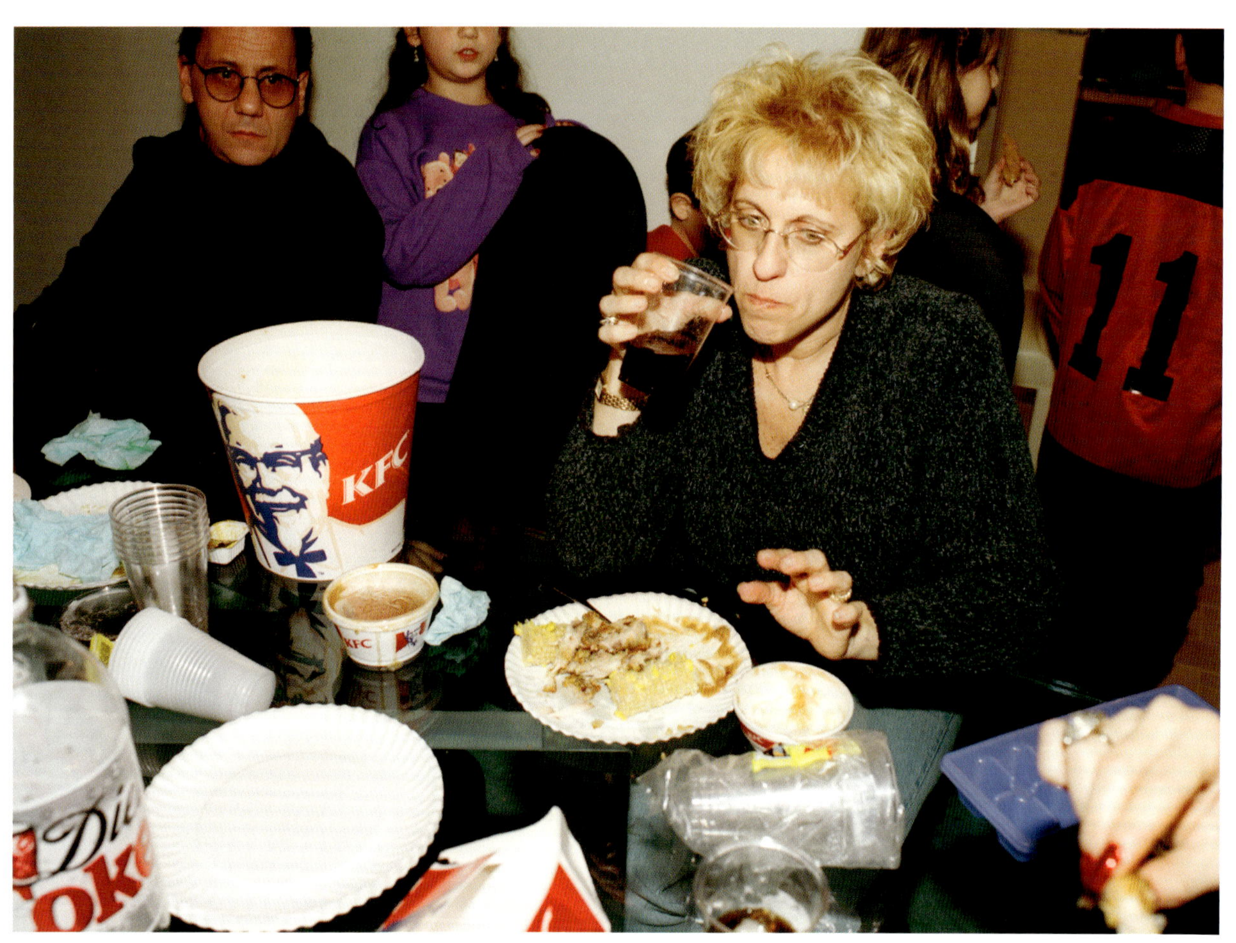

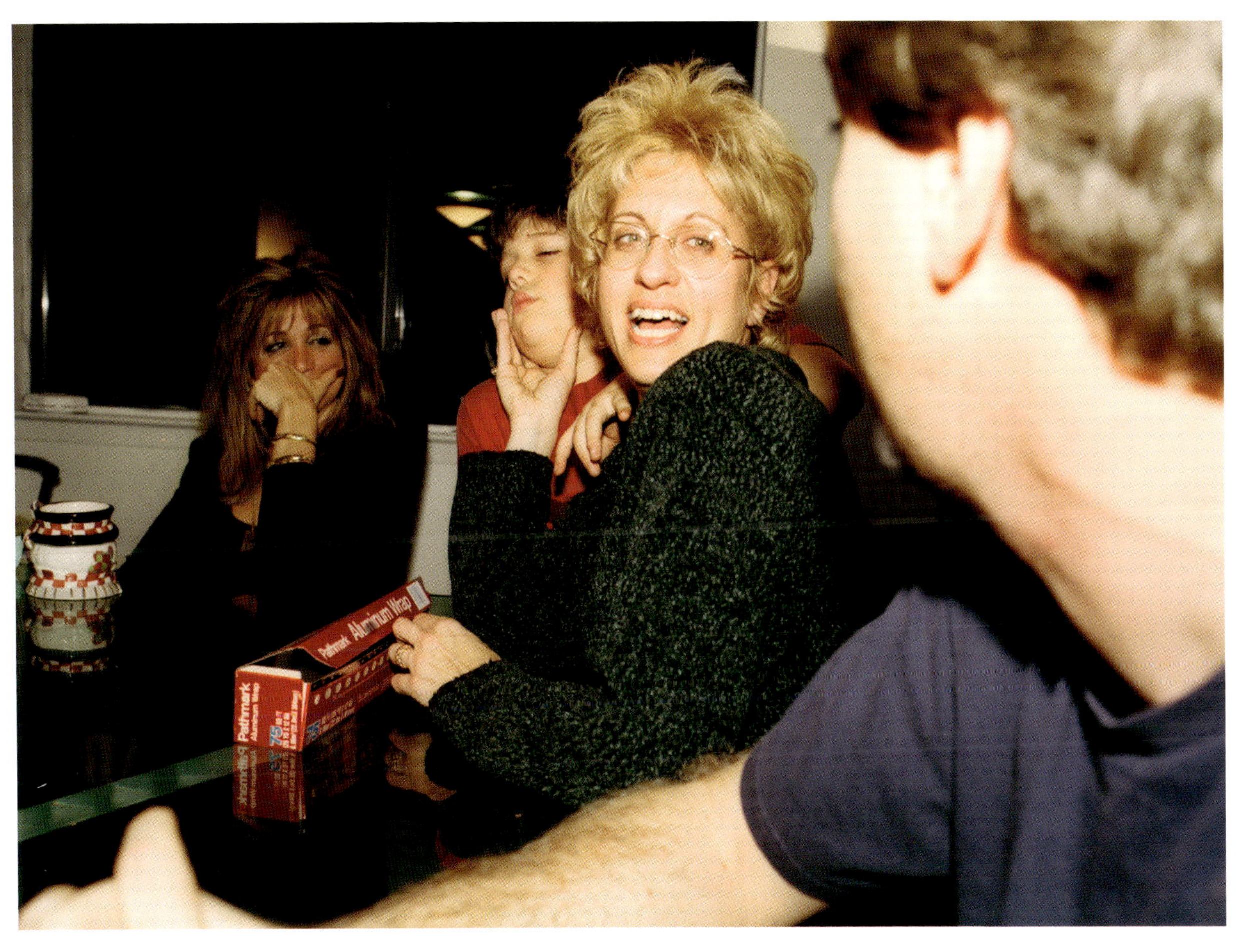

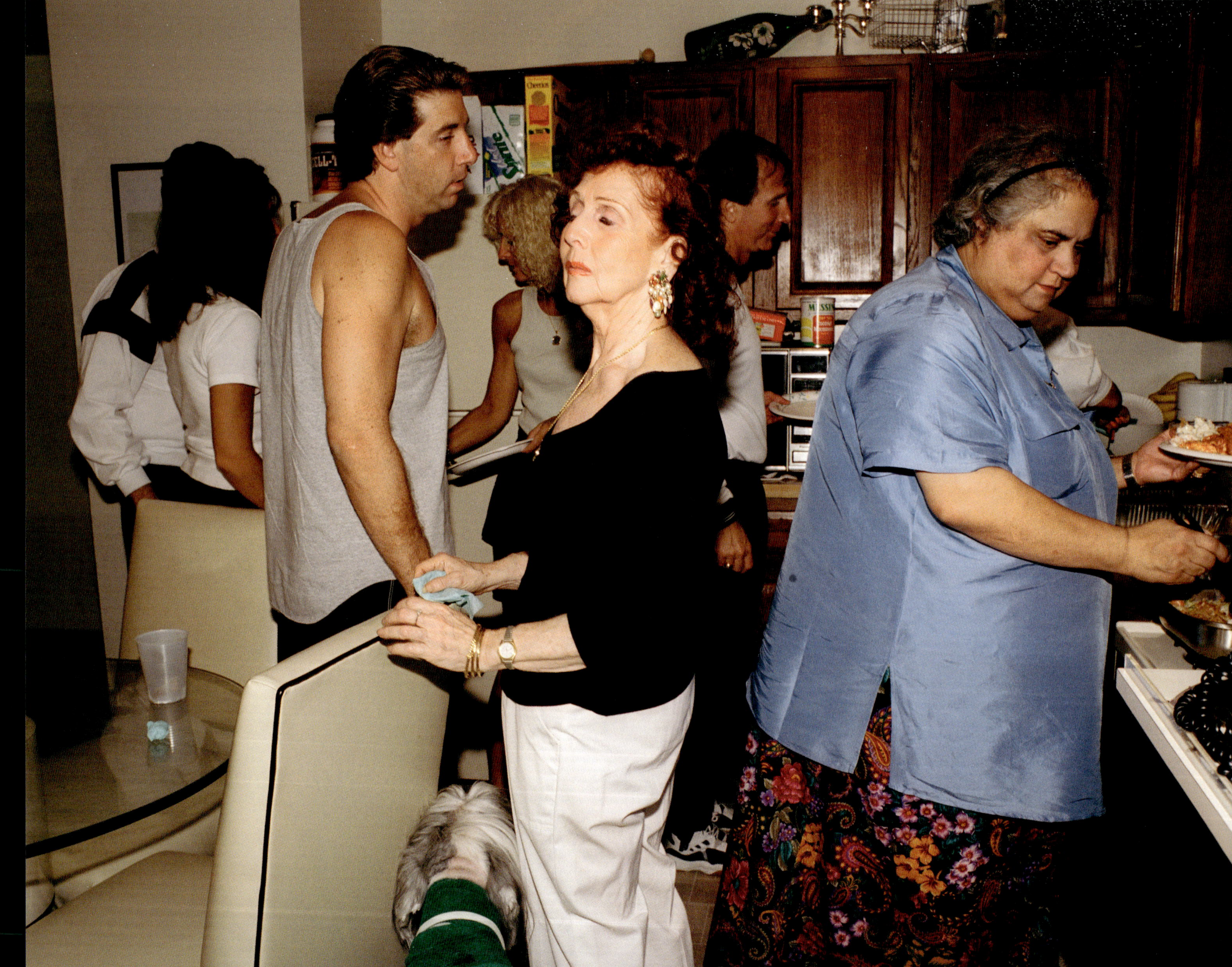

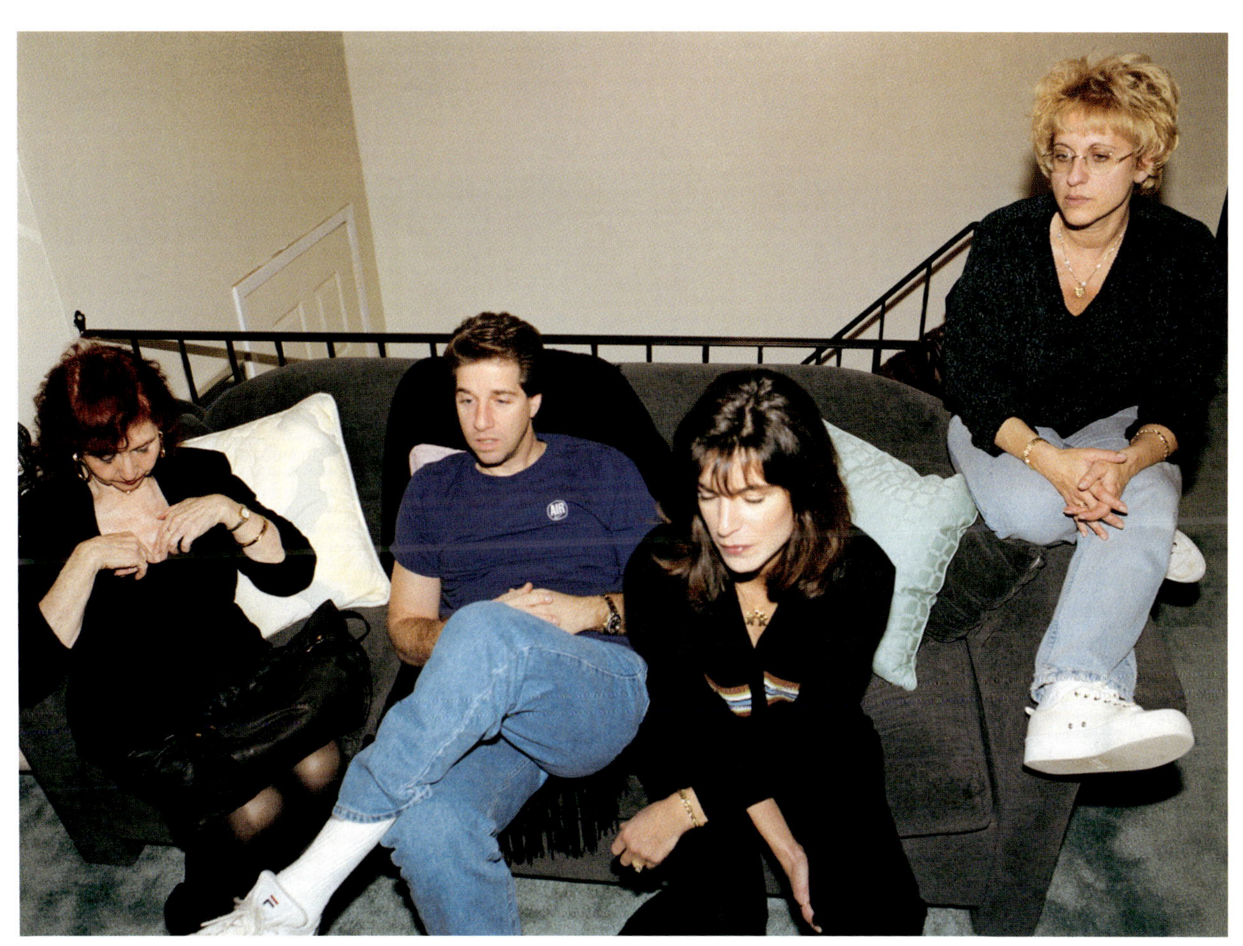

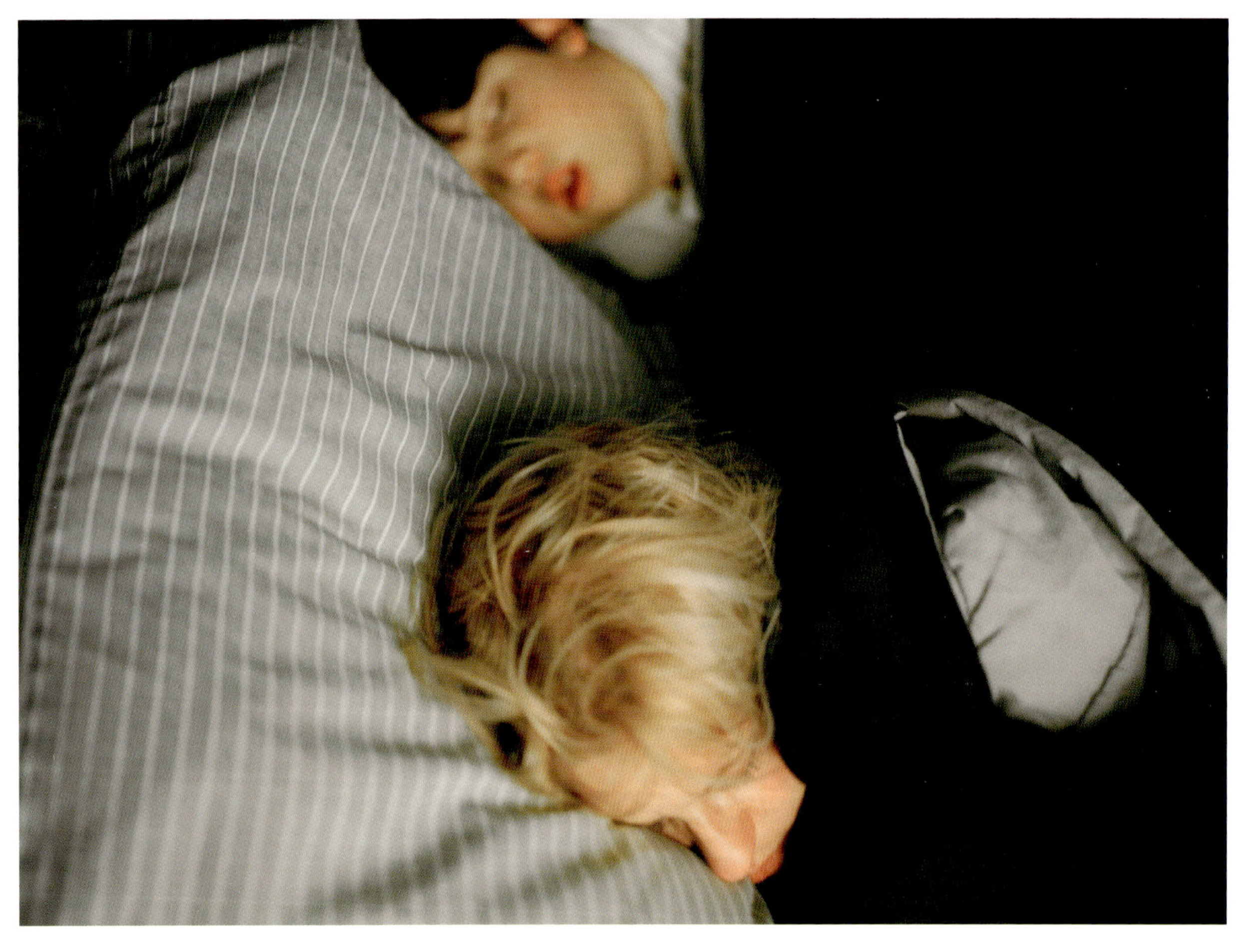

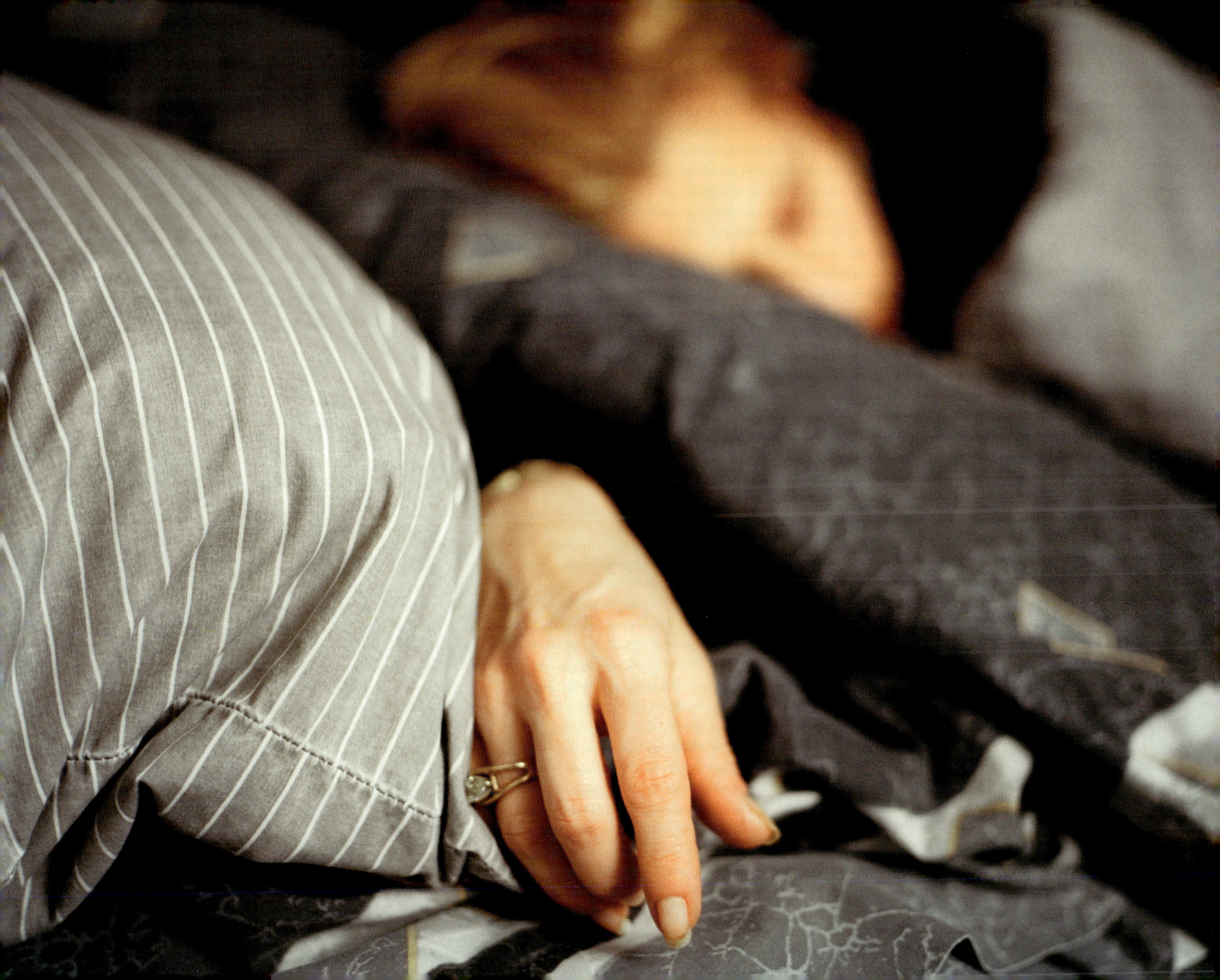

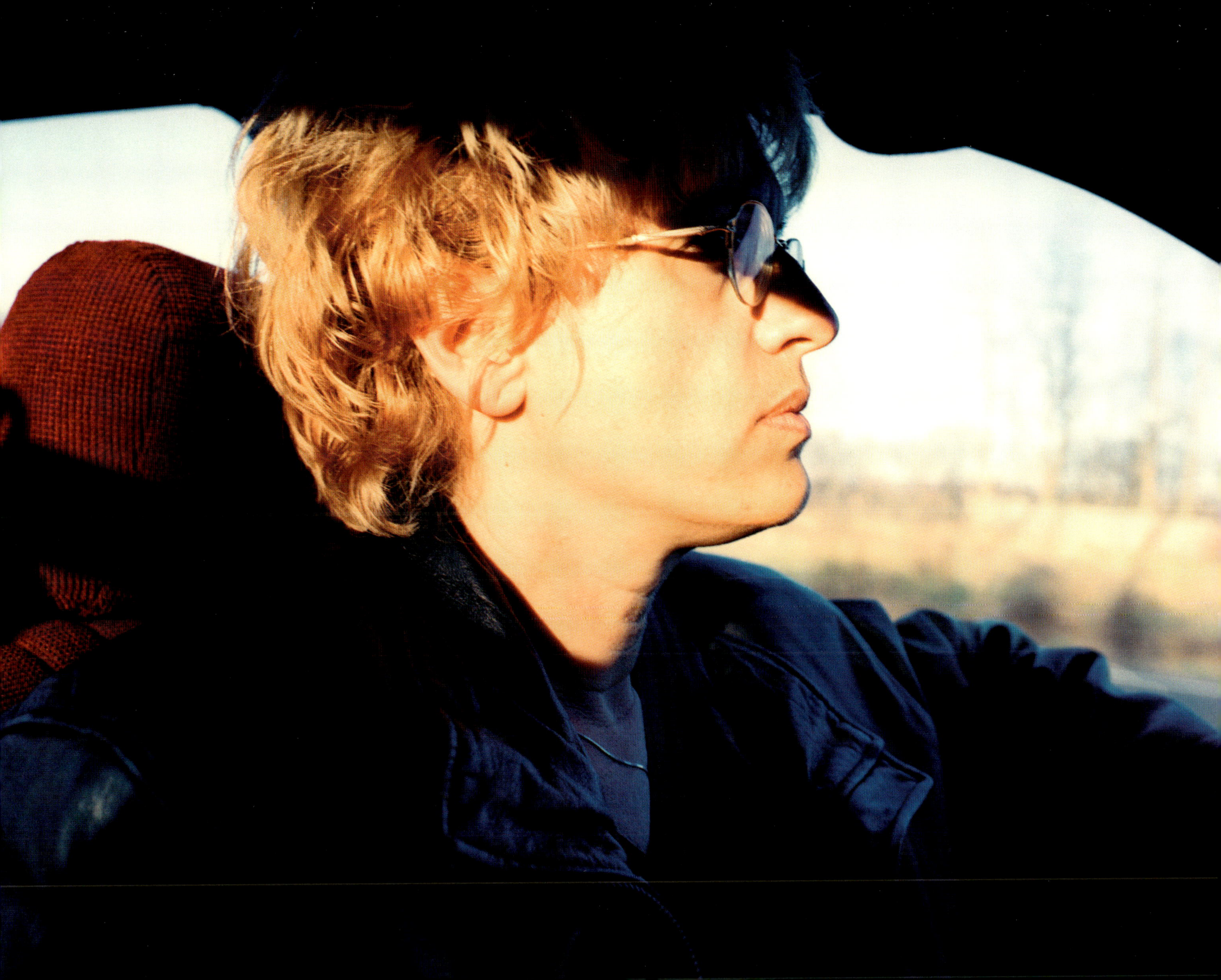

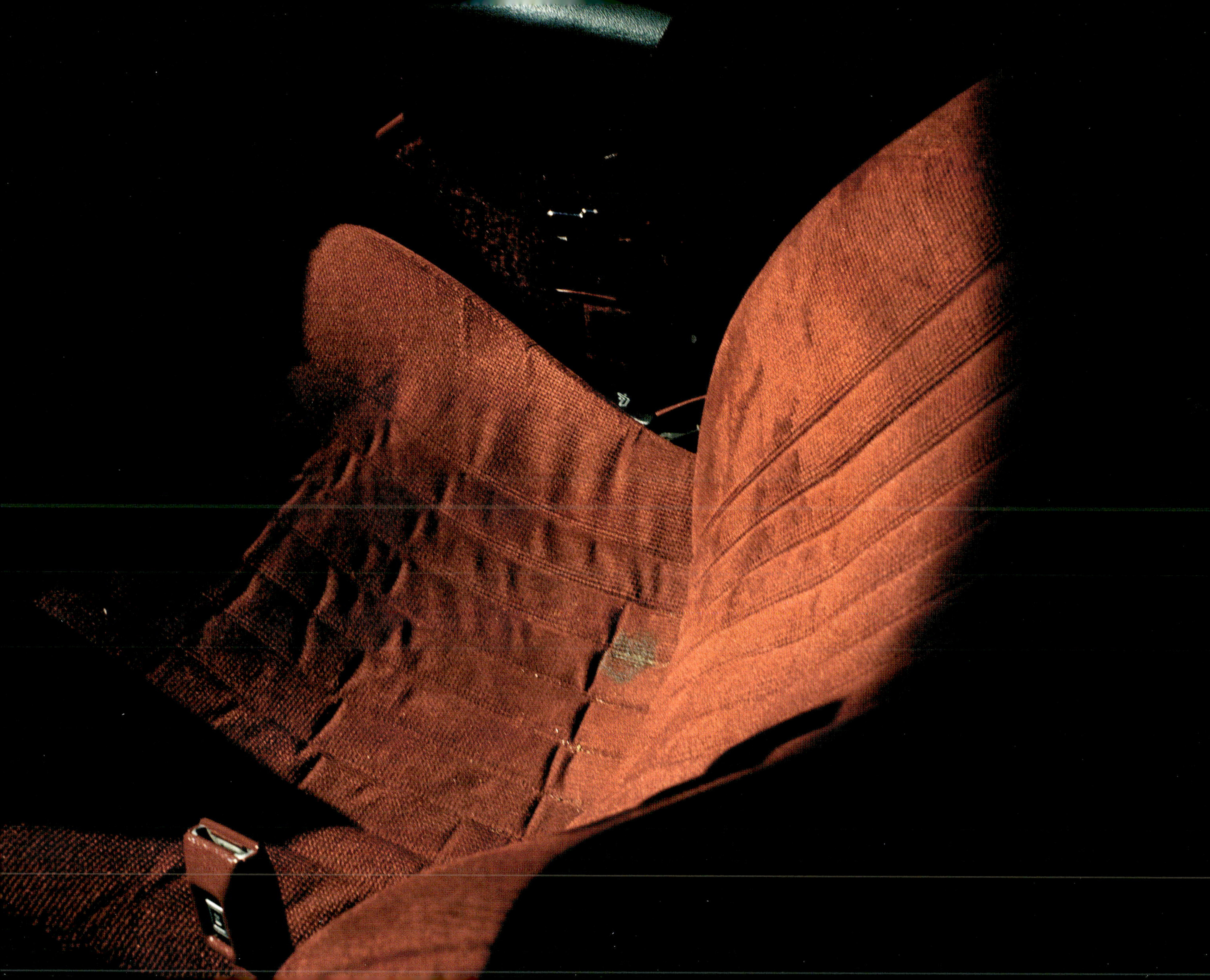

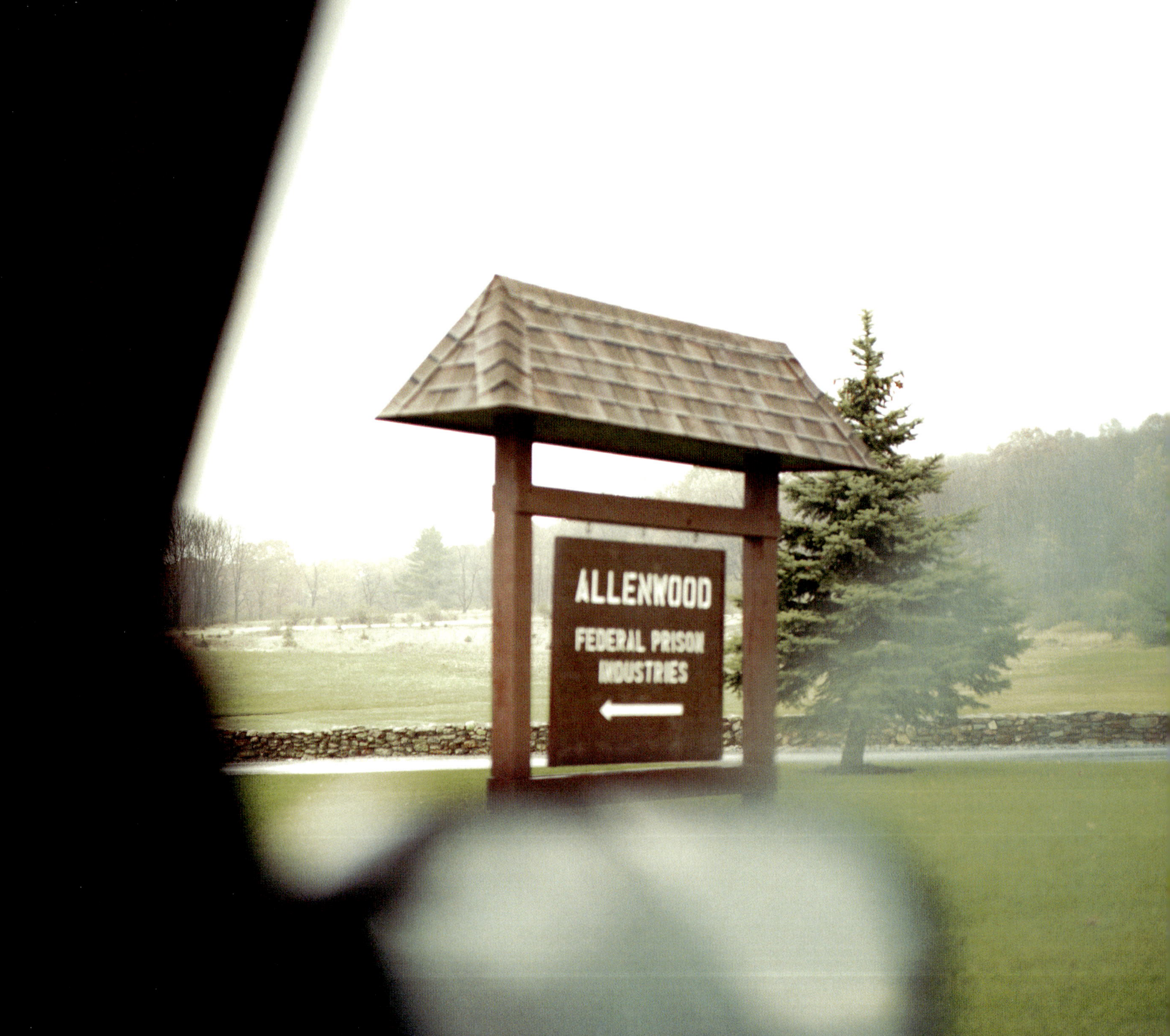

ALLENWOOD
FEDERAL PRISON
INDUSTRIES

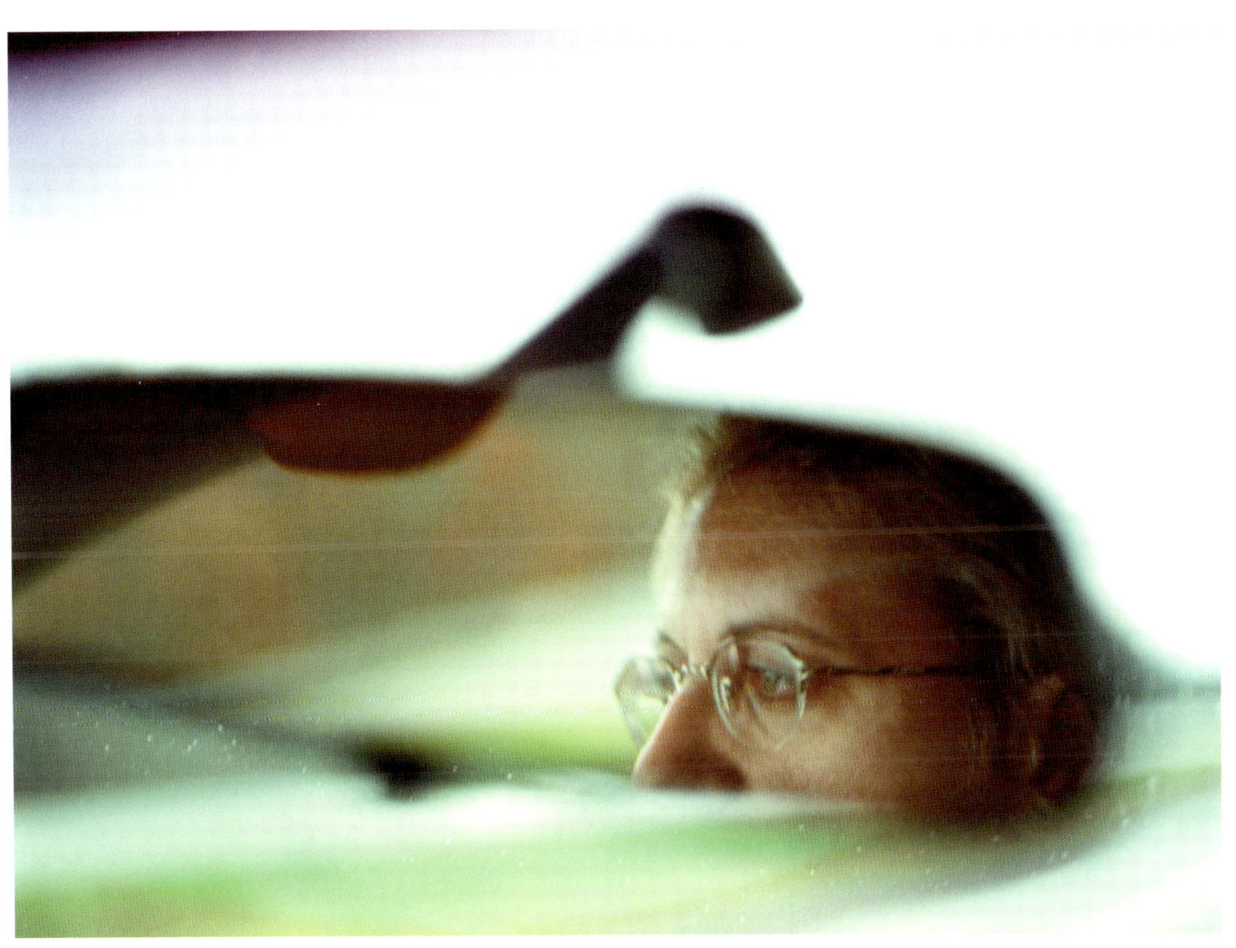

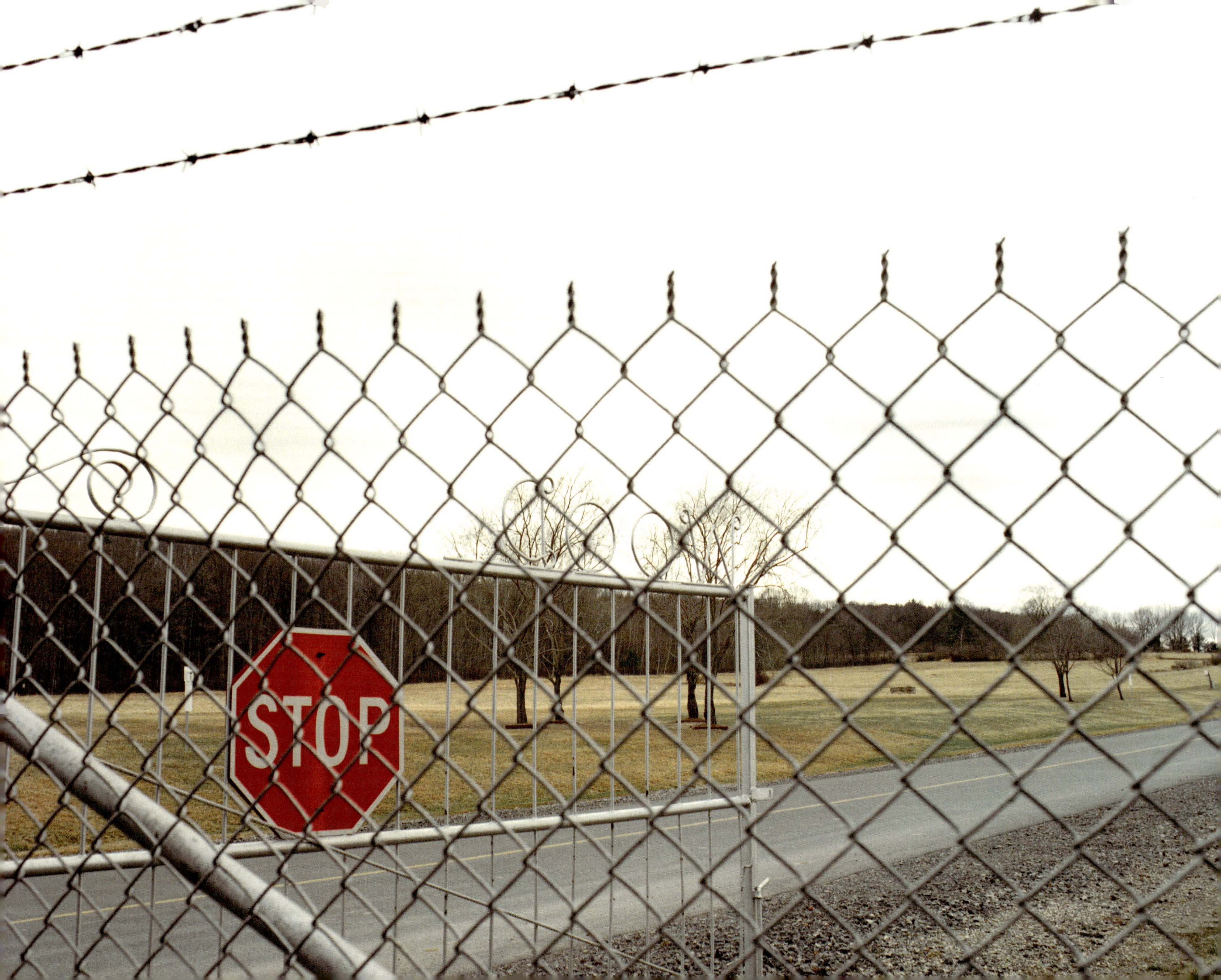
STOP

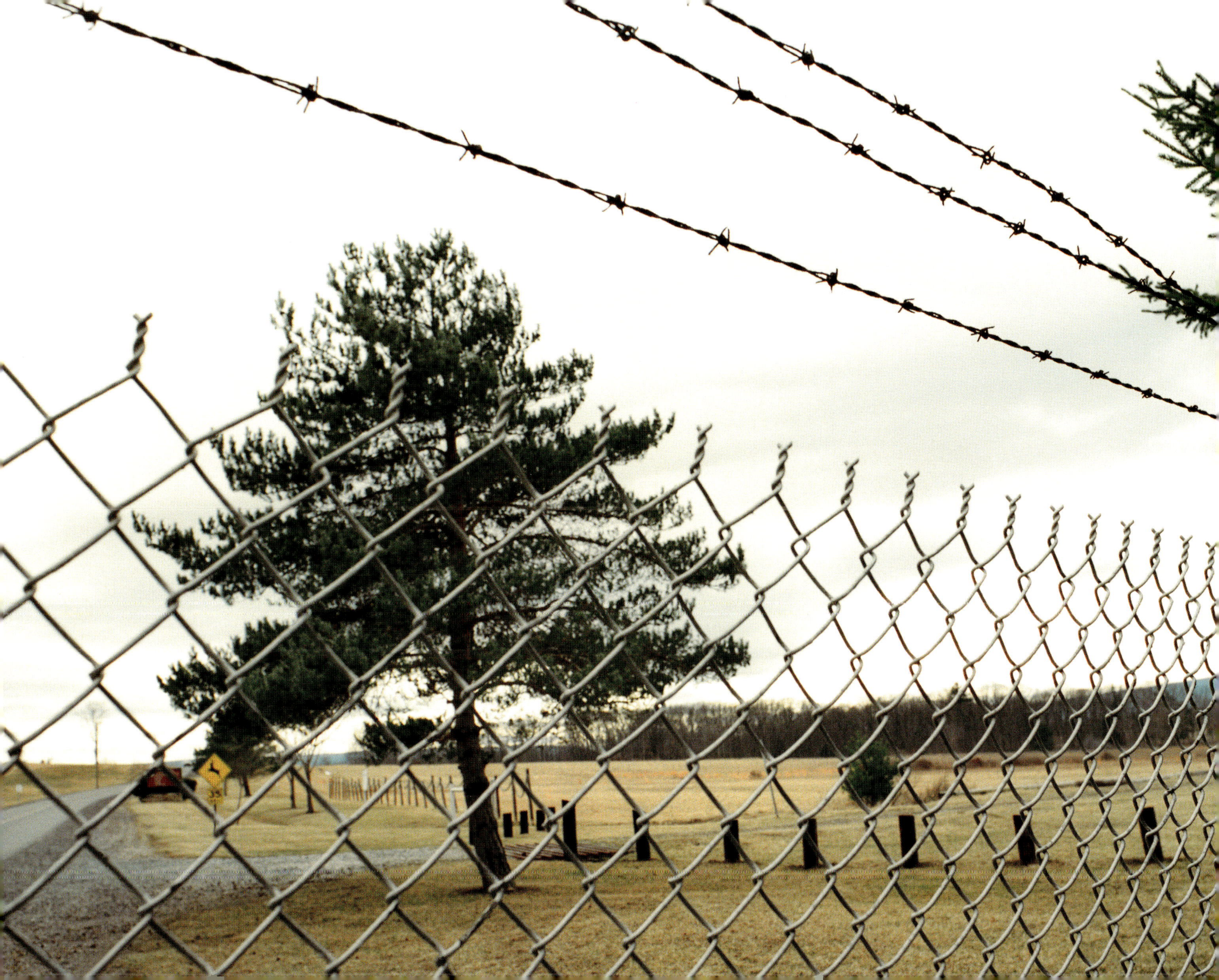

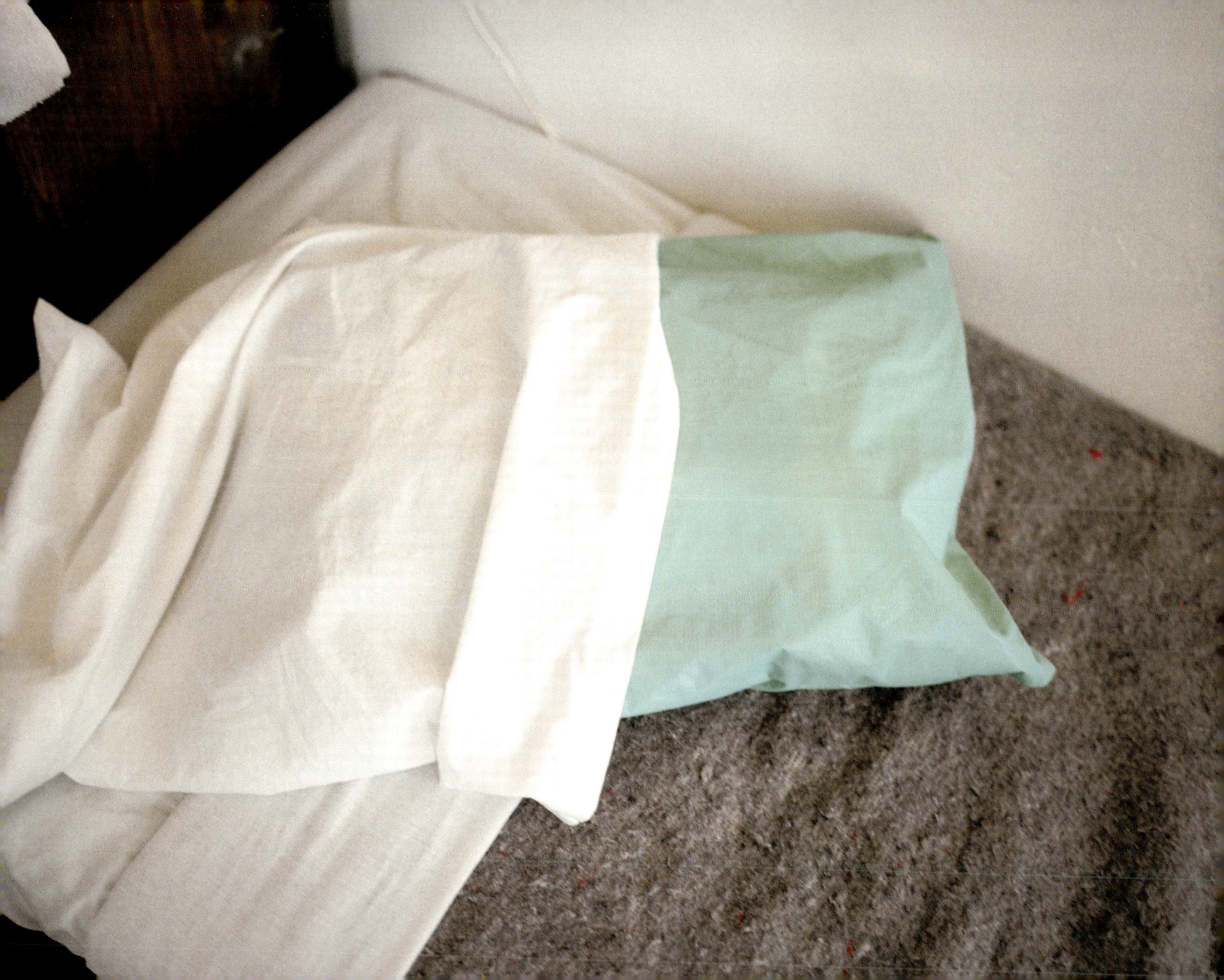

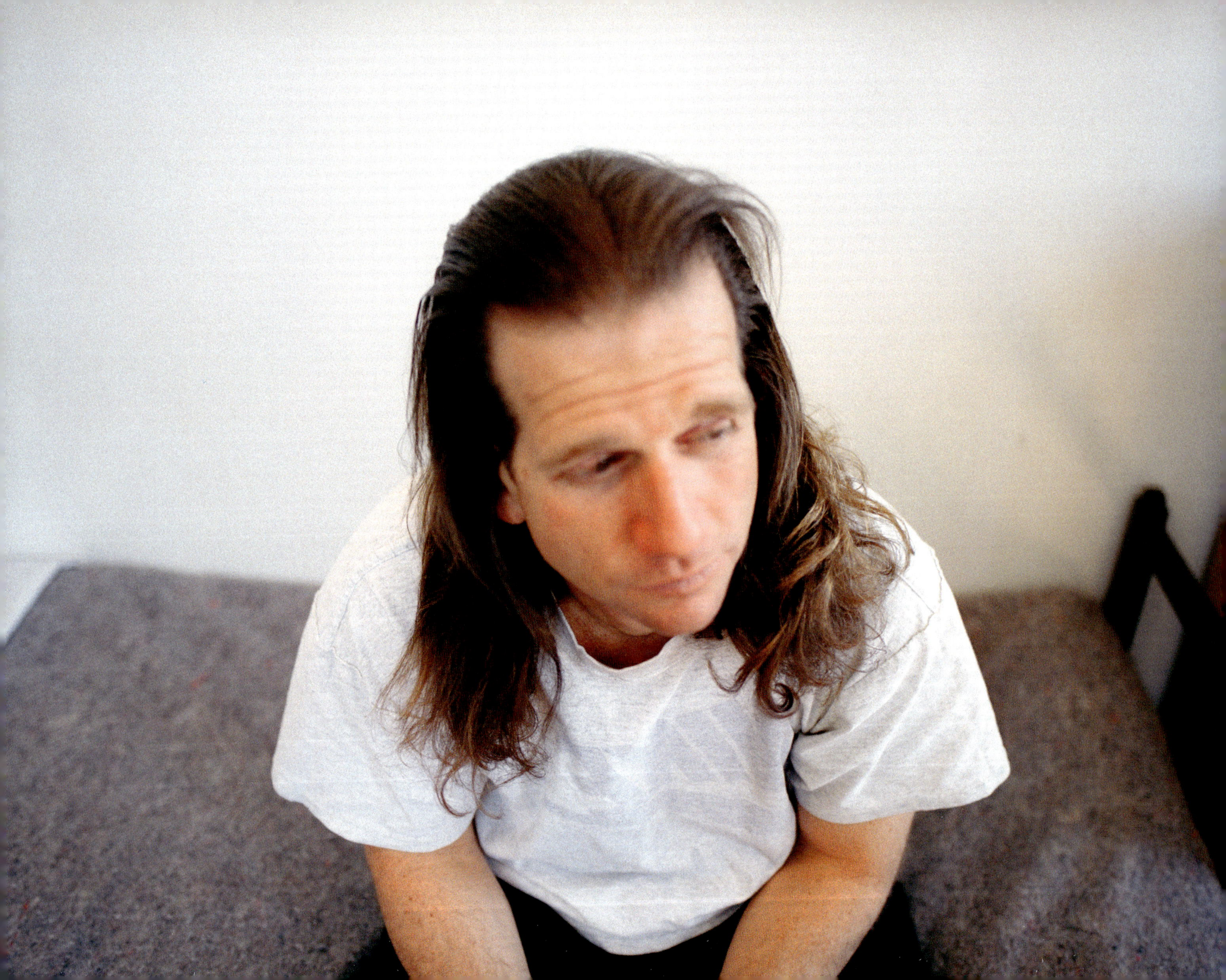

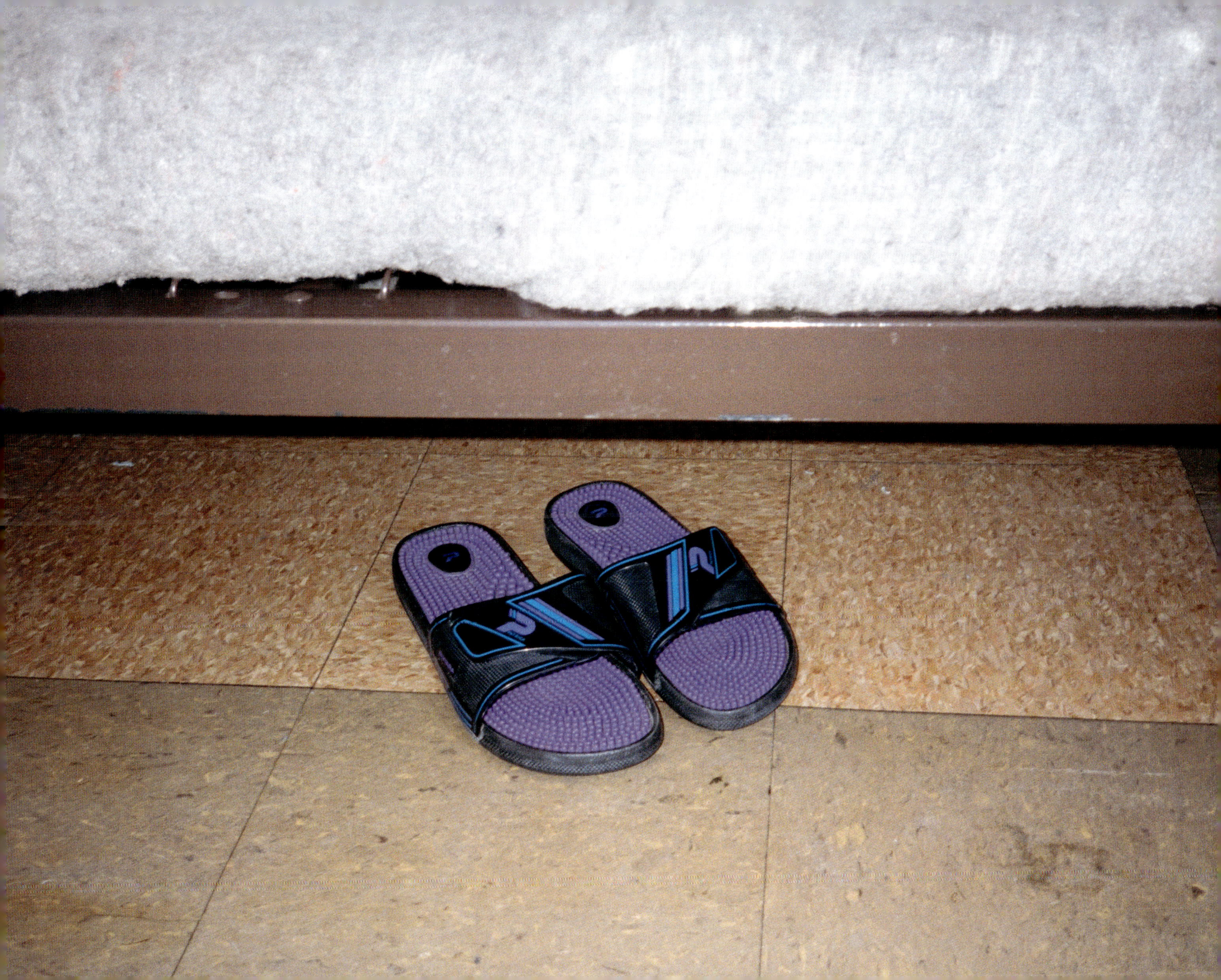

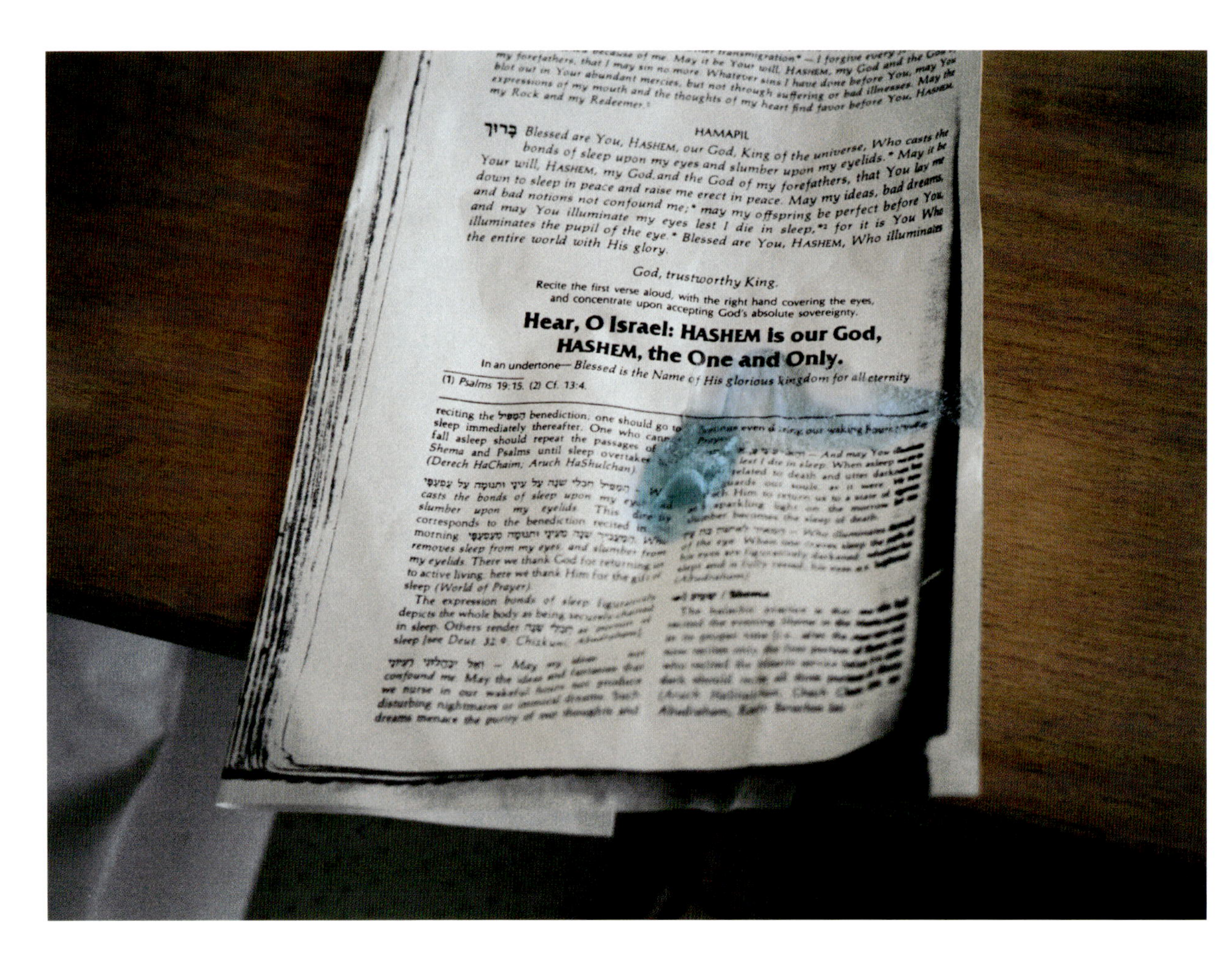

my forefathers, that I may sin no more. Whatever sins I have done before You, may You blot out in Your abundant mercies, but not through suffering or bad illnesses. May the expressions of my mouth and the thoughts of my heart find favor before You, HASHEM, my Rock and my Redeemer.¹

HAMAPIL

בָּרוּךְ Blessed are You, HASHEM, our God, King of the universe, Who casts the bonds of sleep upon my eyes and slumber upon my eyelids. * May it be Your will, HASHEM, my God, and the God of my forefathers, that You lay me down to sleep in peace and raise me erect in peace. May my ideas, bad dreams, and bad notions not confound me; * may my offspring be perfect before You, and may You illuminate my eyes lest I die in sleep,*² for it is You Who illuminates the pupil of the eye. * Blessed are You, HASHEM, Who illuminates the entire world with His glory.

God, trustworthy King.

Recite the first verse aloud, with the right hand covering the eyes, and concentrate upon accepting God's absolute sovereignty.

Hear, O Israel: HASHEM is our God, HASHEM, the One and Only.

In an undertone— Blessed is the Name of His glorious kingdom for all eternity

(1) Psalms 19:15. (2) Cf. 13:4.

reciting the הַמַּפִּיל benediction, one should go to sleep immediately thereafter. One who cannot fall asleep should repeat the passages of Shema and Psalms until sleep overtakes him (Derech HaChaim; Aruch HaShulchan).

הַמַּפִּיל חֶבְלֵי שֵׁנָה עַל עֵינַי וּתְנוּמָה עַל עַפְעַפָּי — casts the bonds of sleep upon my eyes and slumber upon my eyelids. This directly corresponds to the benediction recited in the morning הַמַּעֲבִיר שֵׁנָה מֵעֵינַי וּתְנוּמָה מֵעַפְעַפָּי, Who removes sleep from my eyes and slumber from my eyelids. There we thank God for returning us to active living; here we thank Him for the gift of sleep (World of Prayer).

The expression bonds of sleep figuratively depicts the whole body as being securely chained in sleep. Others render חֶבְלֵי שֵׁנָה as portions of sleep [see Deut. 32:9; Chizkuni, Abudraham].

וְאַל יְבַהֲלוּנִי רַעְיוֹנַי — May my ideas ... not confound me. May the ideas and fantasies that we nurse in our wakeful hours not produce disturbing nightmares or immoral dreams. Such dreams menace the purity of our thoughts and ...

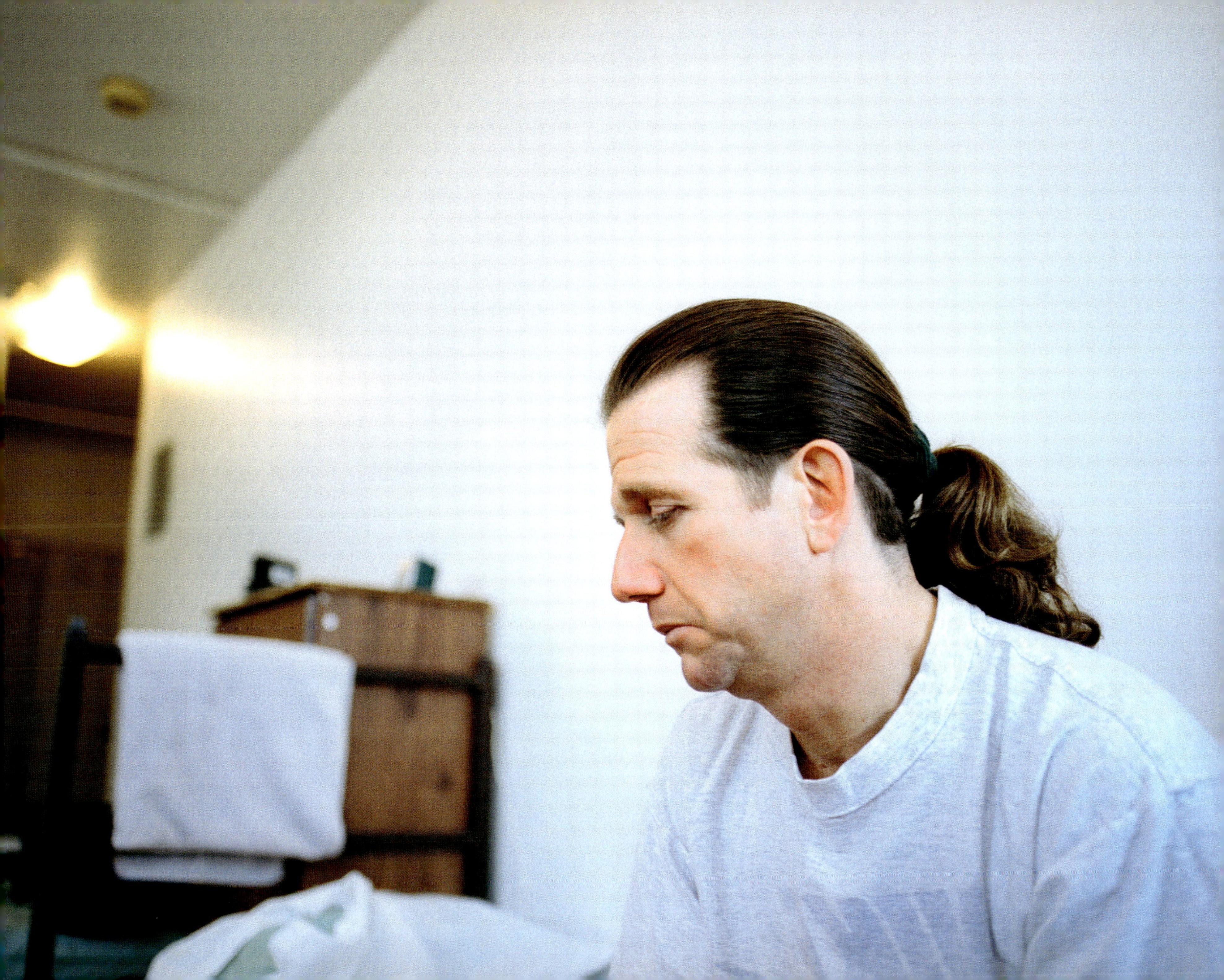

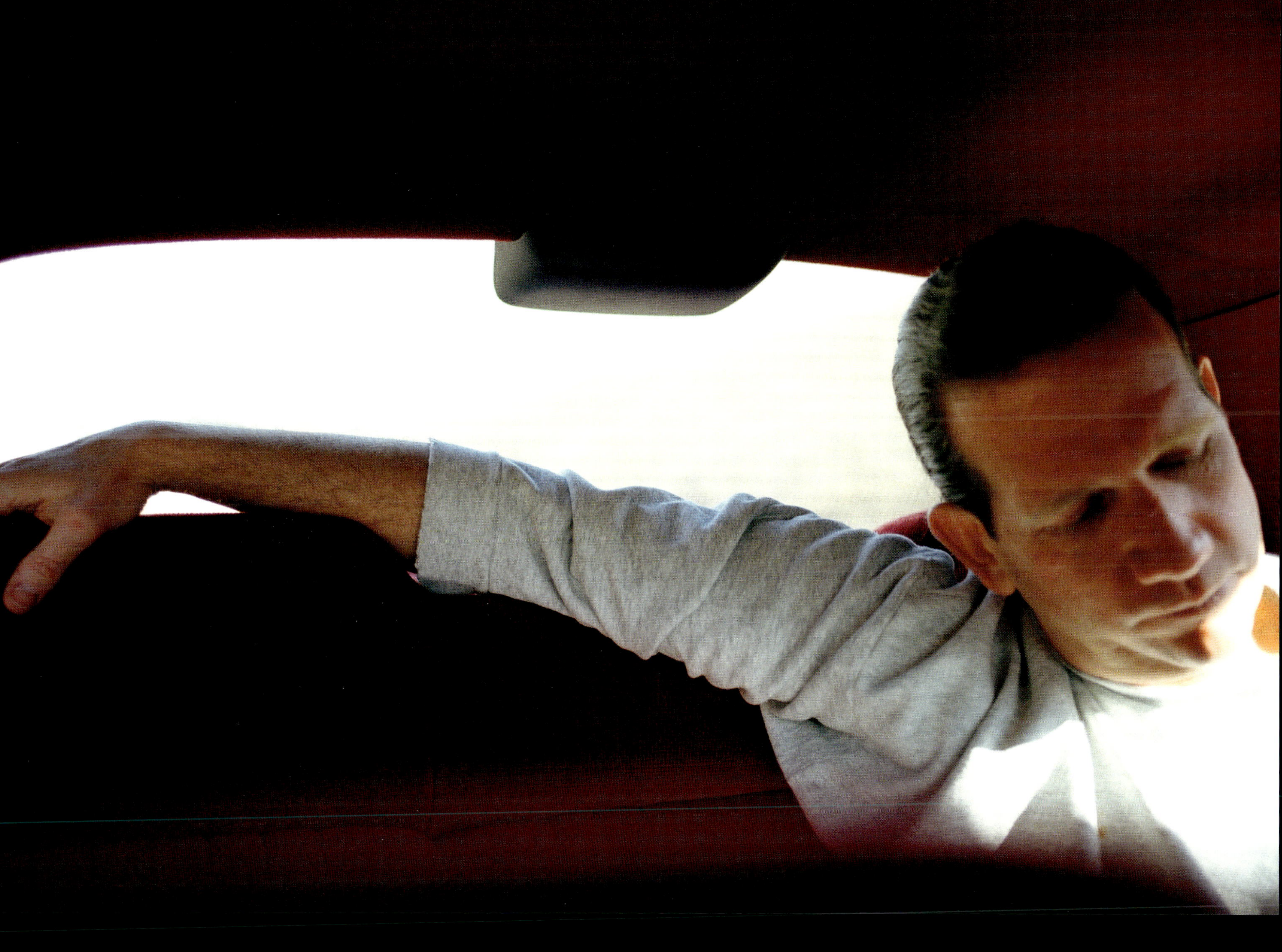

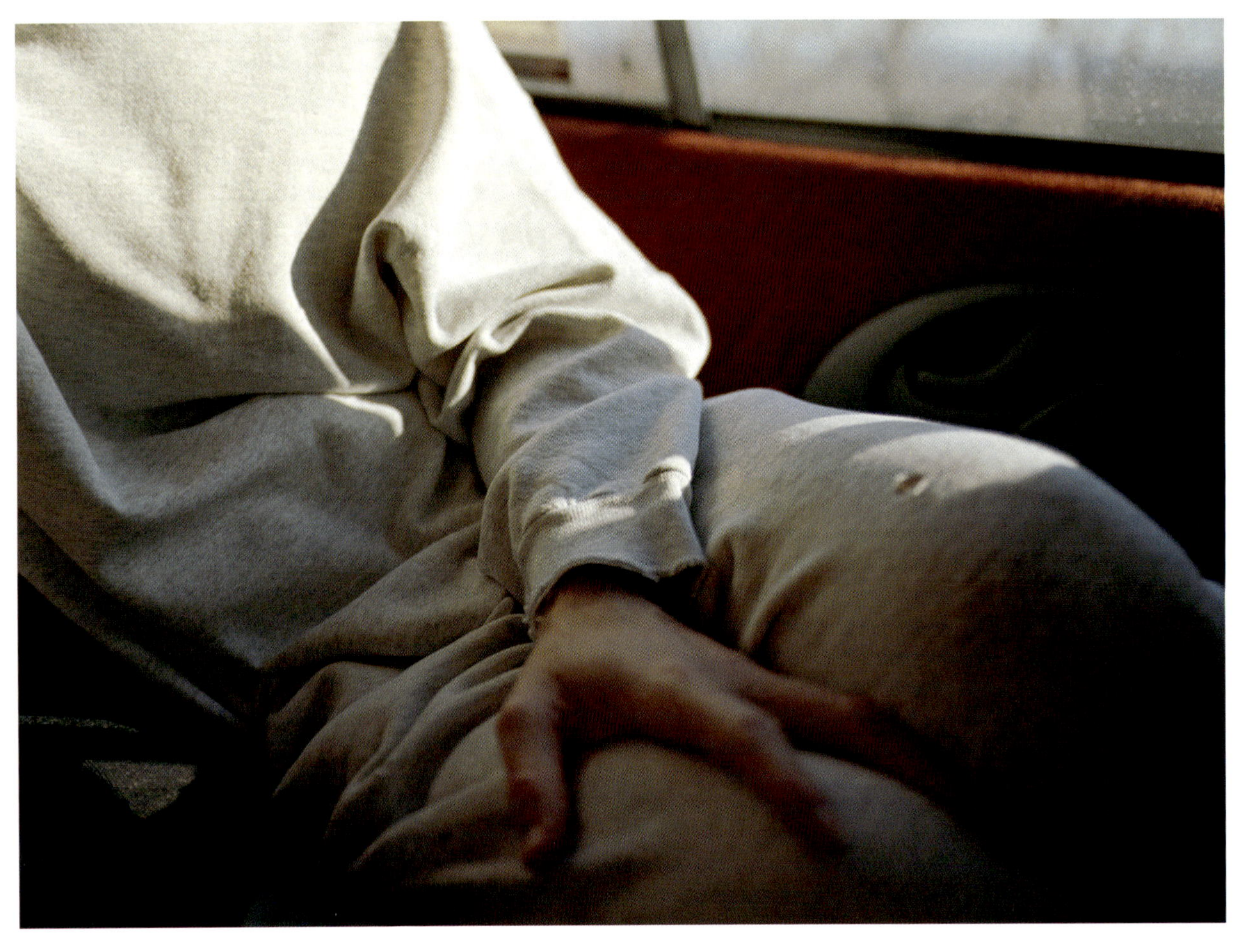

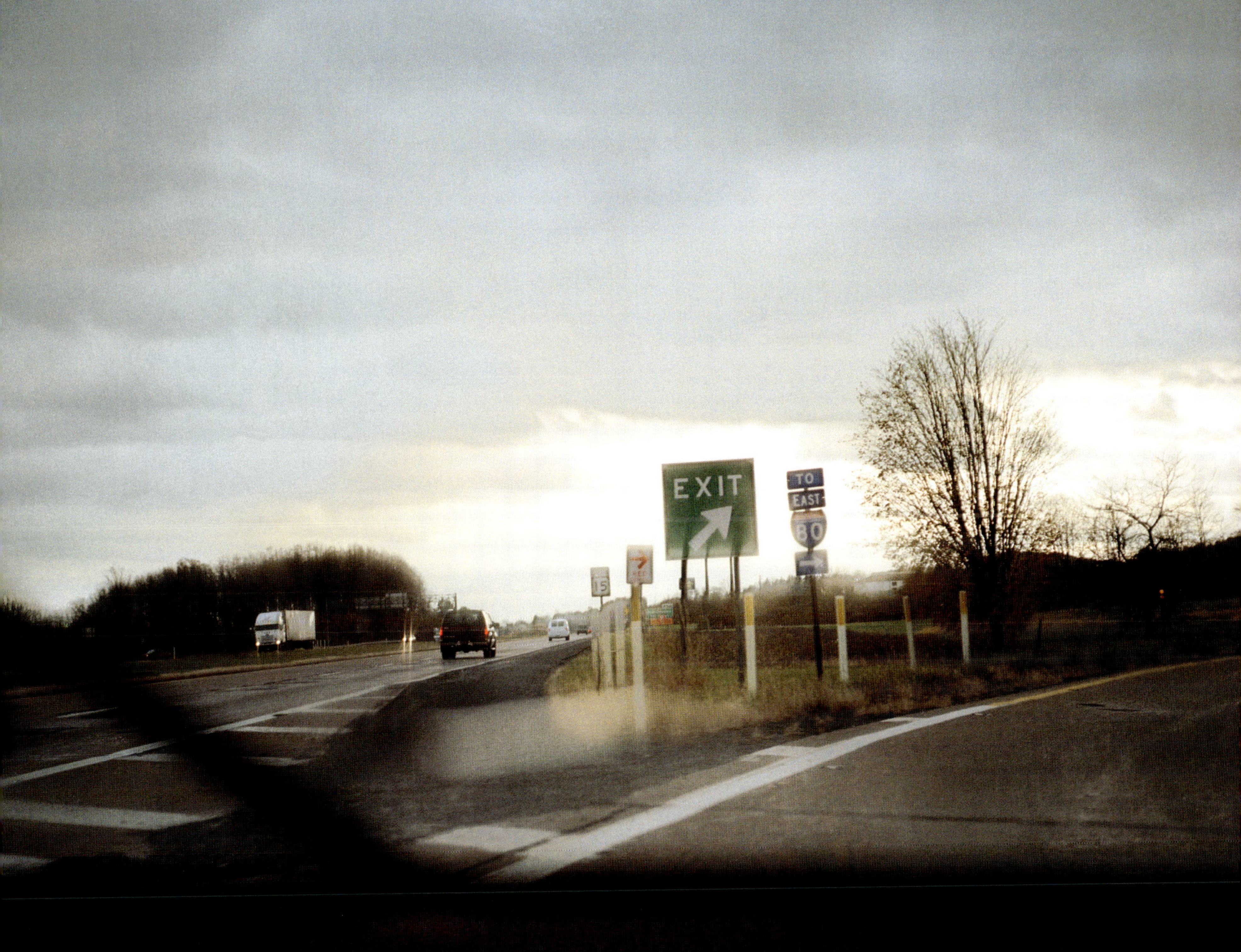

EXIT
TO
EAST
80
15

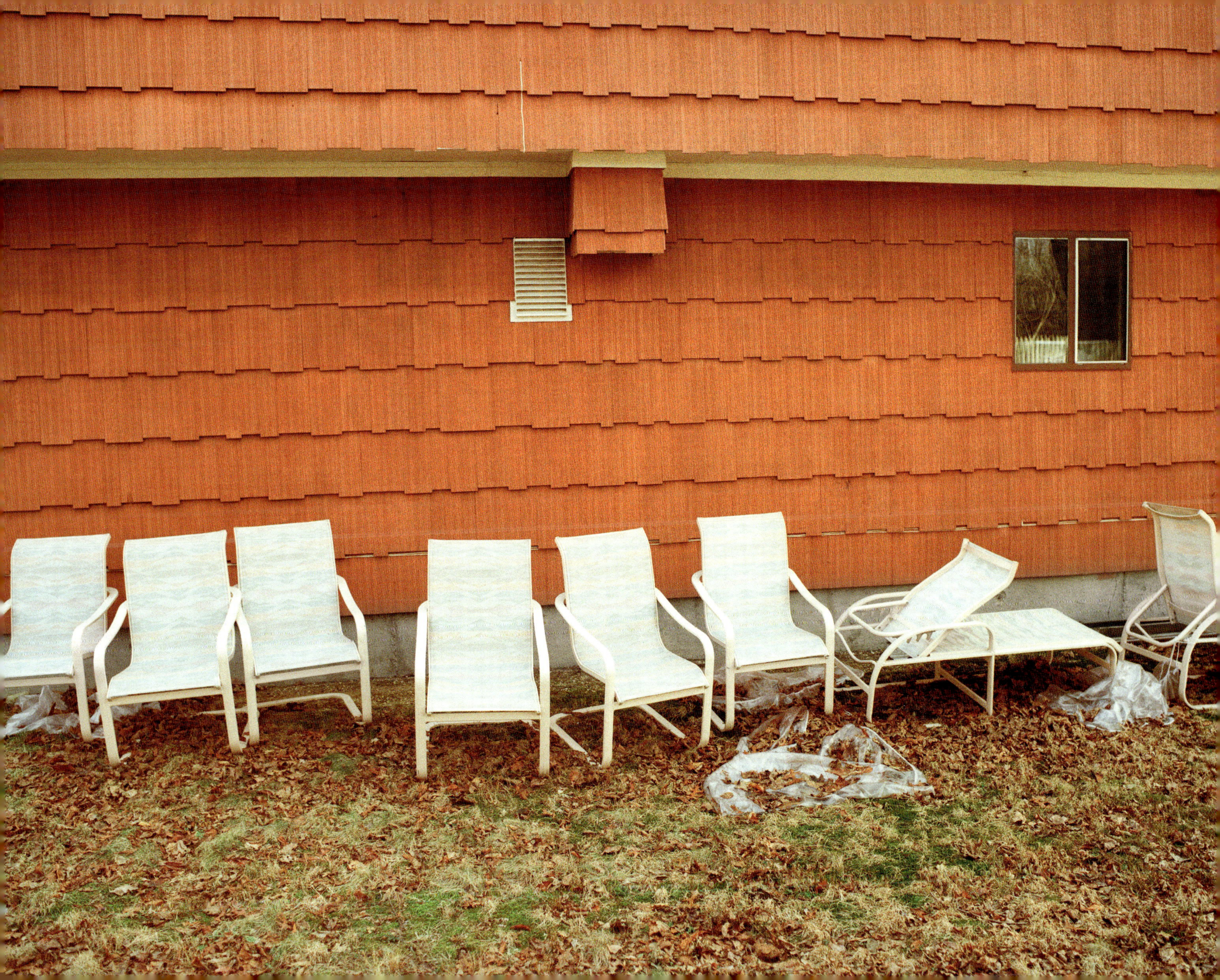

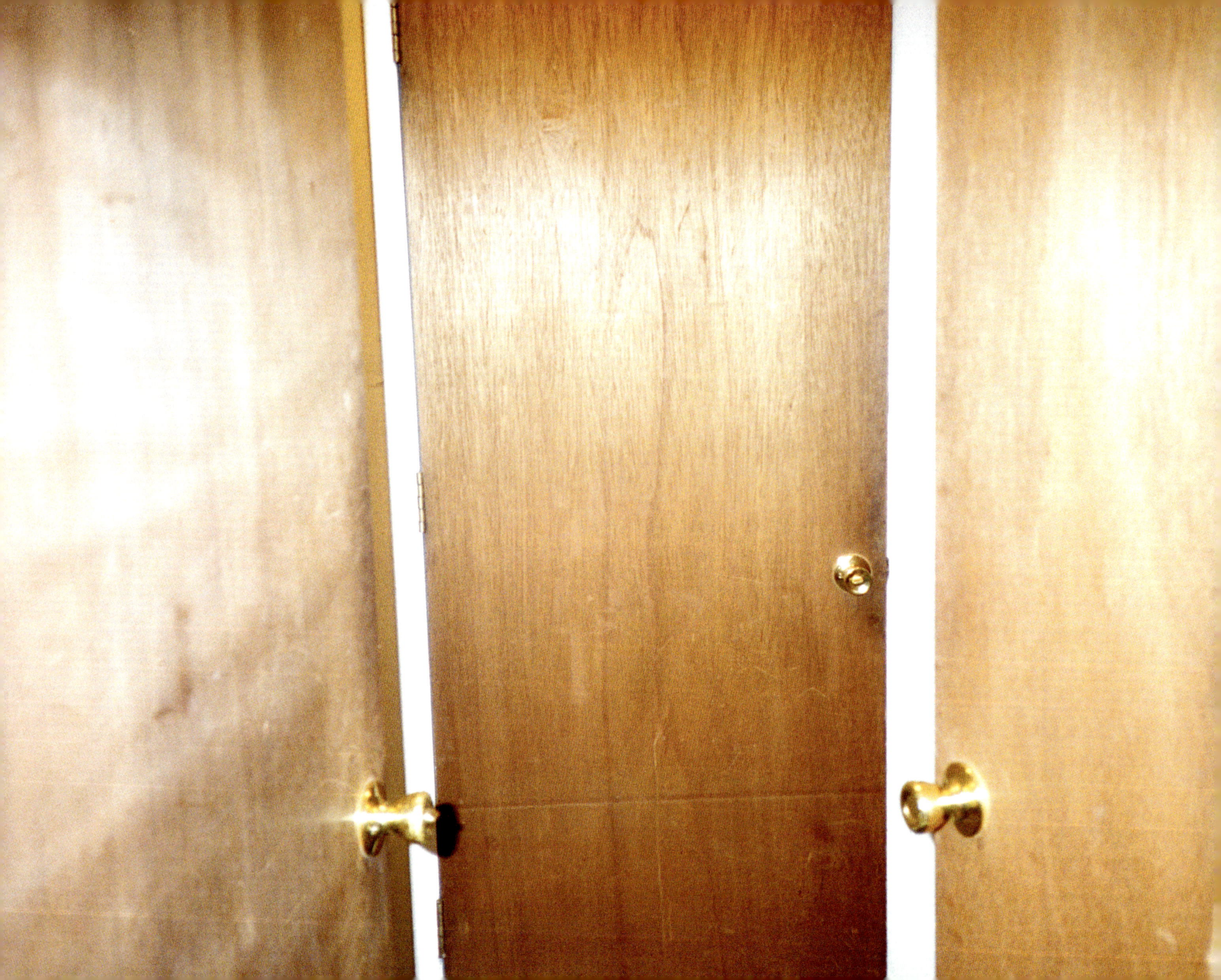

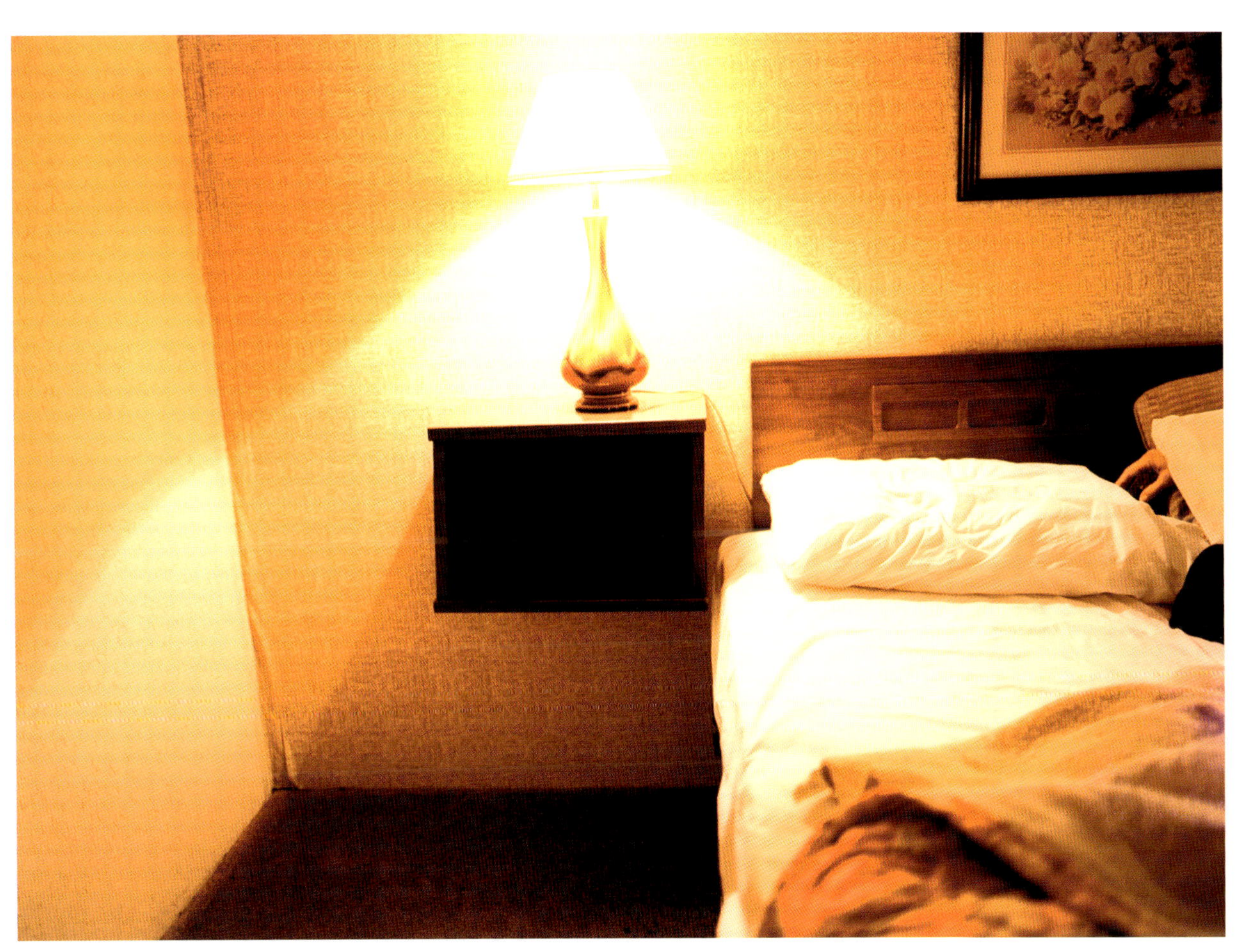

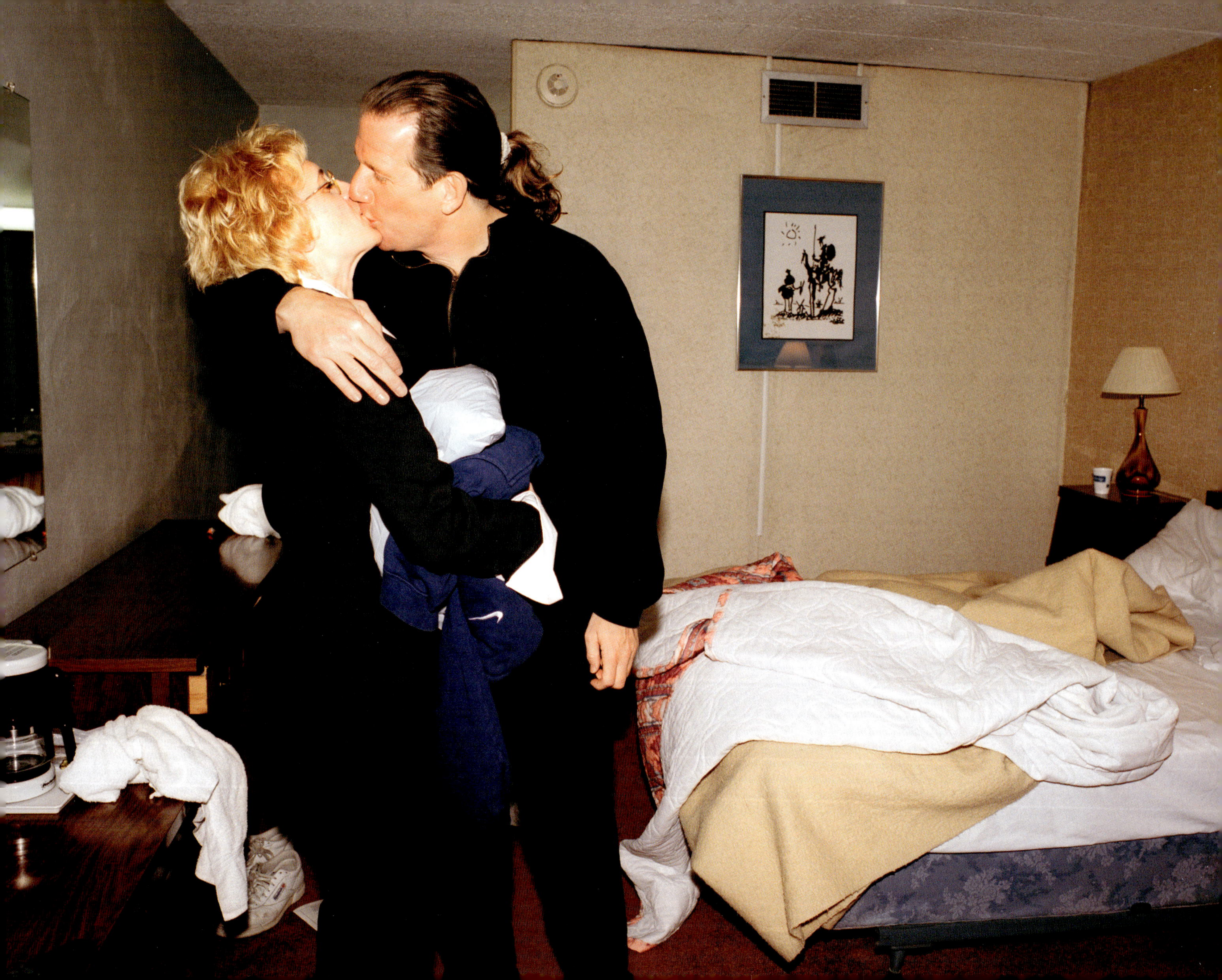

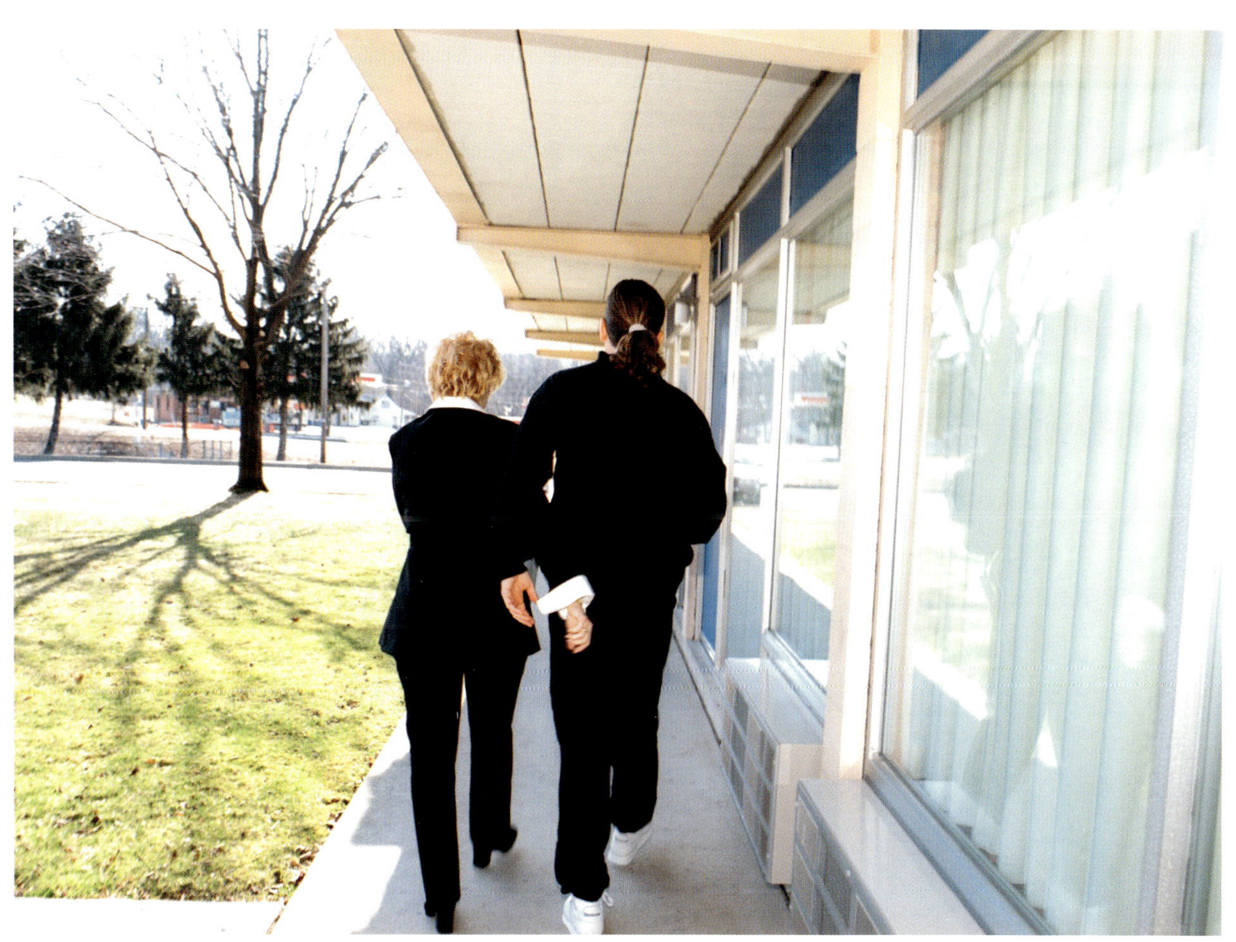

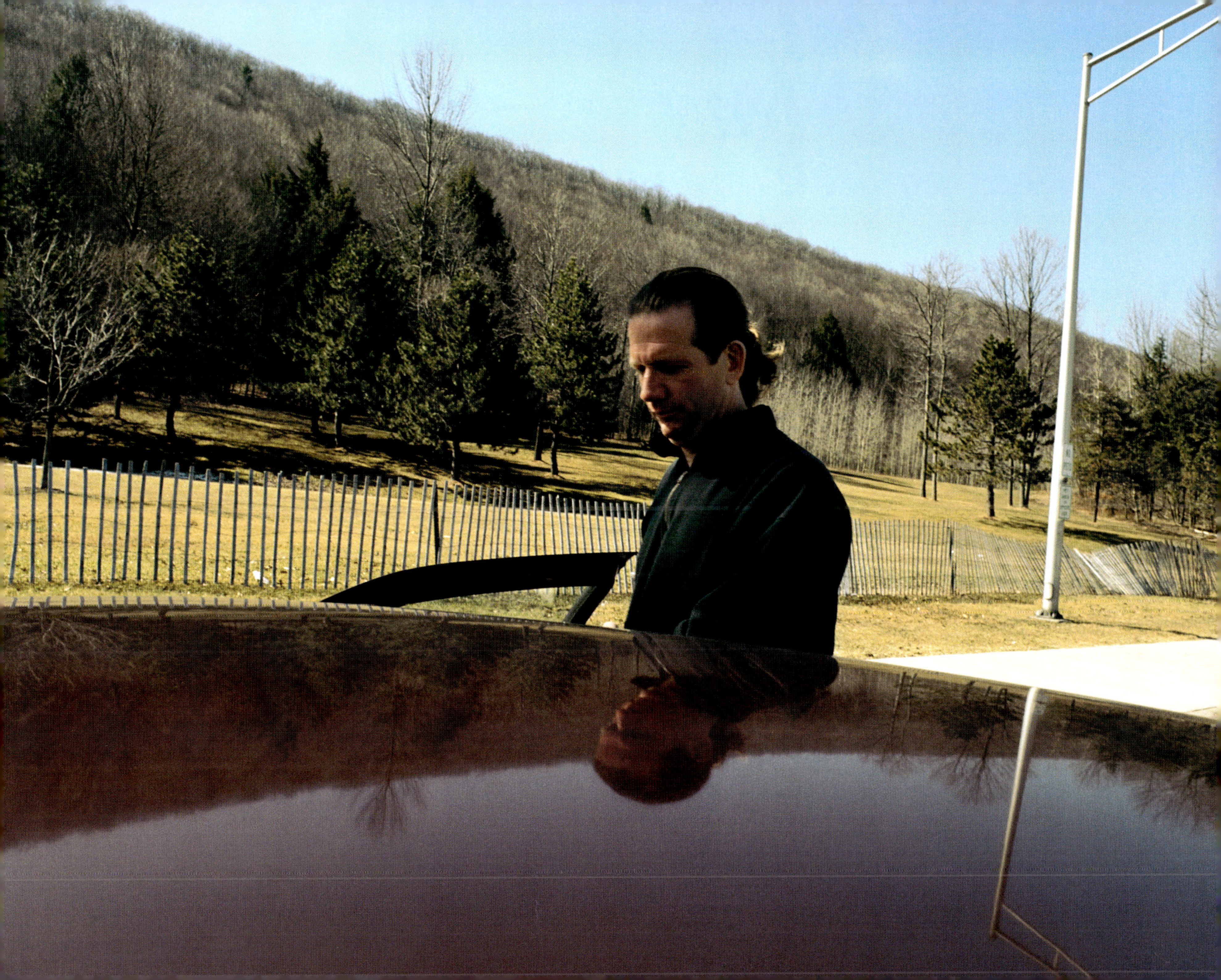

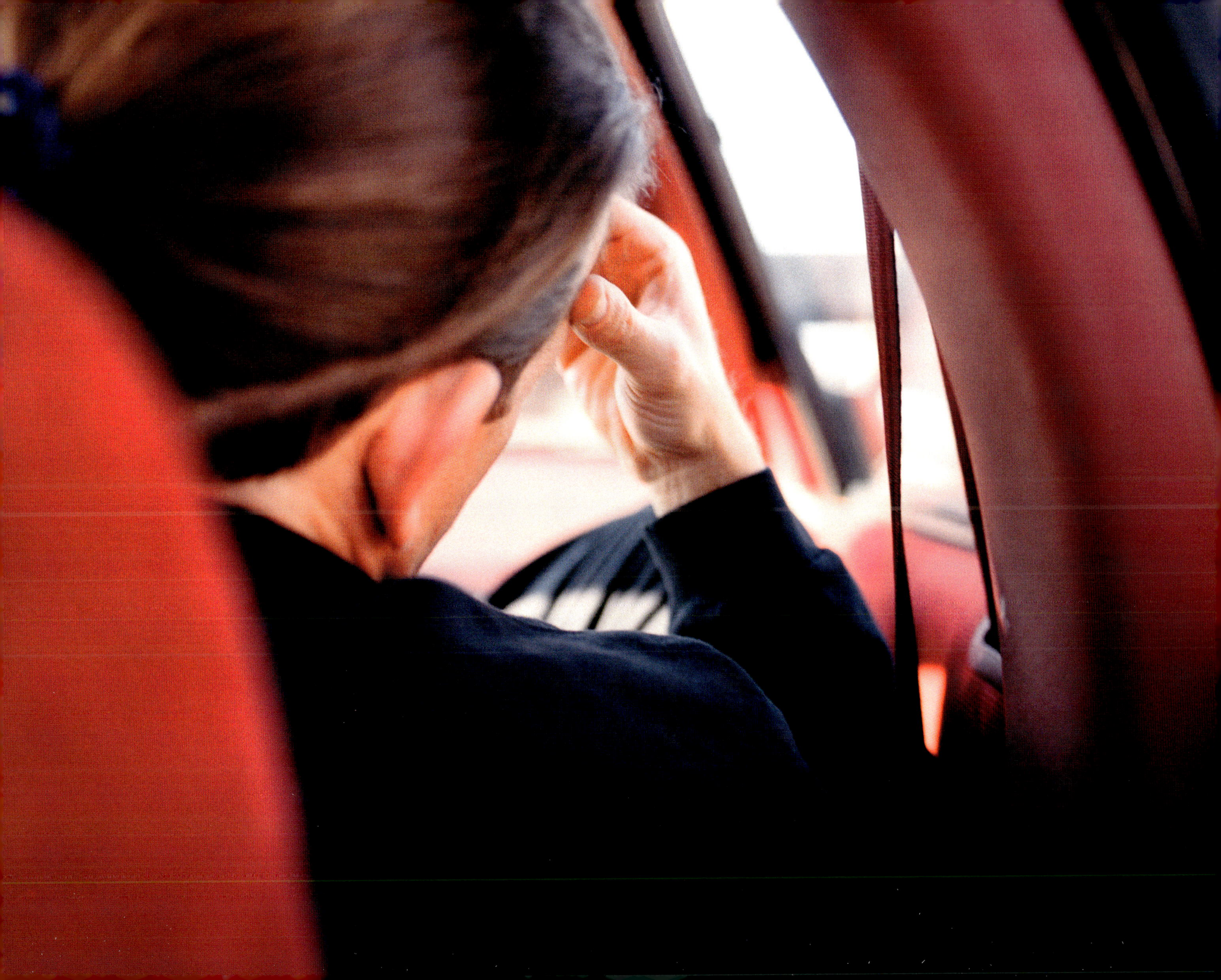

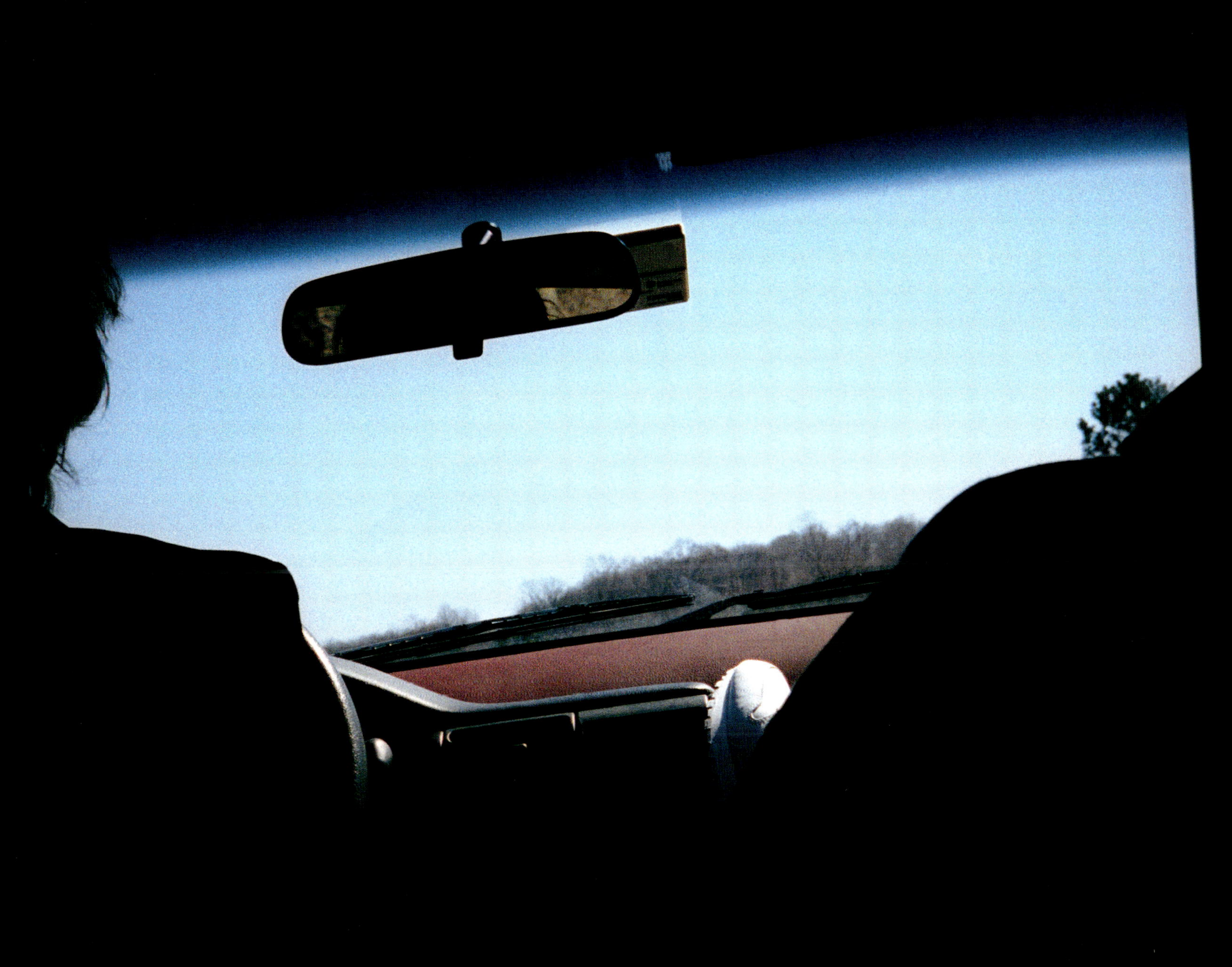

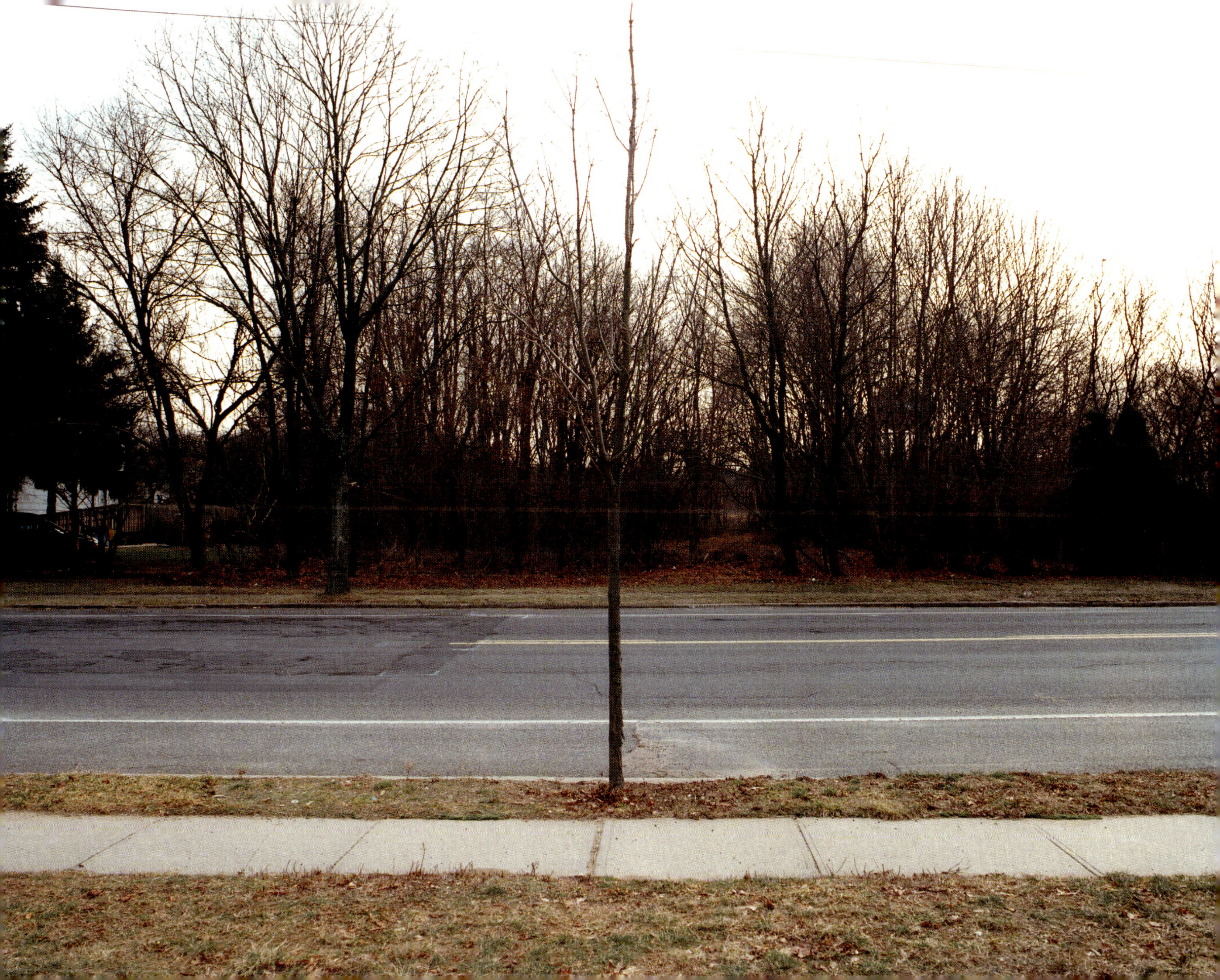

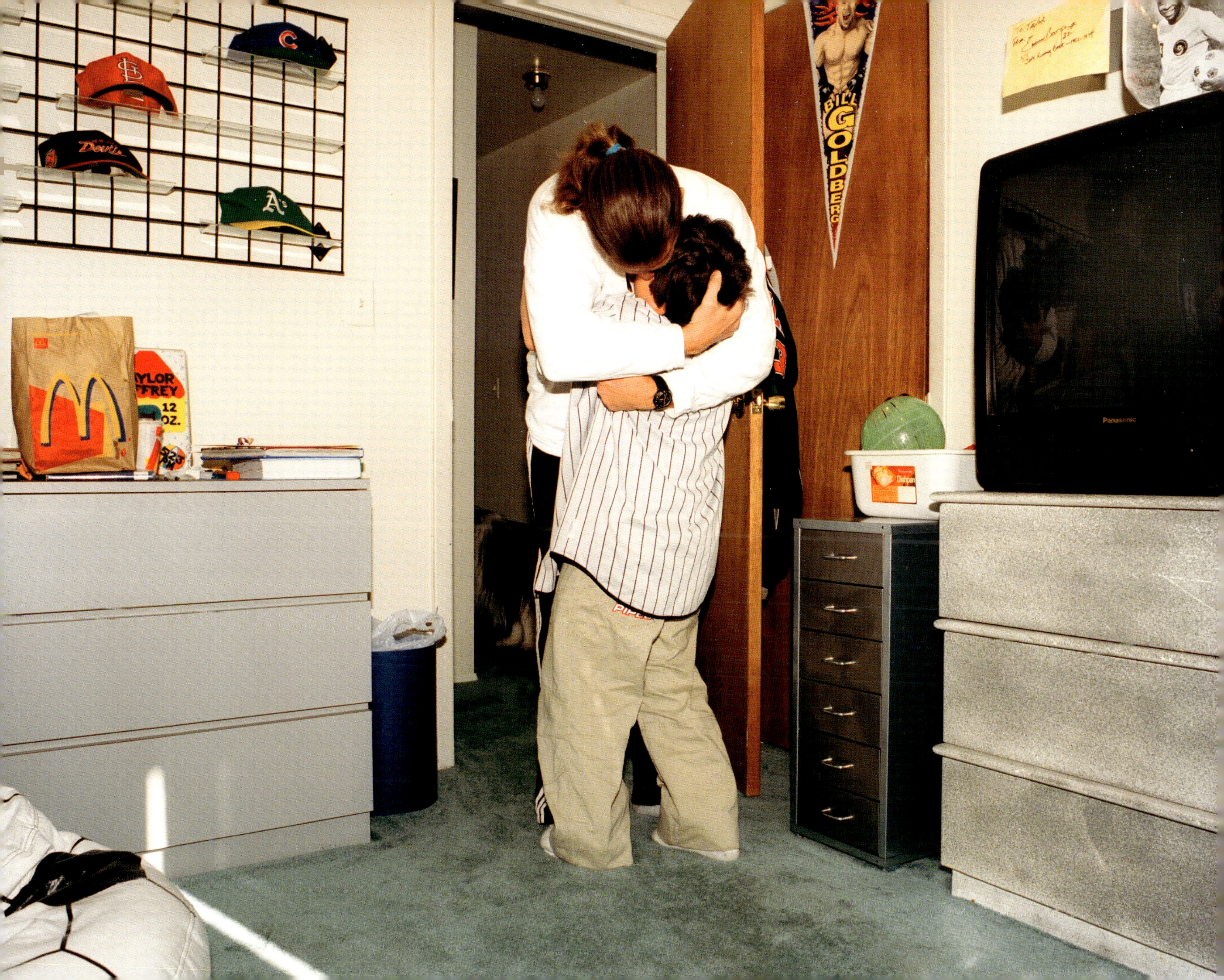

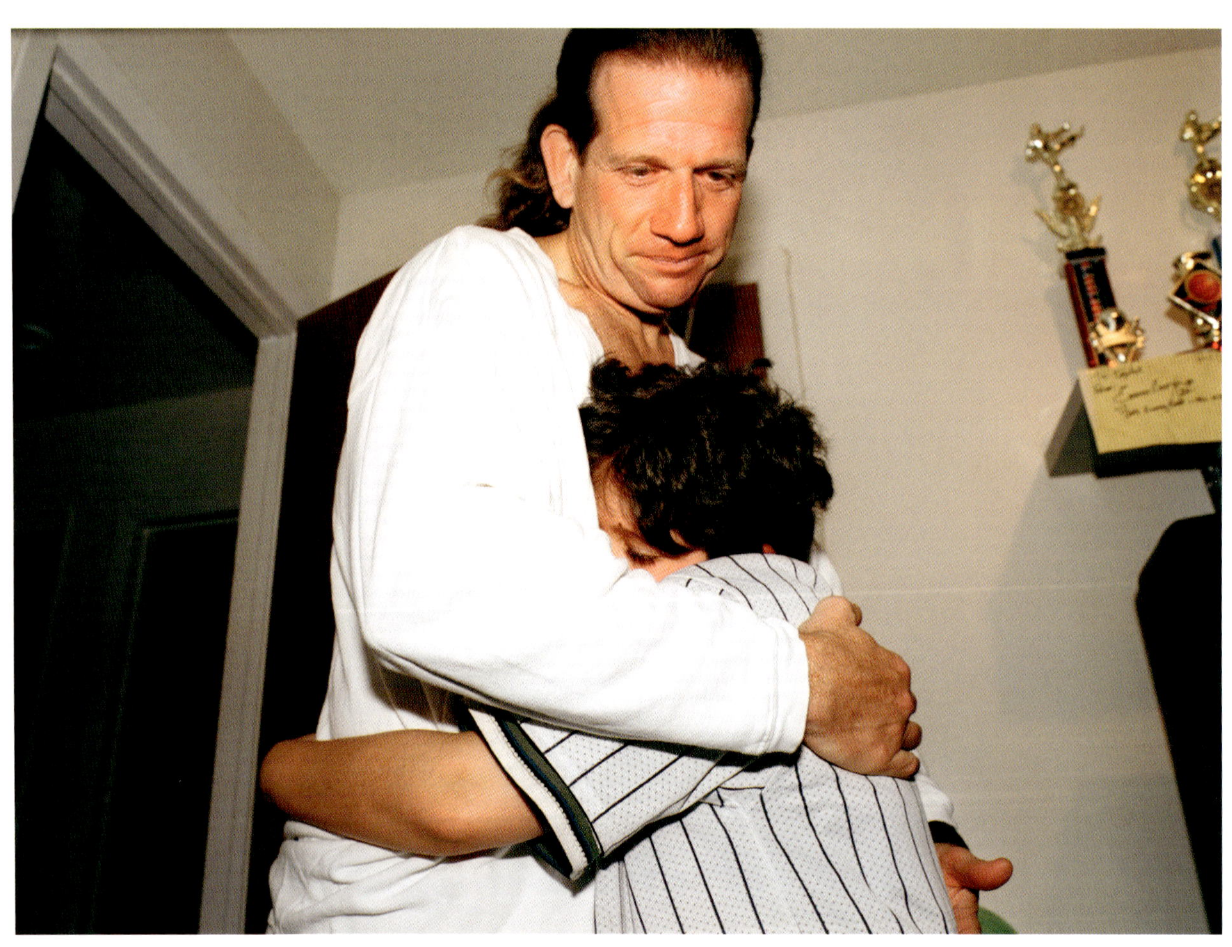

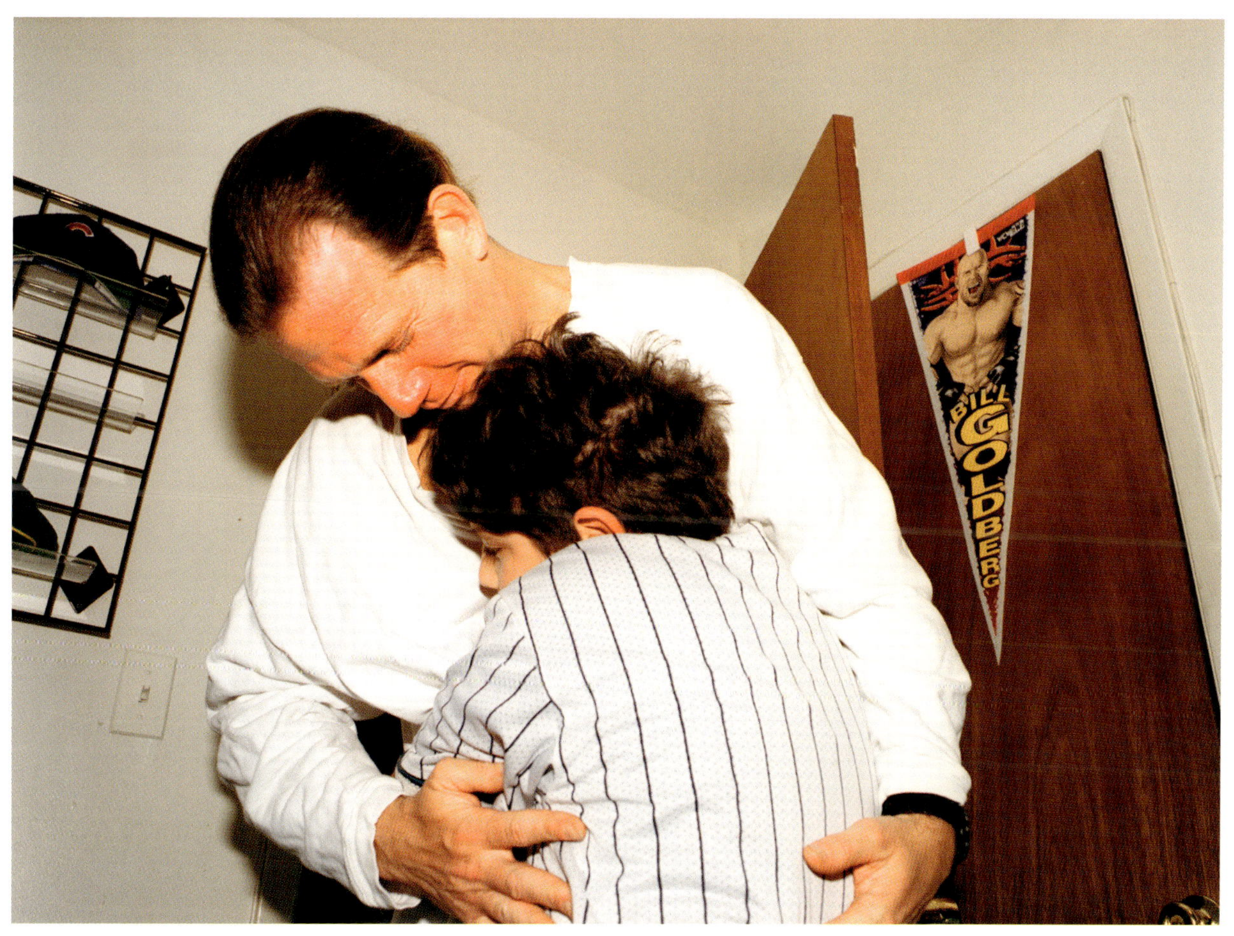
BILL
GOLDBERG

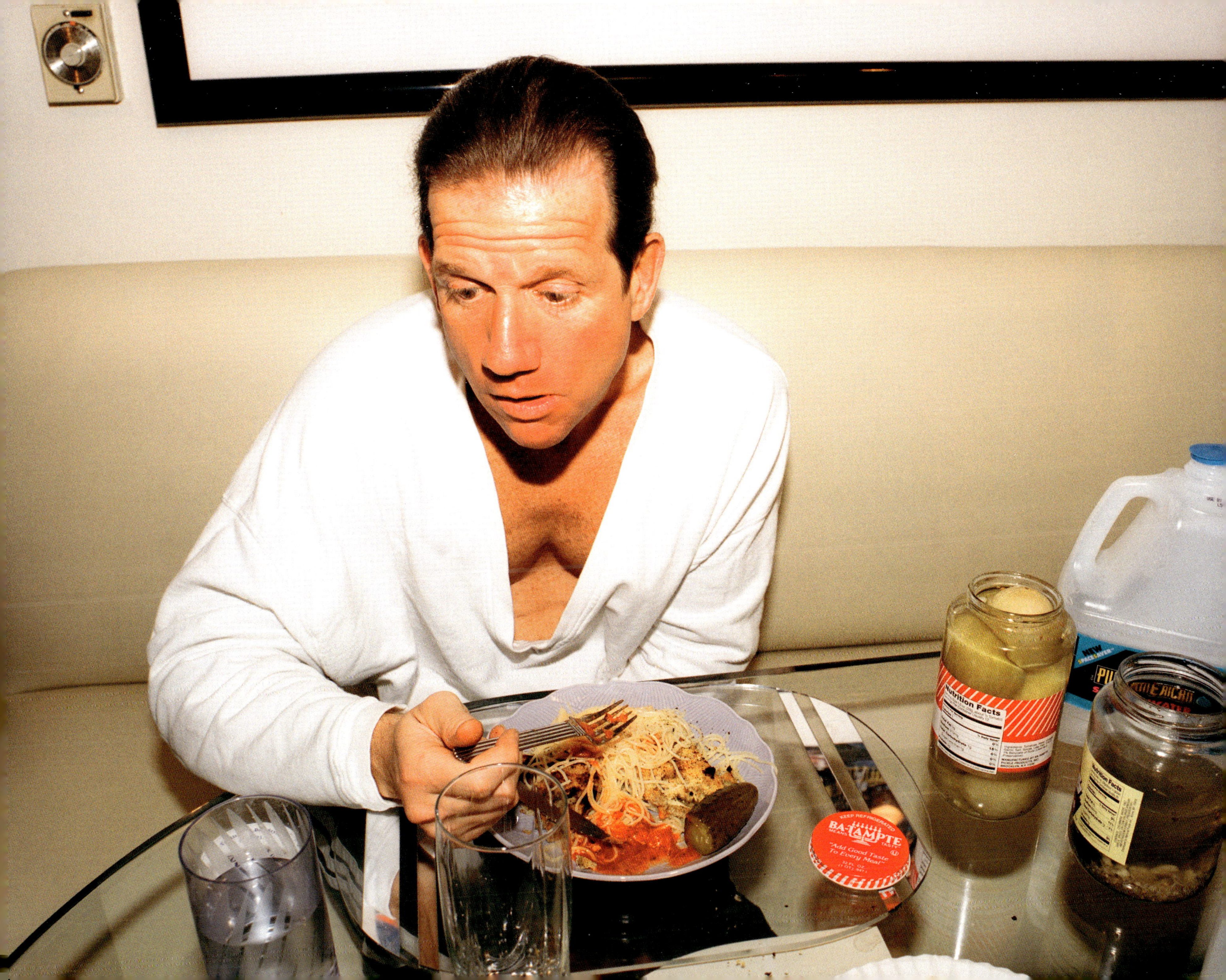

Nutrition Facts
KEEP REFRIGERATED
BA-TAMPTE
BRAND
"Add Good Taste
To Every Meal!"
Nutrition Facts

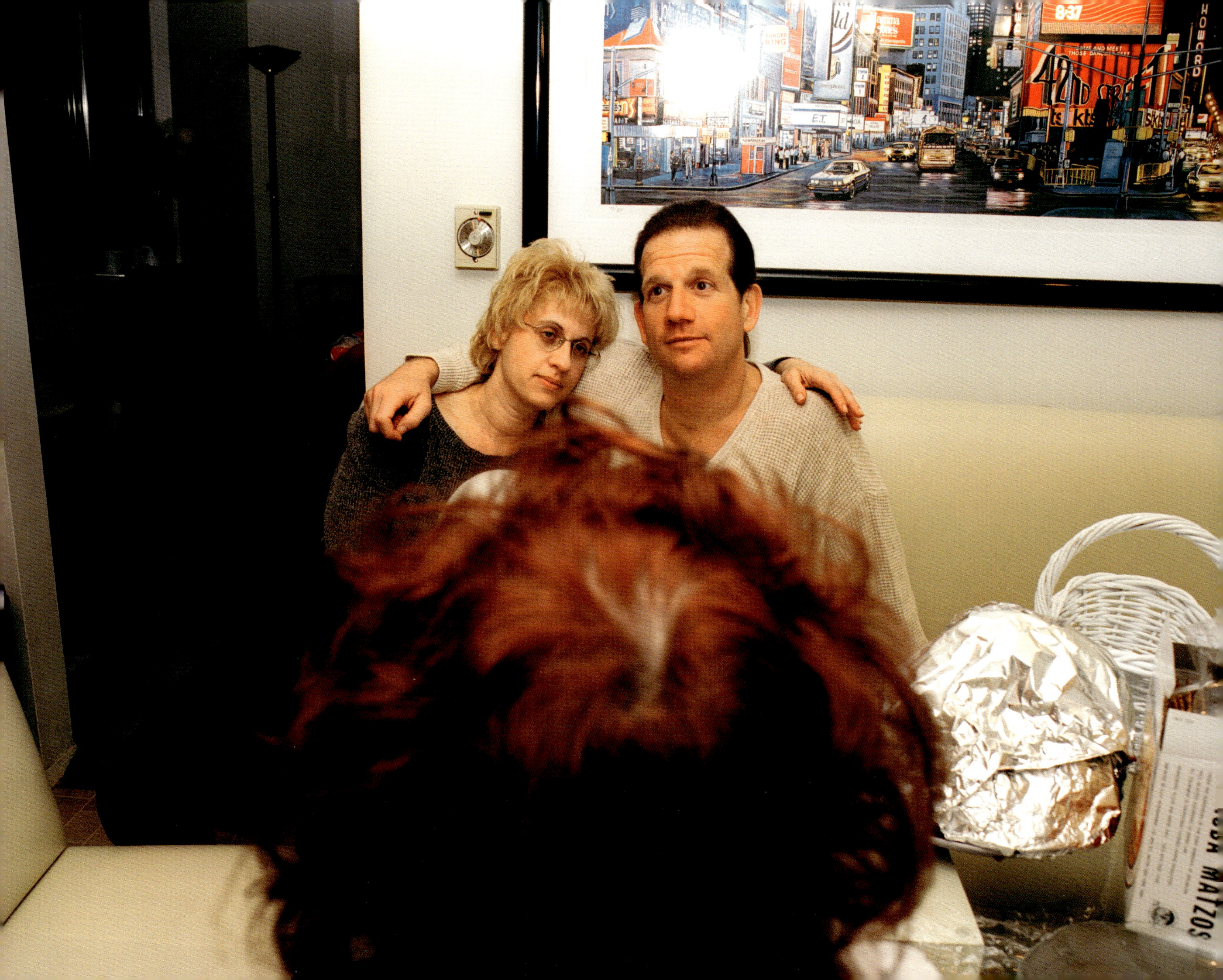

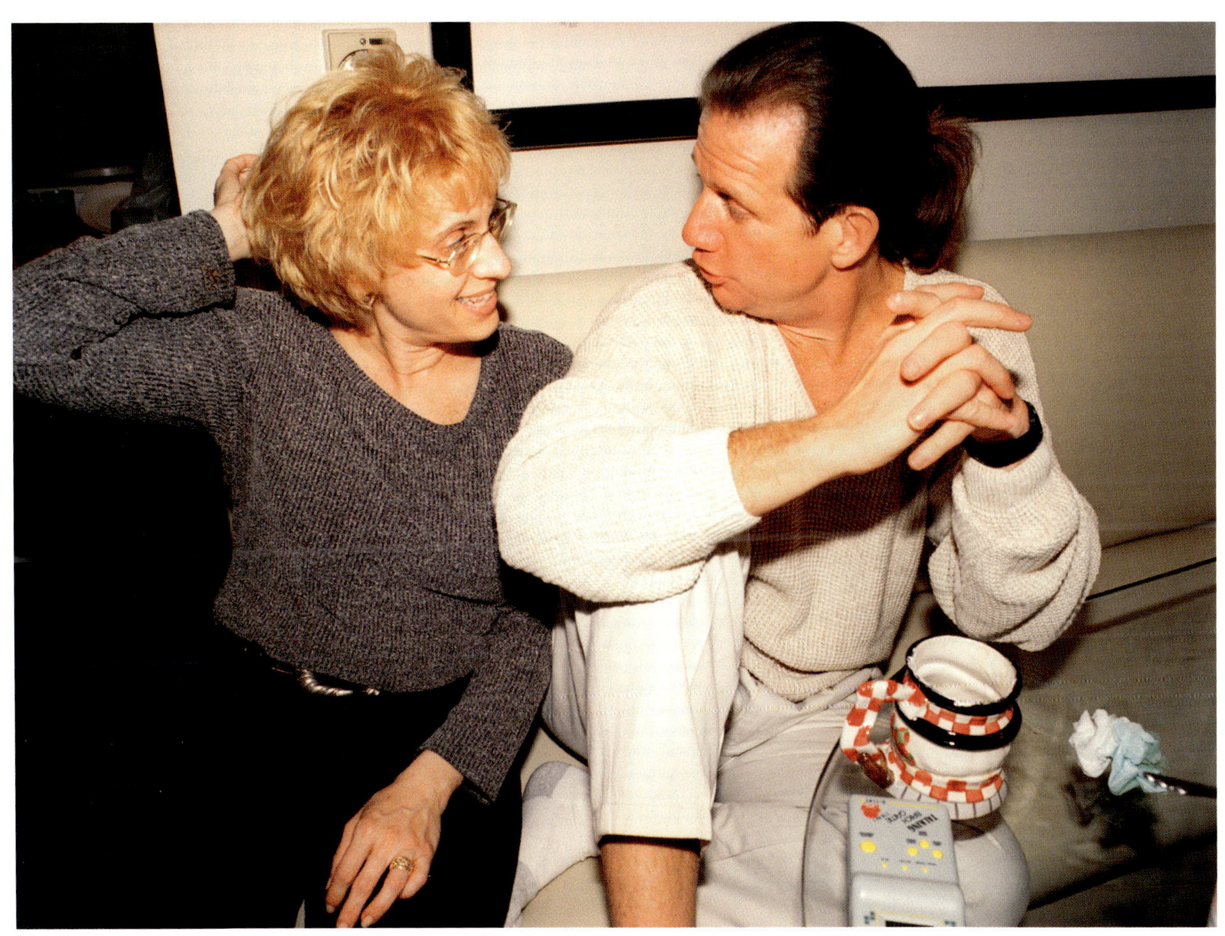

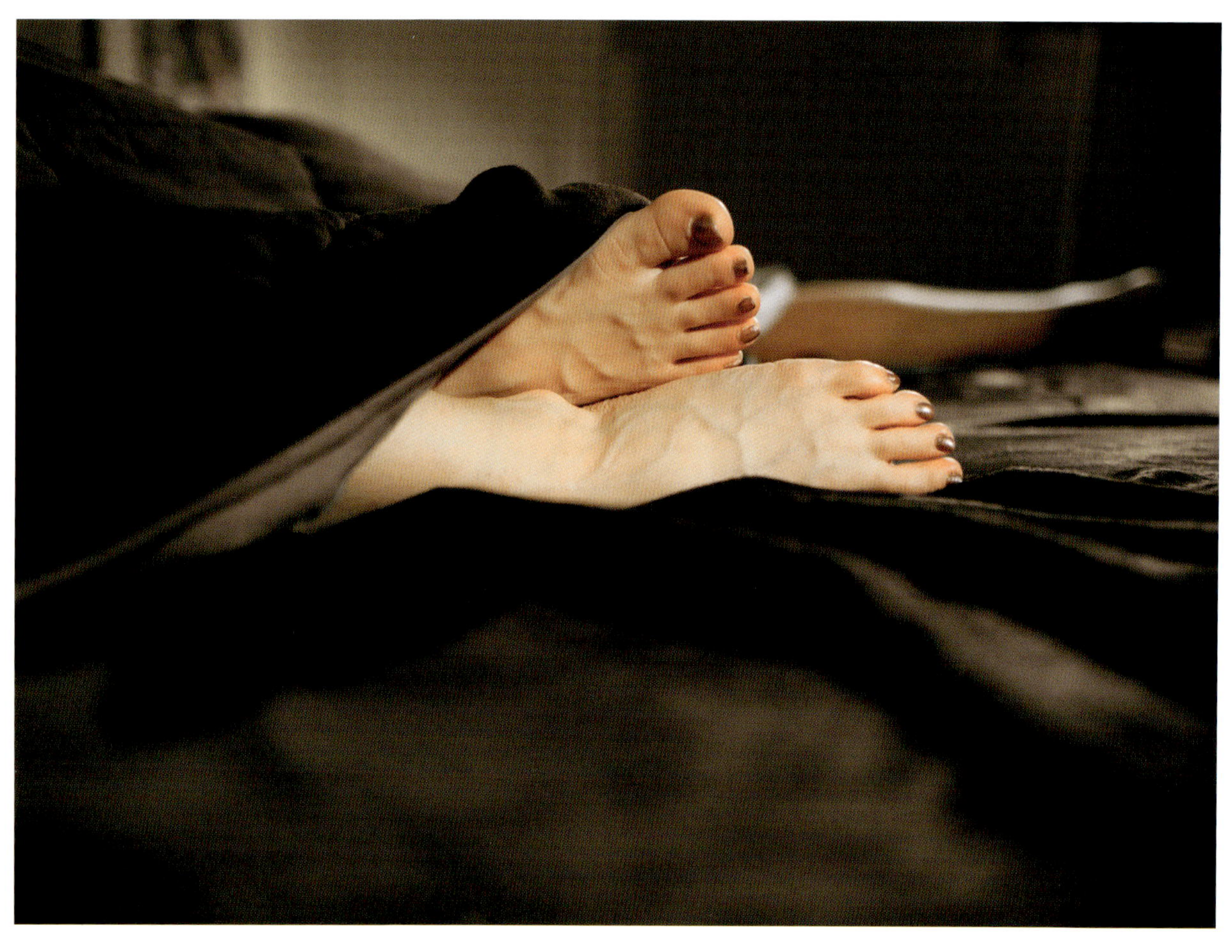

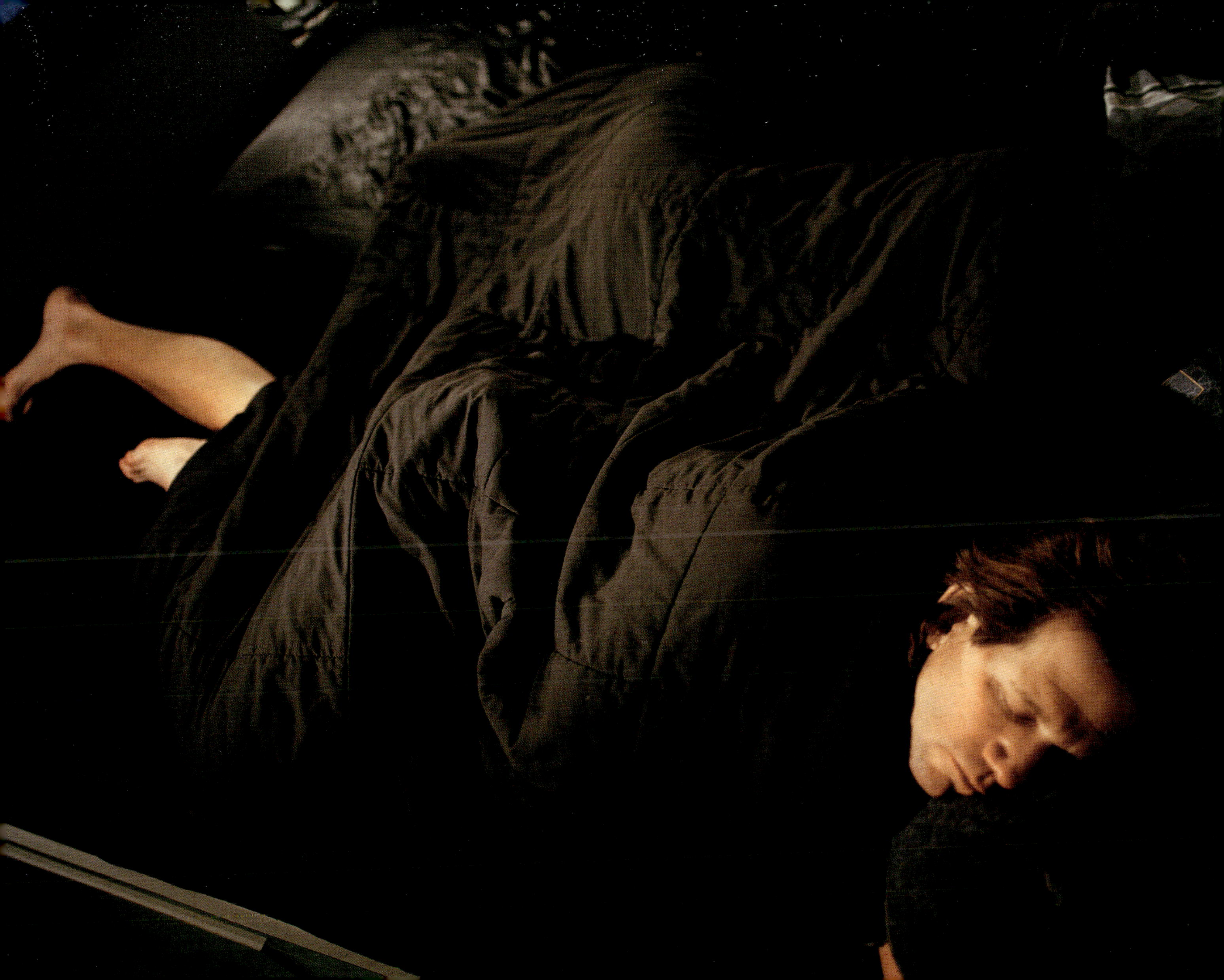

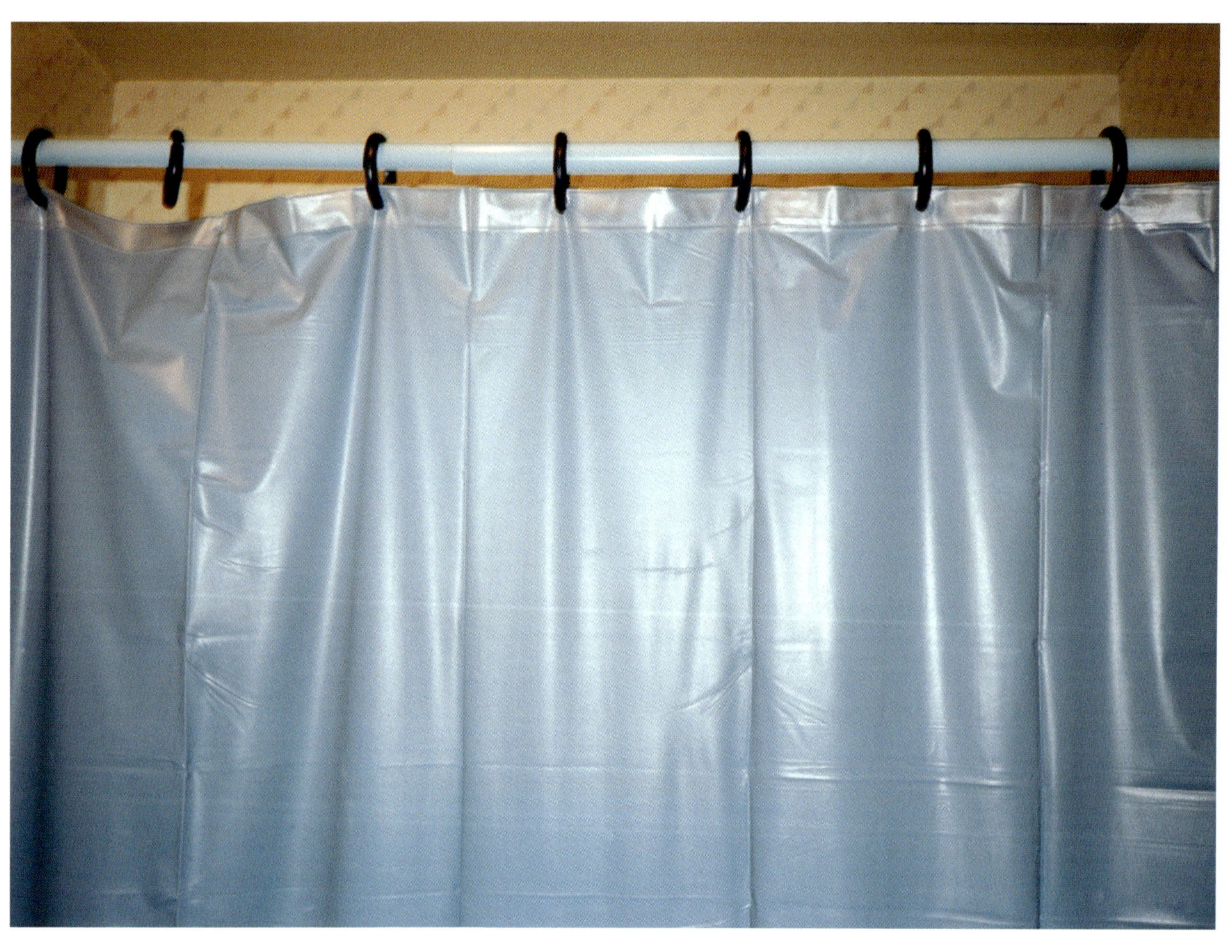

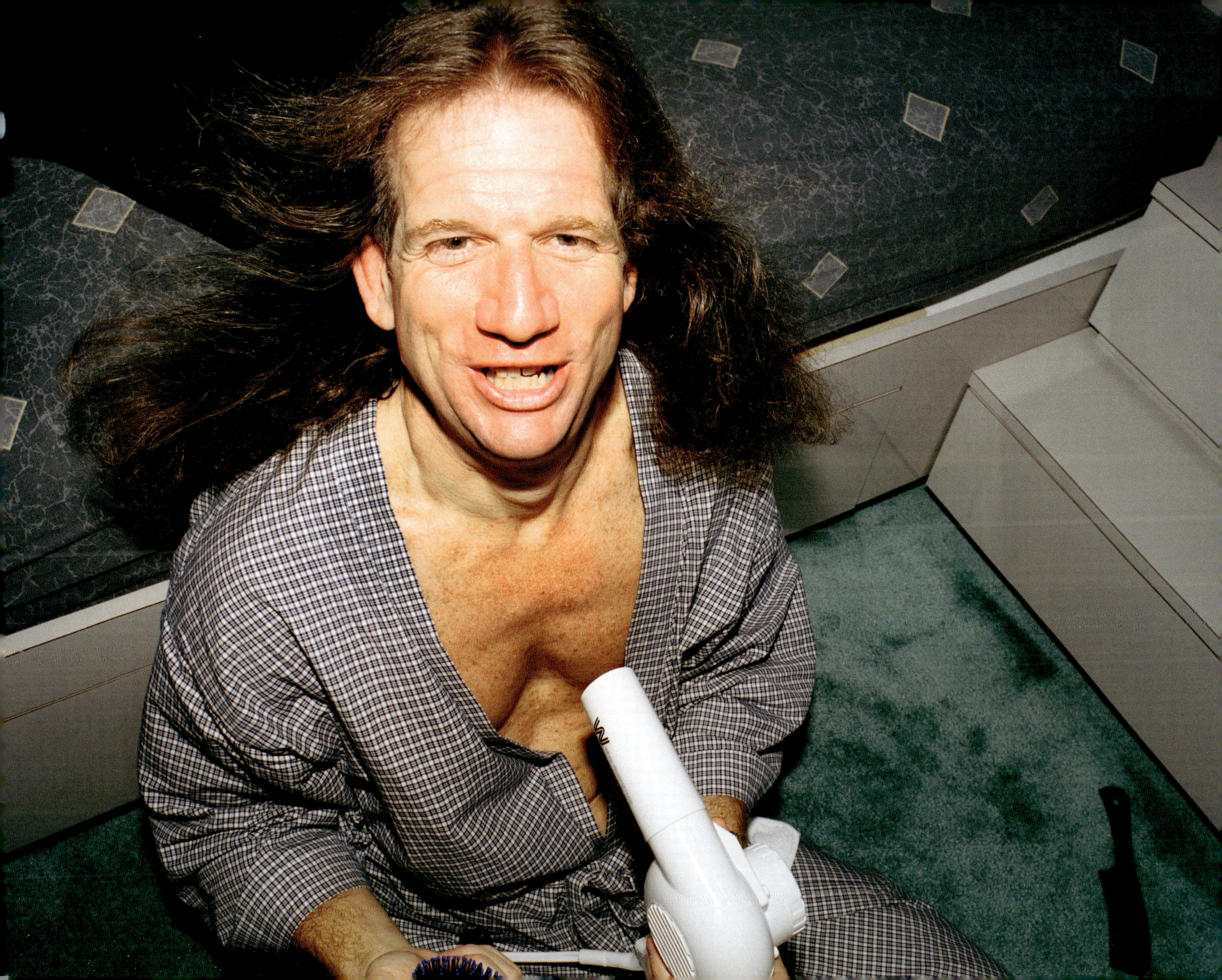

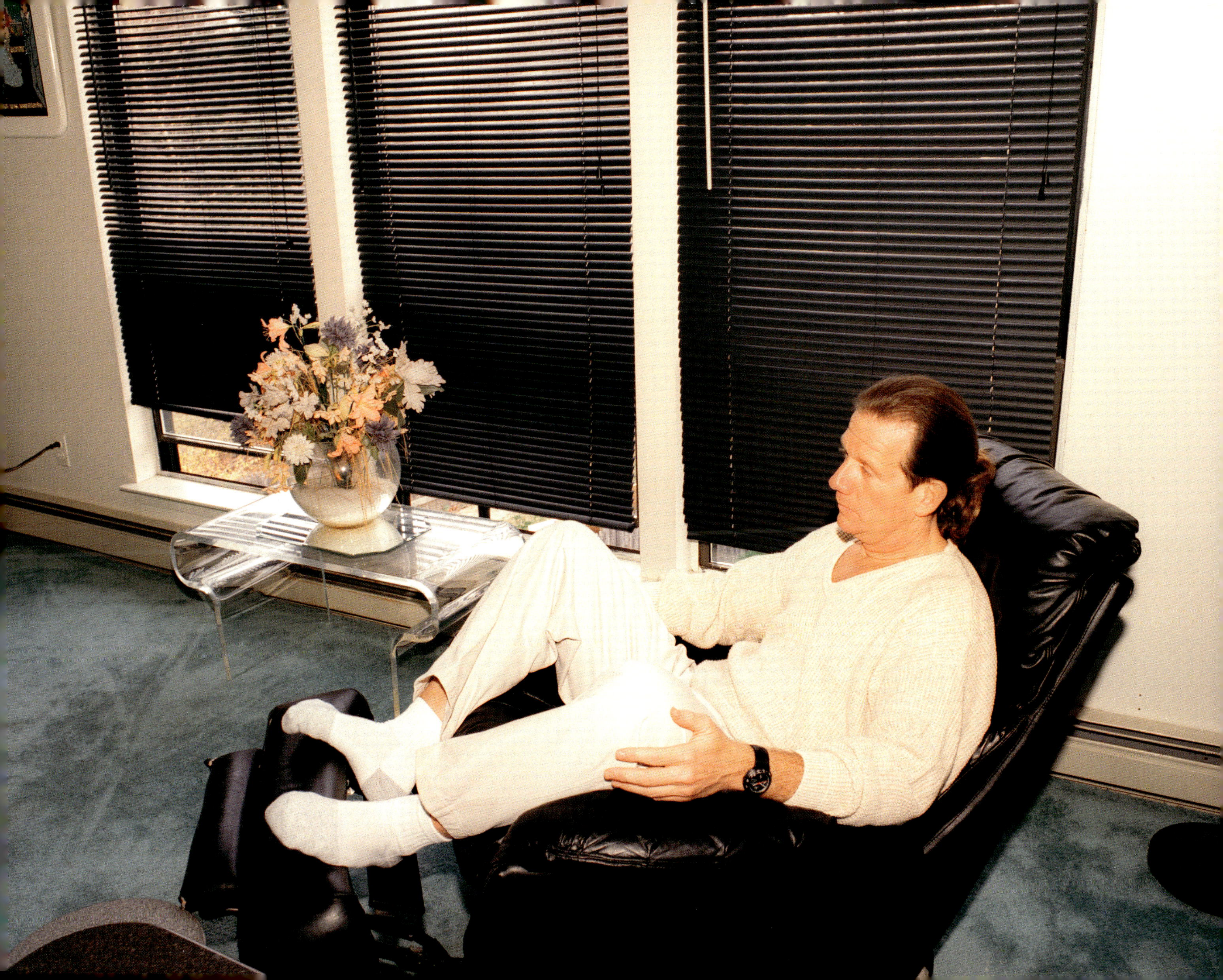

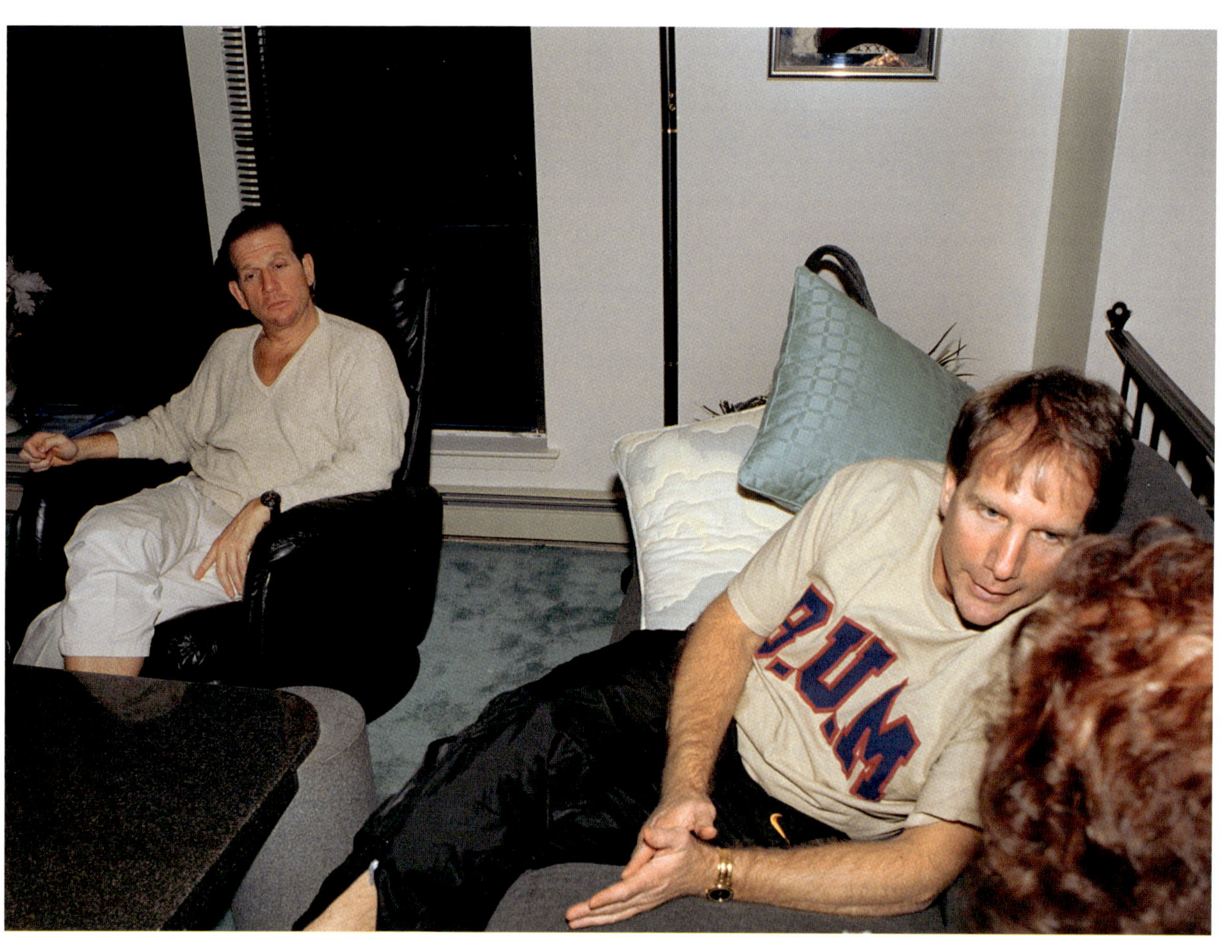

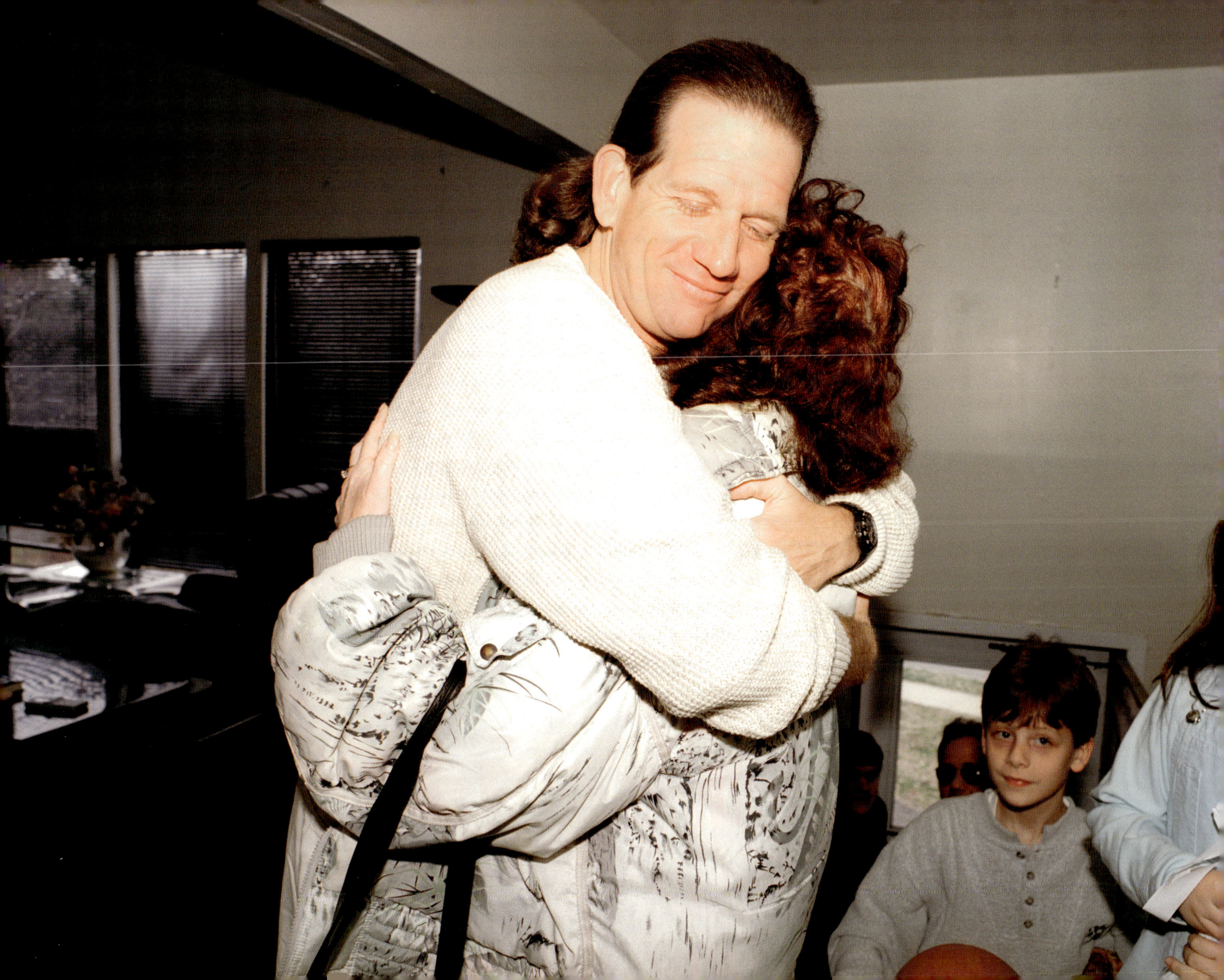

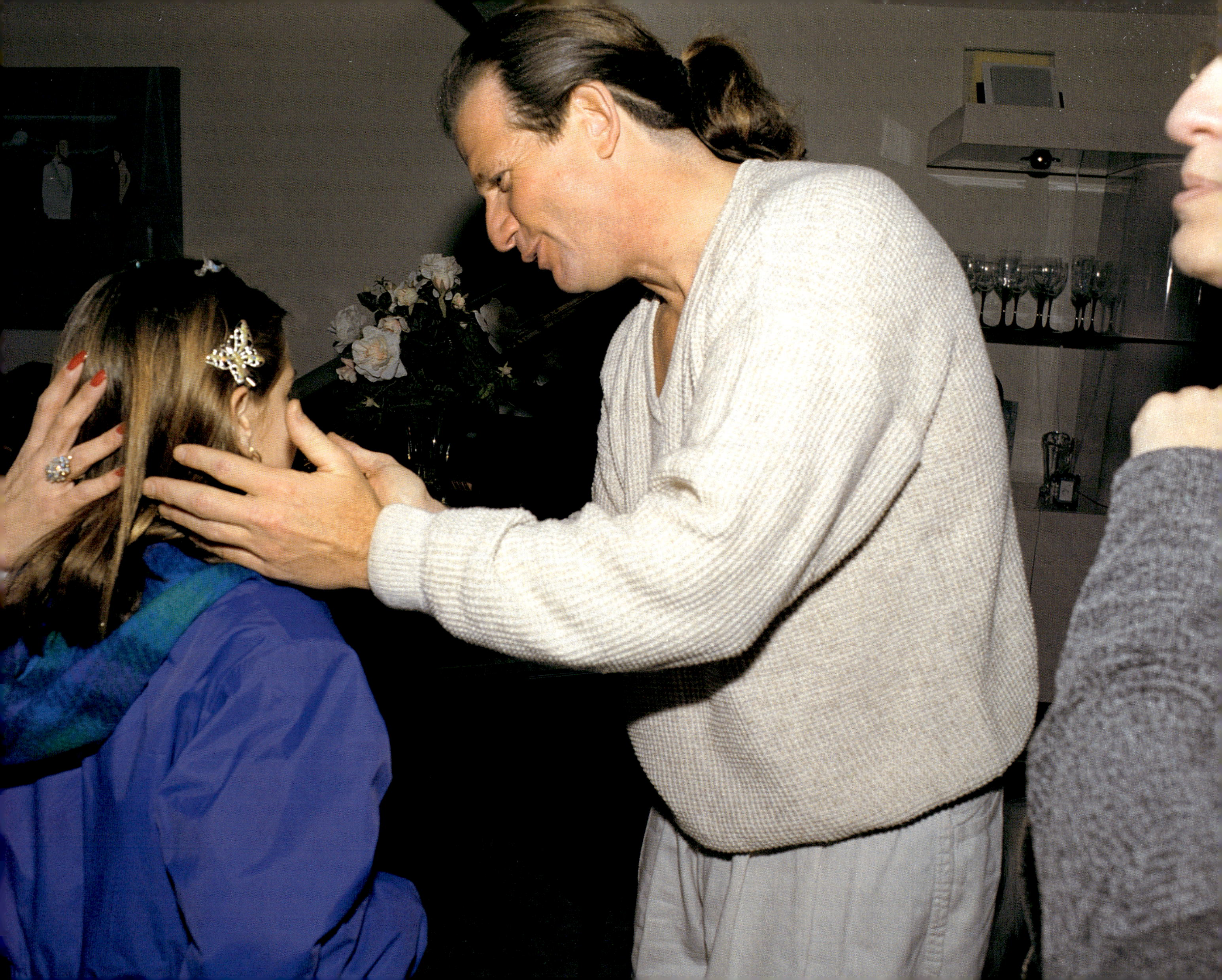

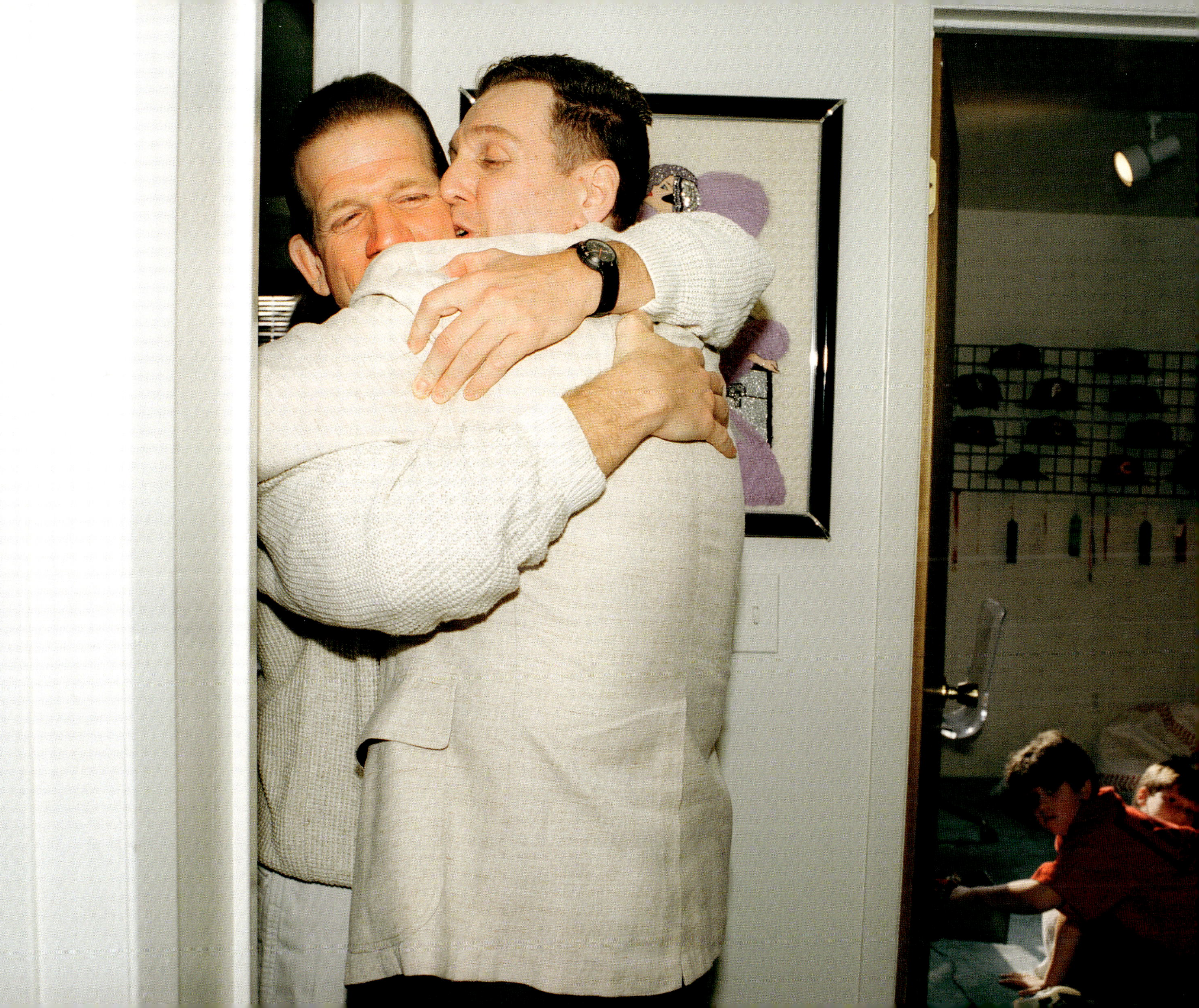

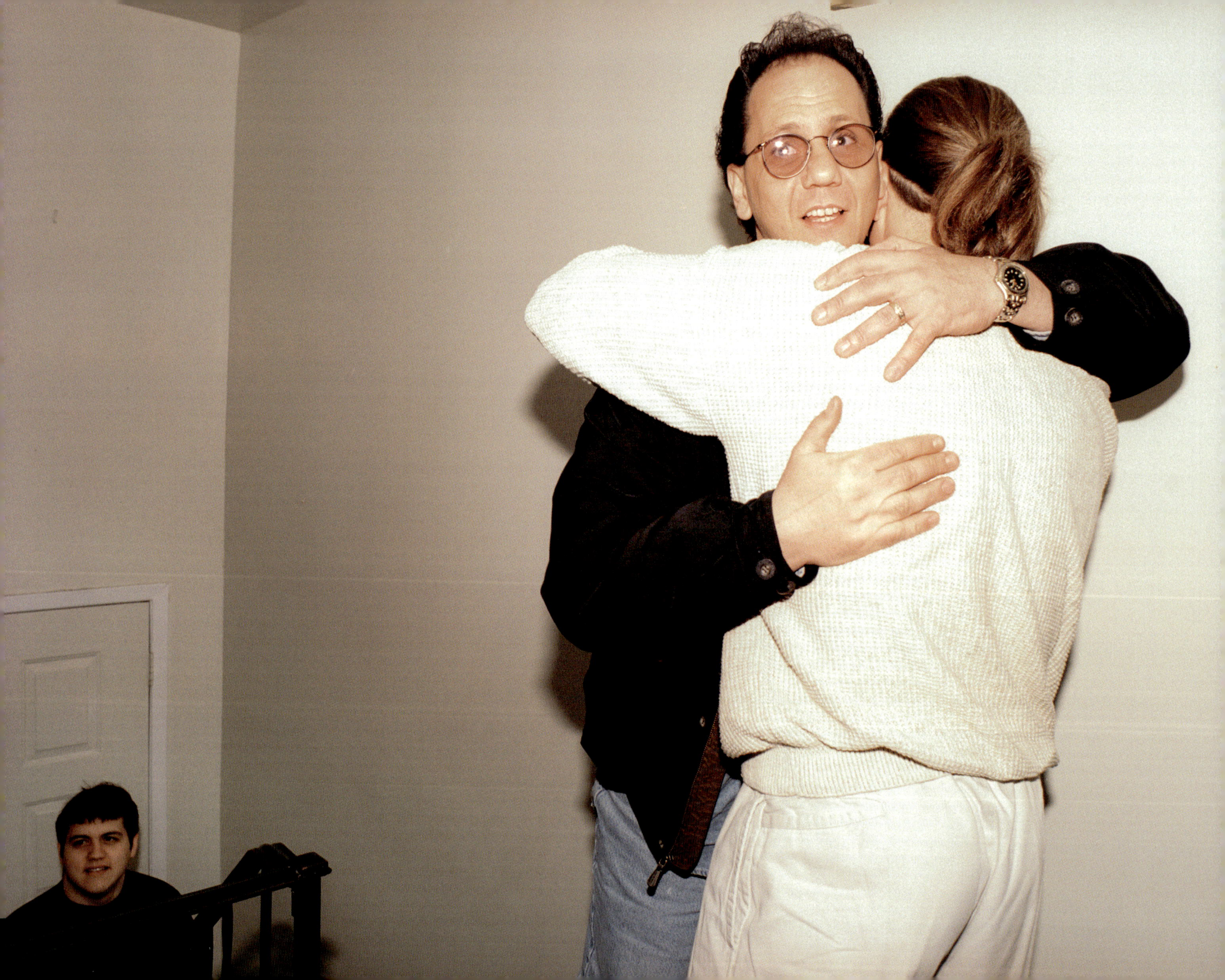

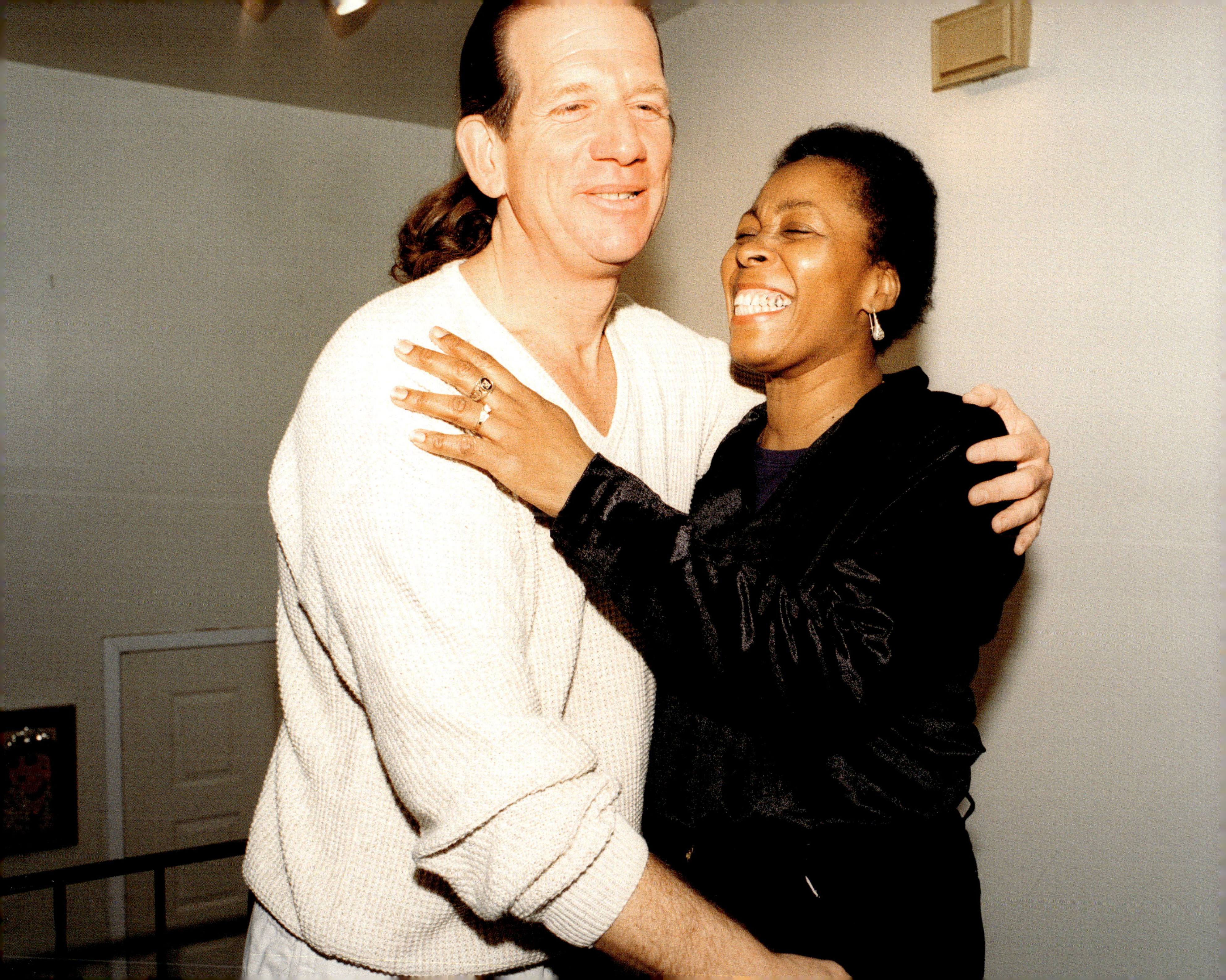

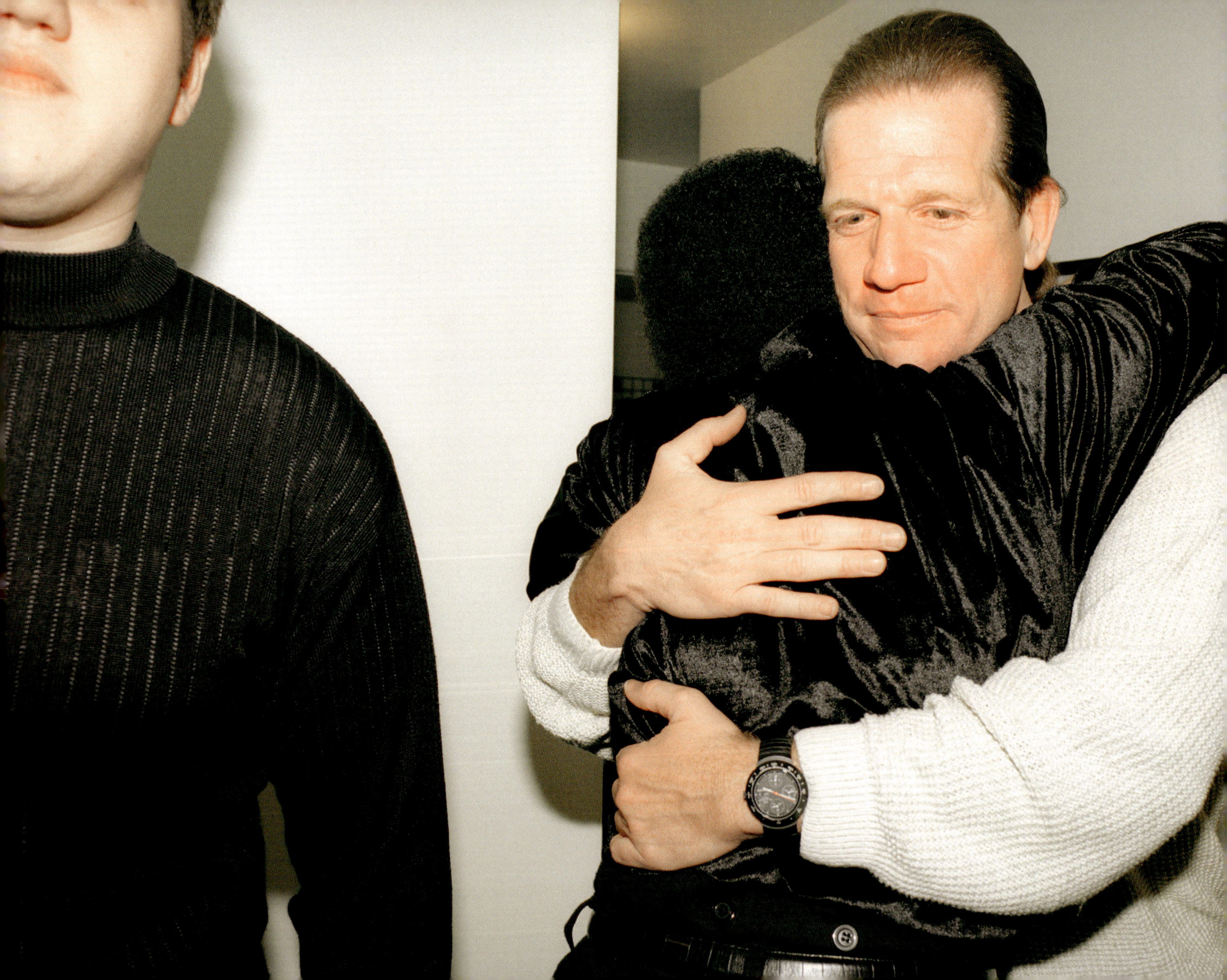

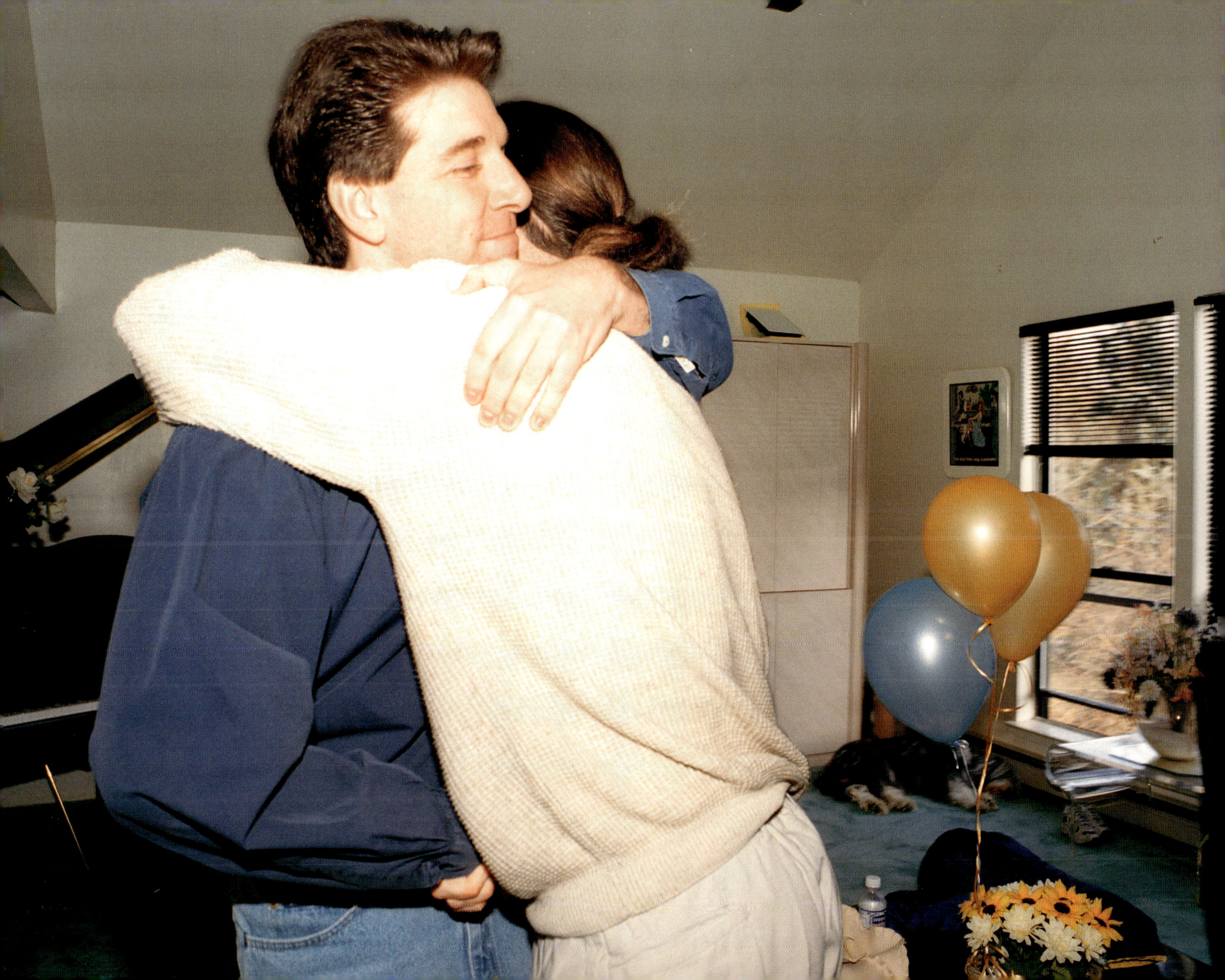

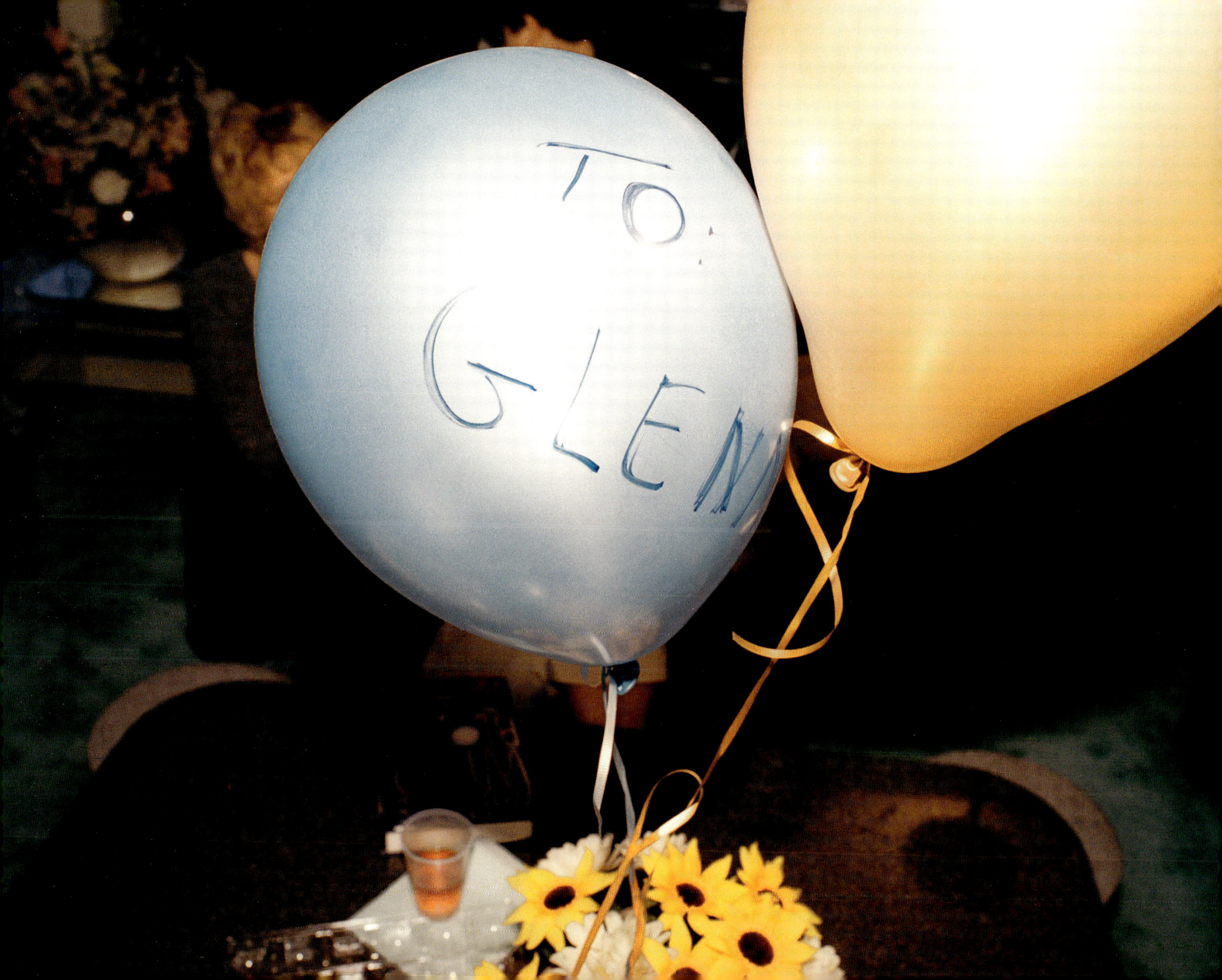
TO:
GLEN

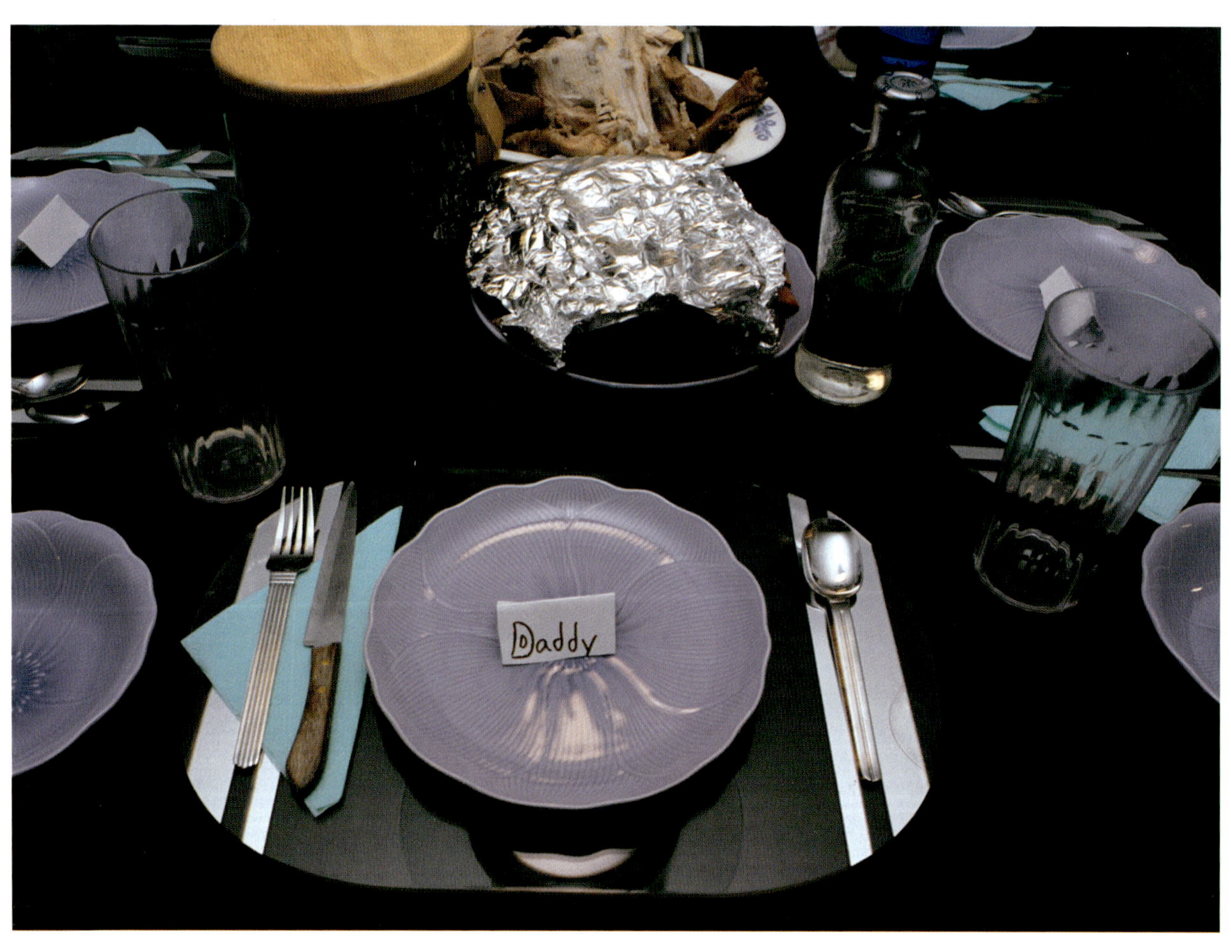
Daddy

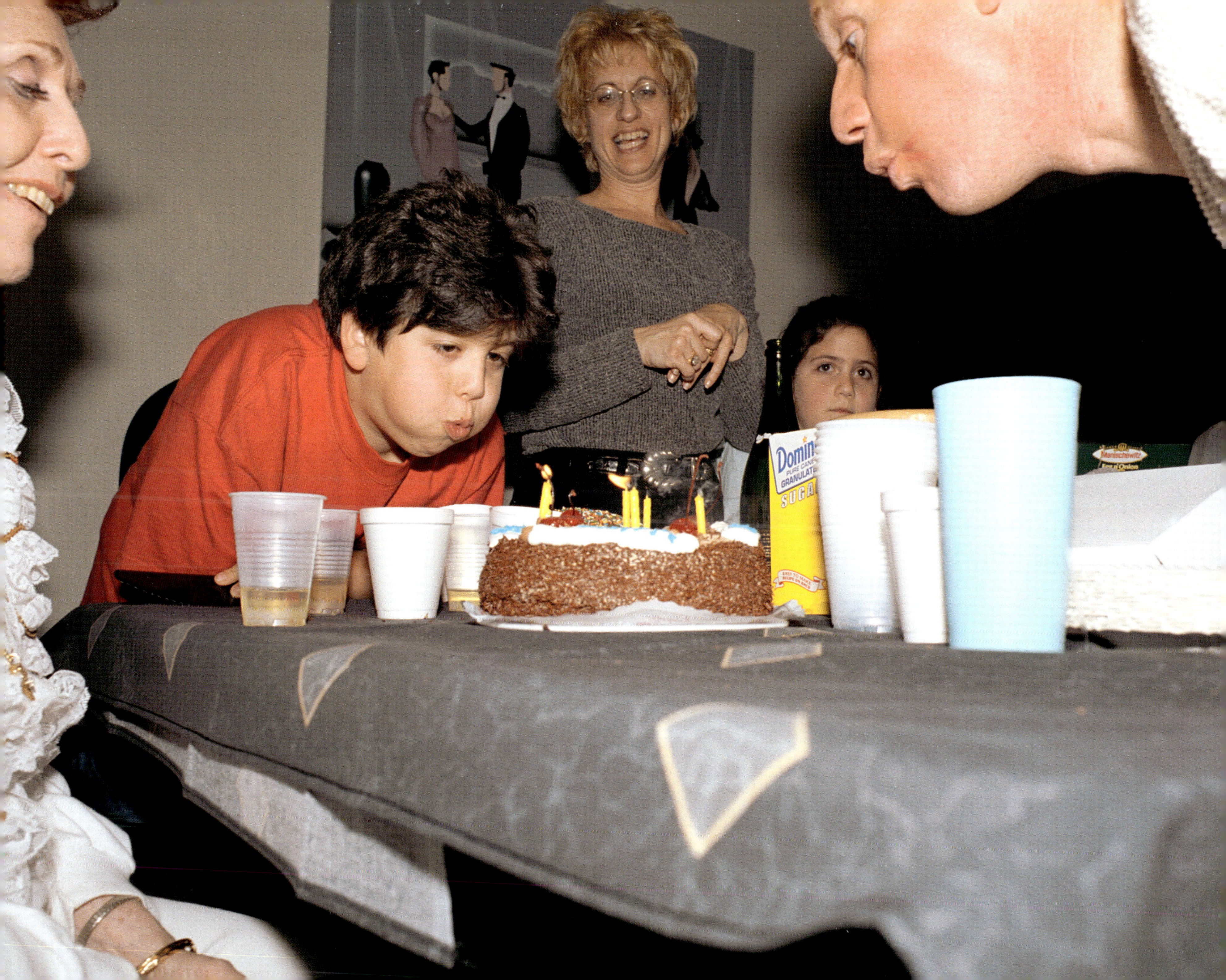

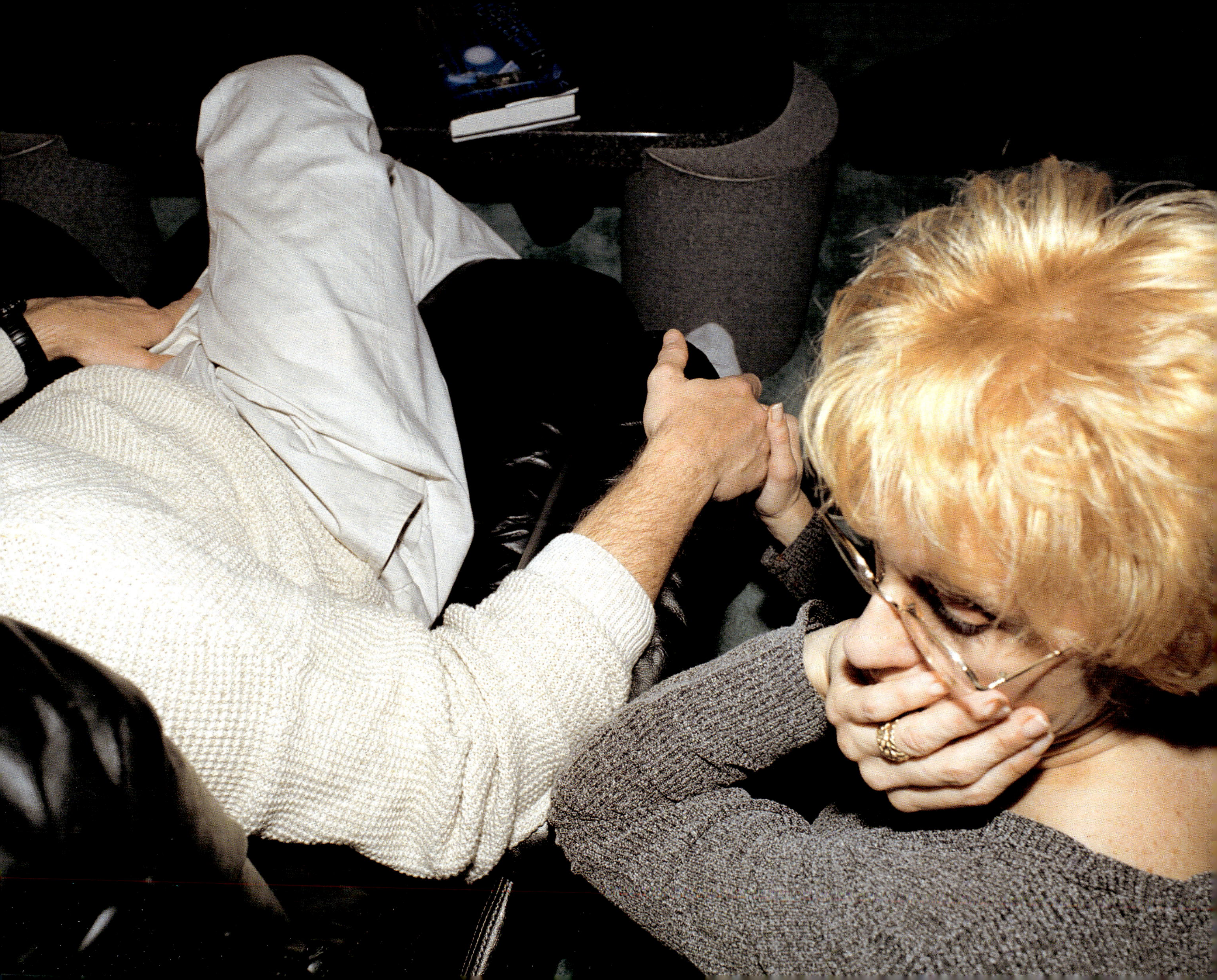

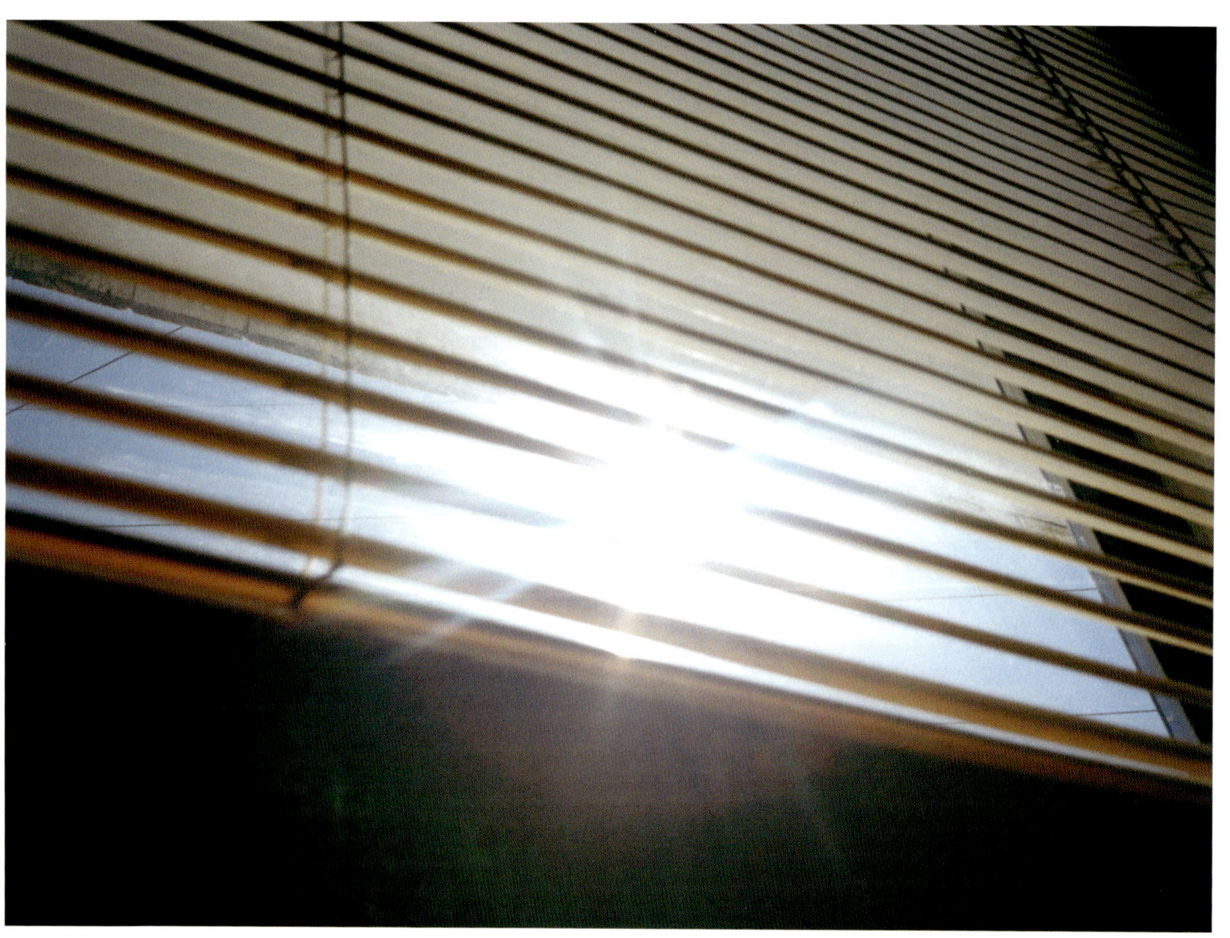

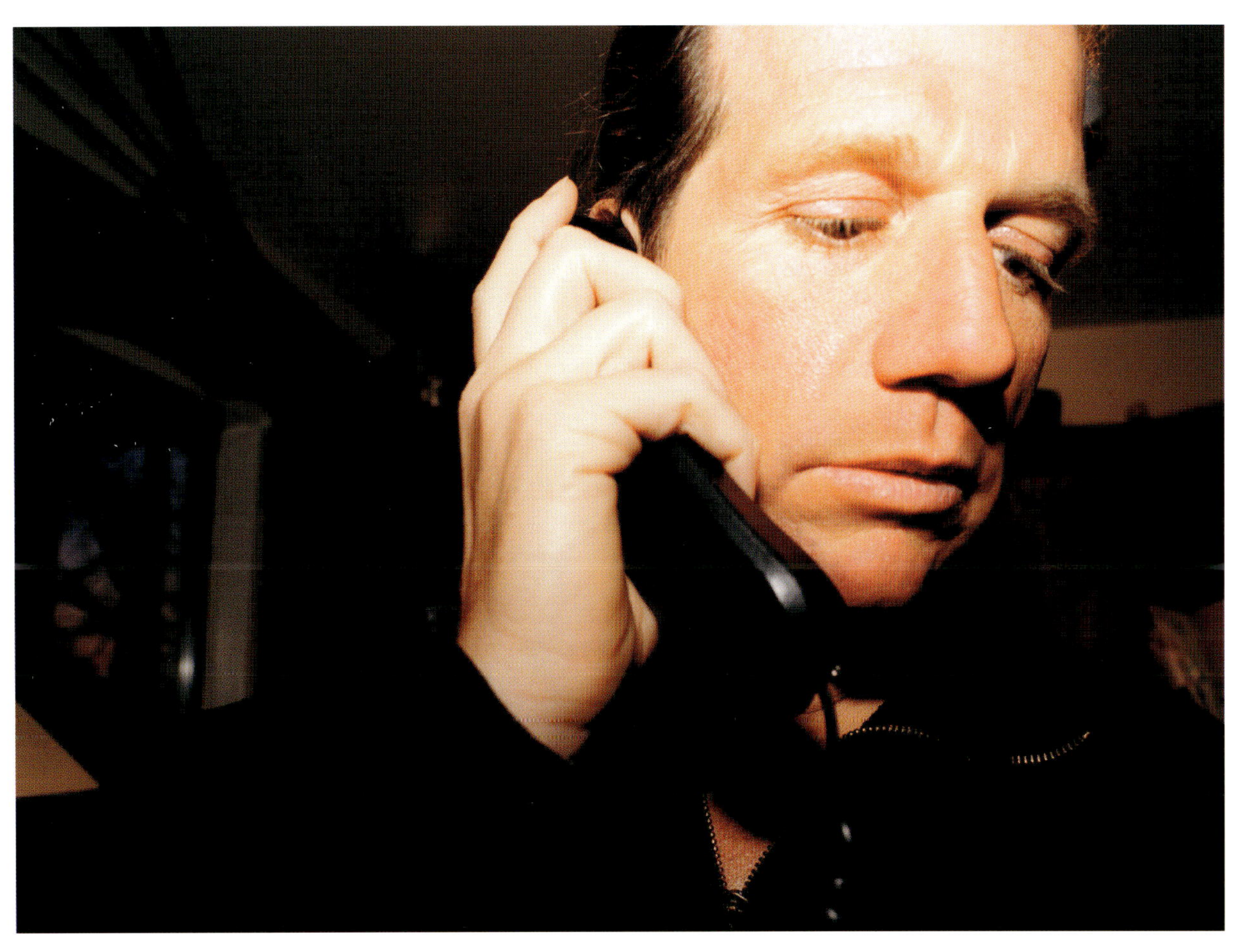

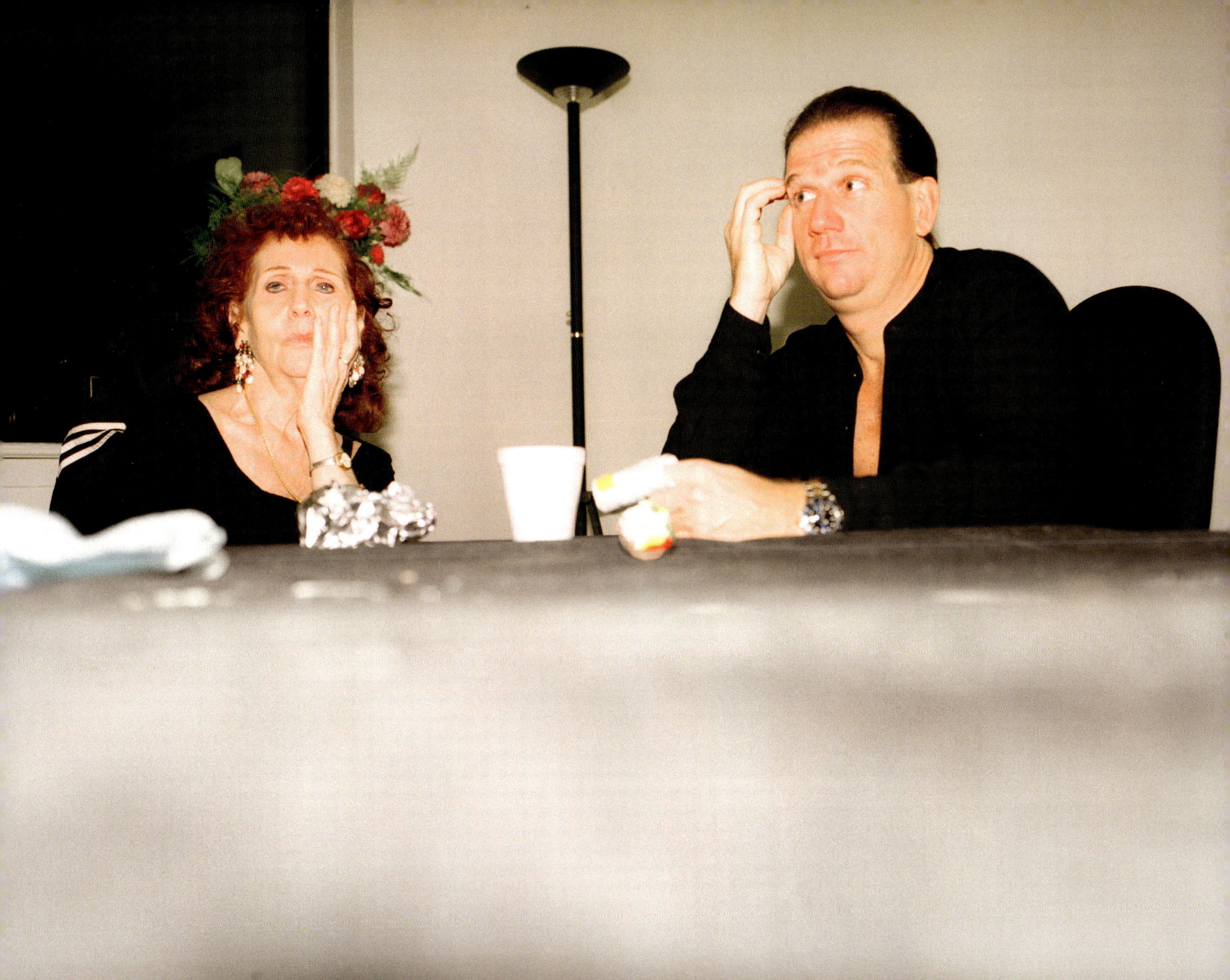

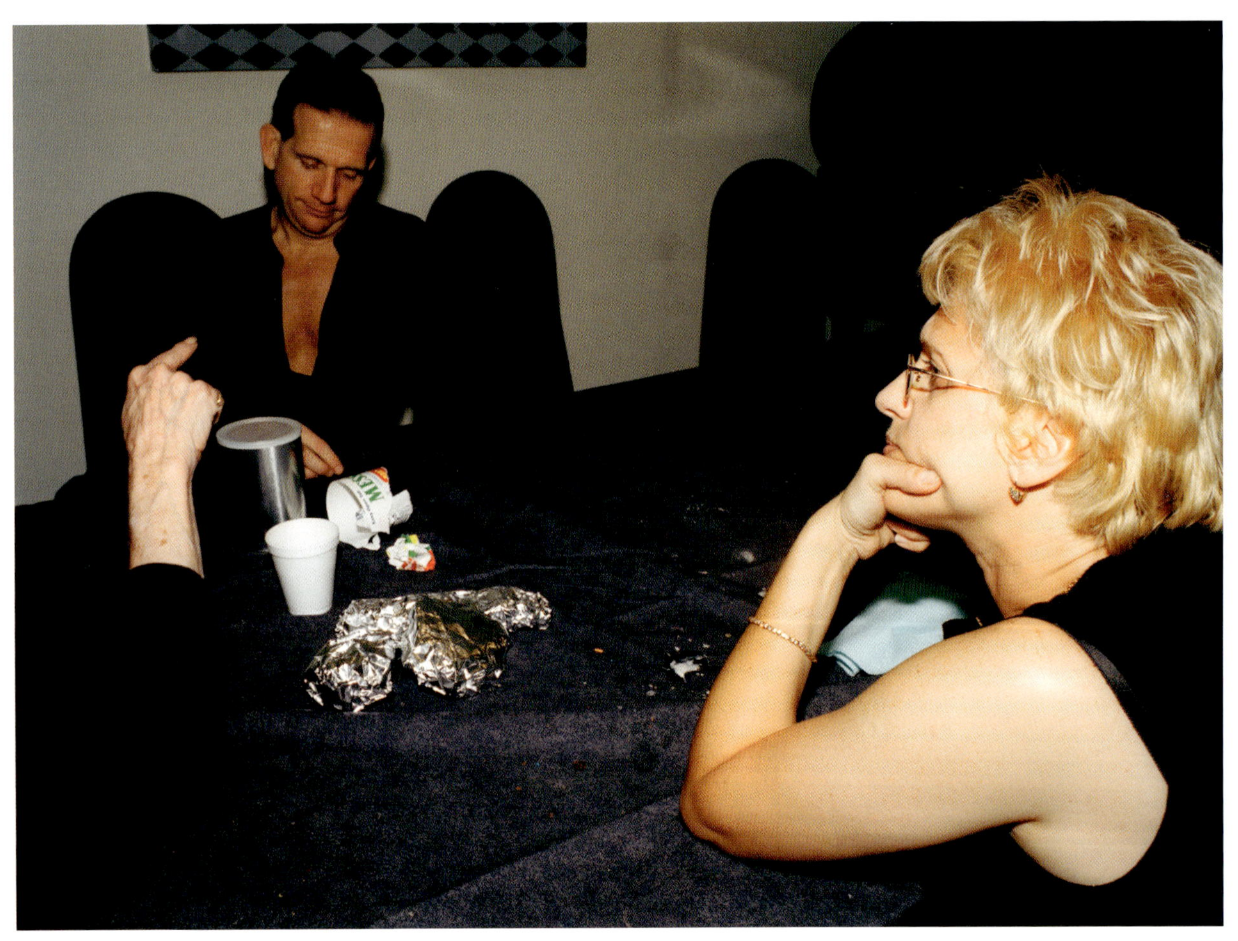

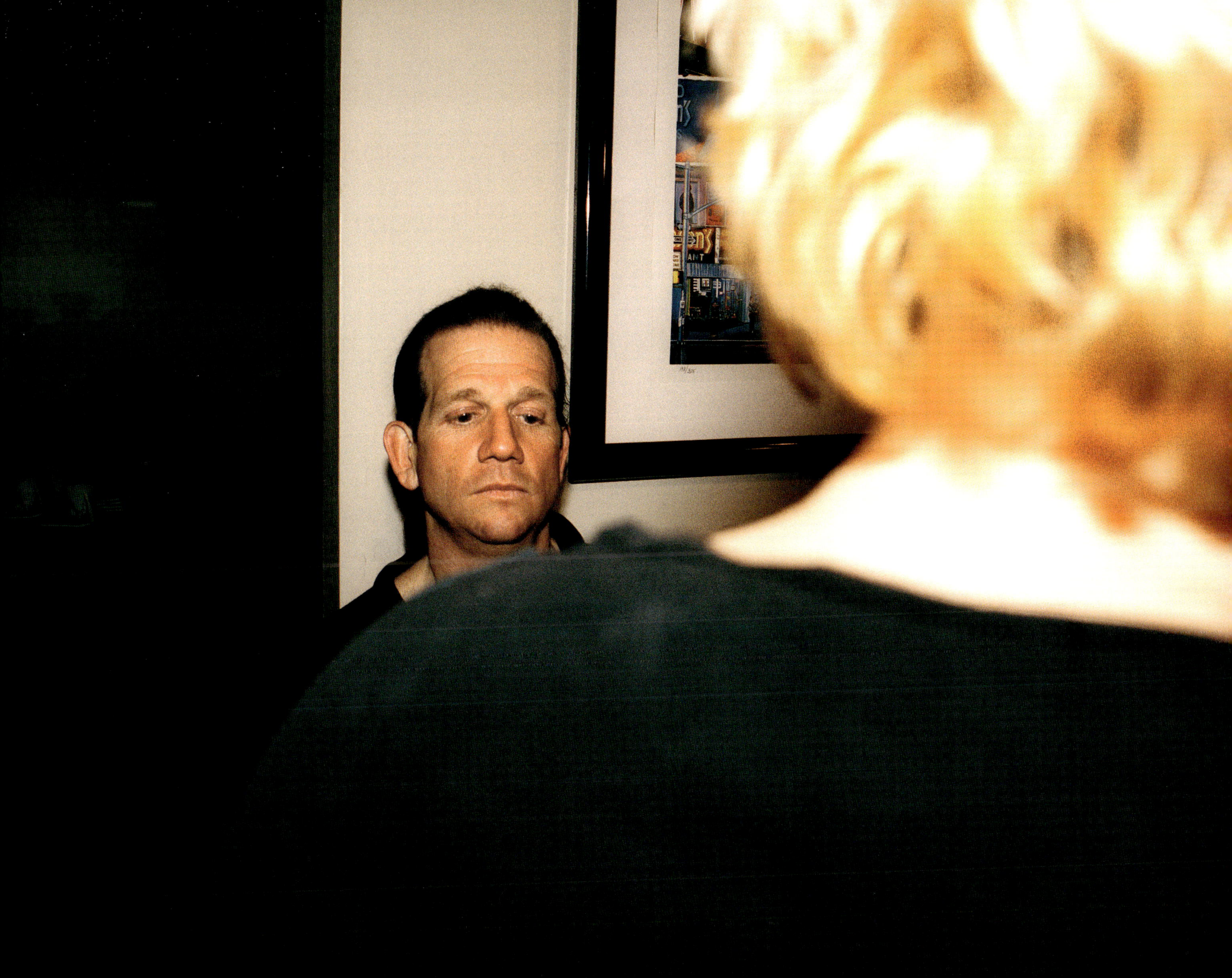

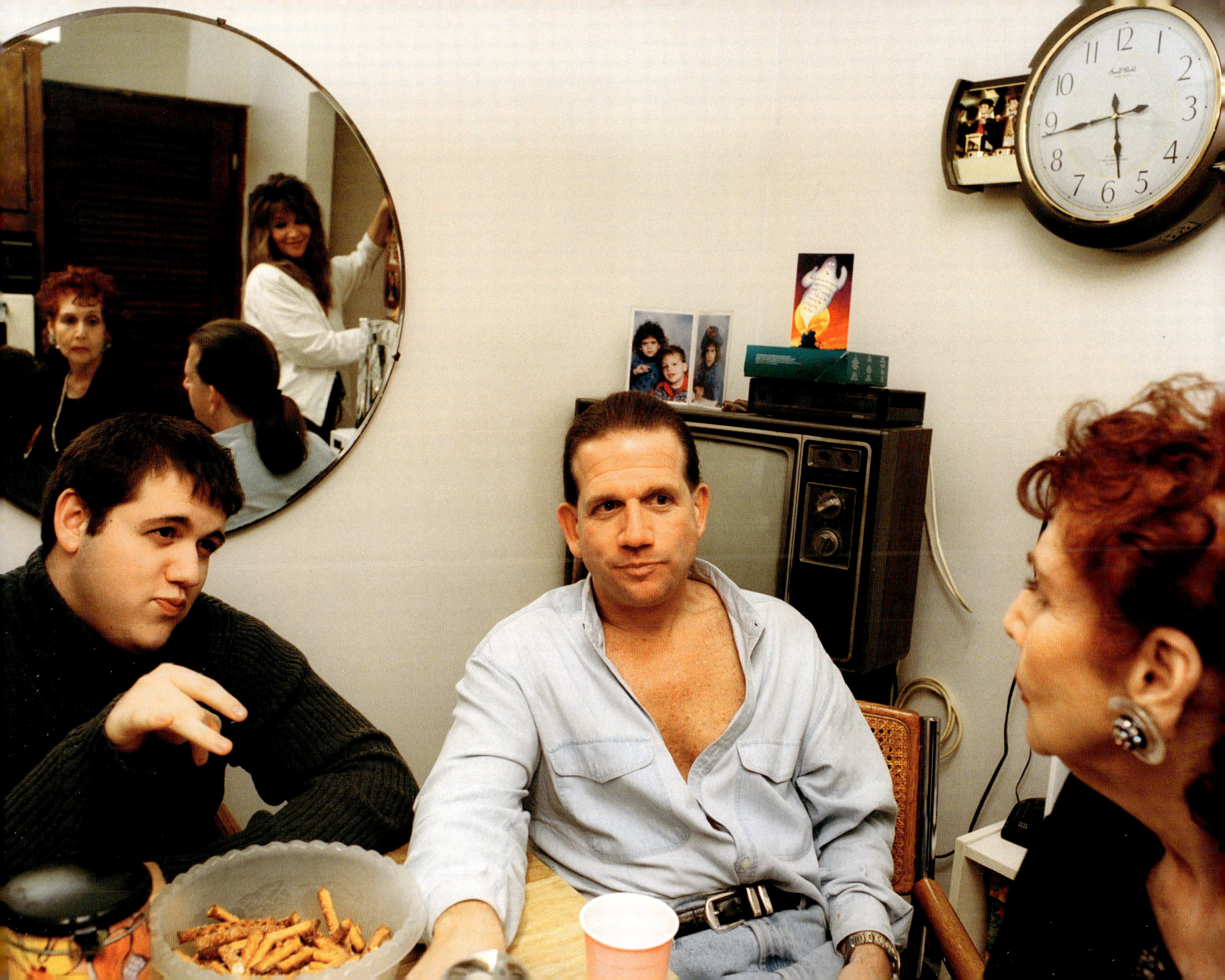

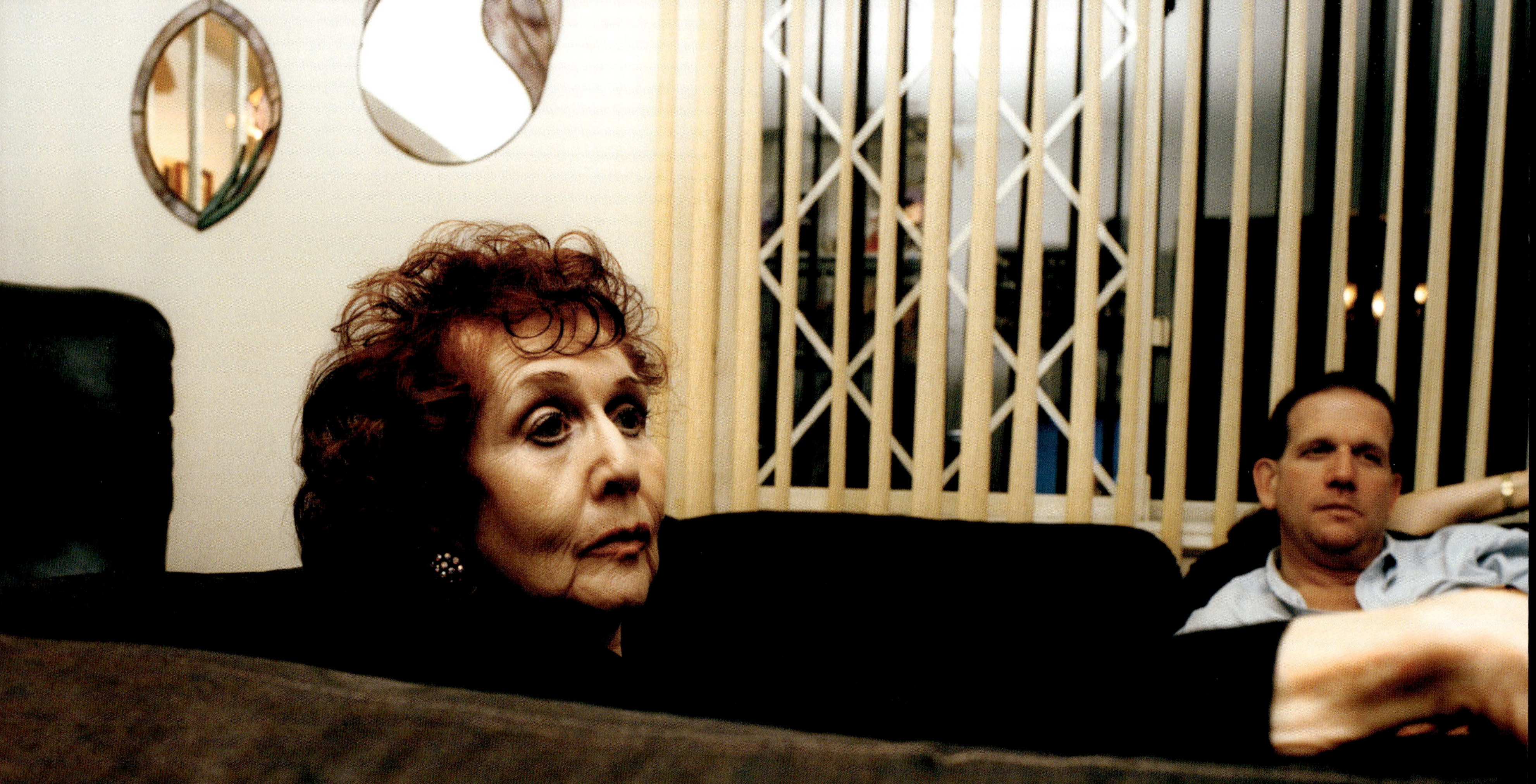

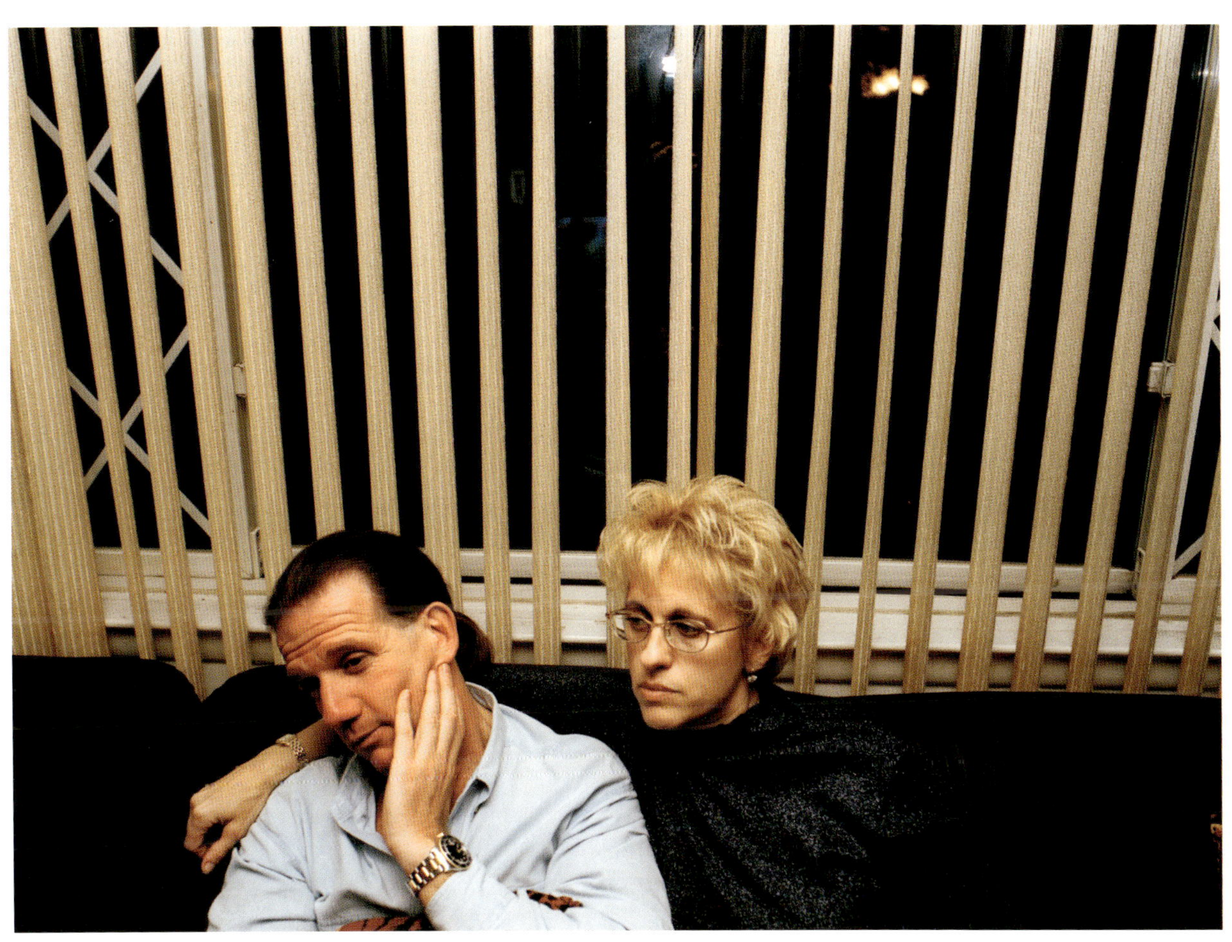

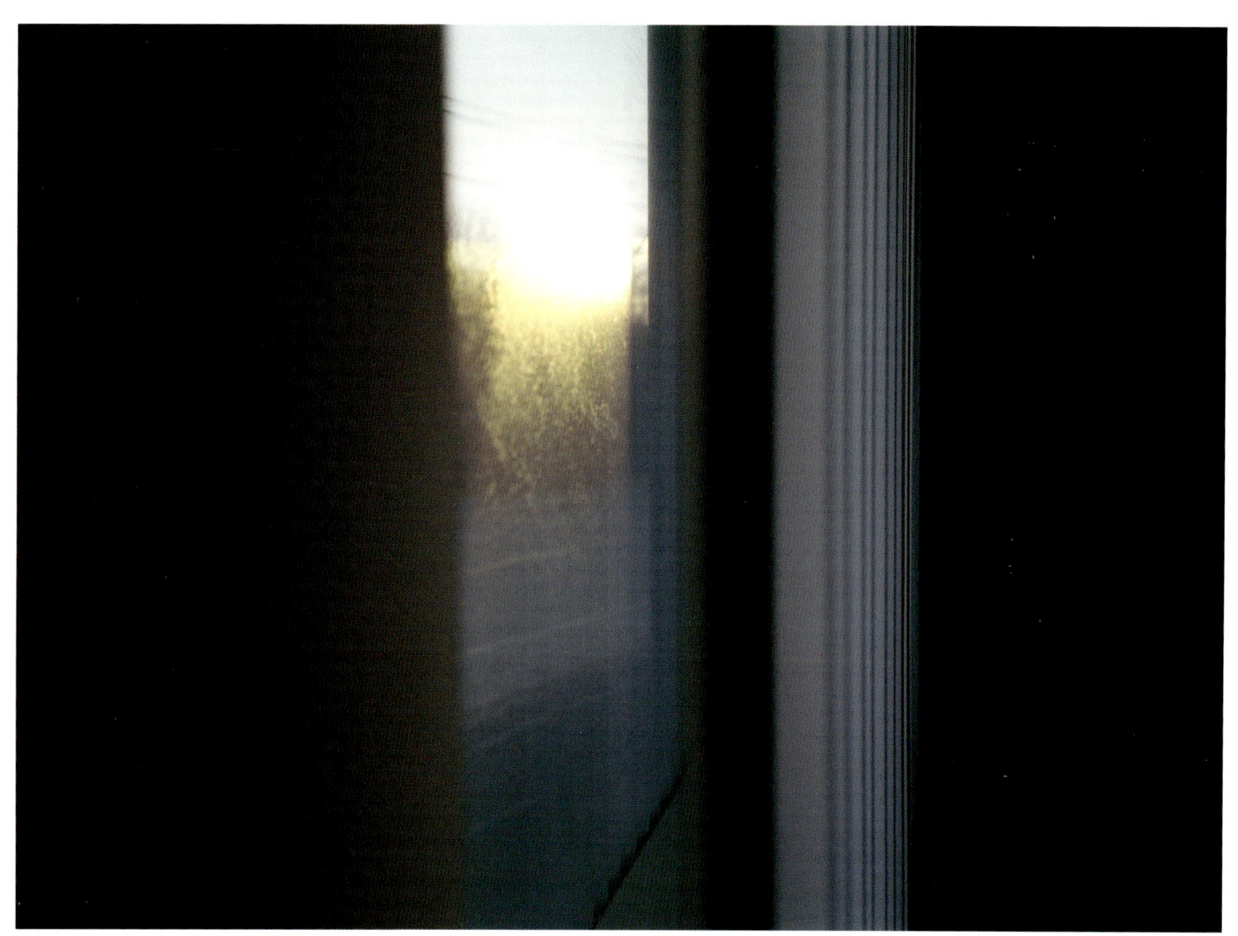

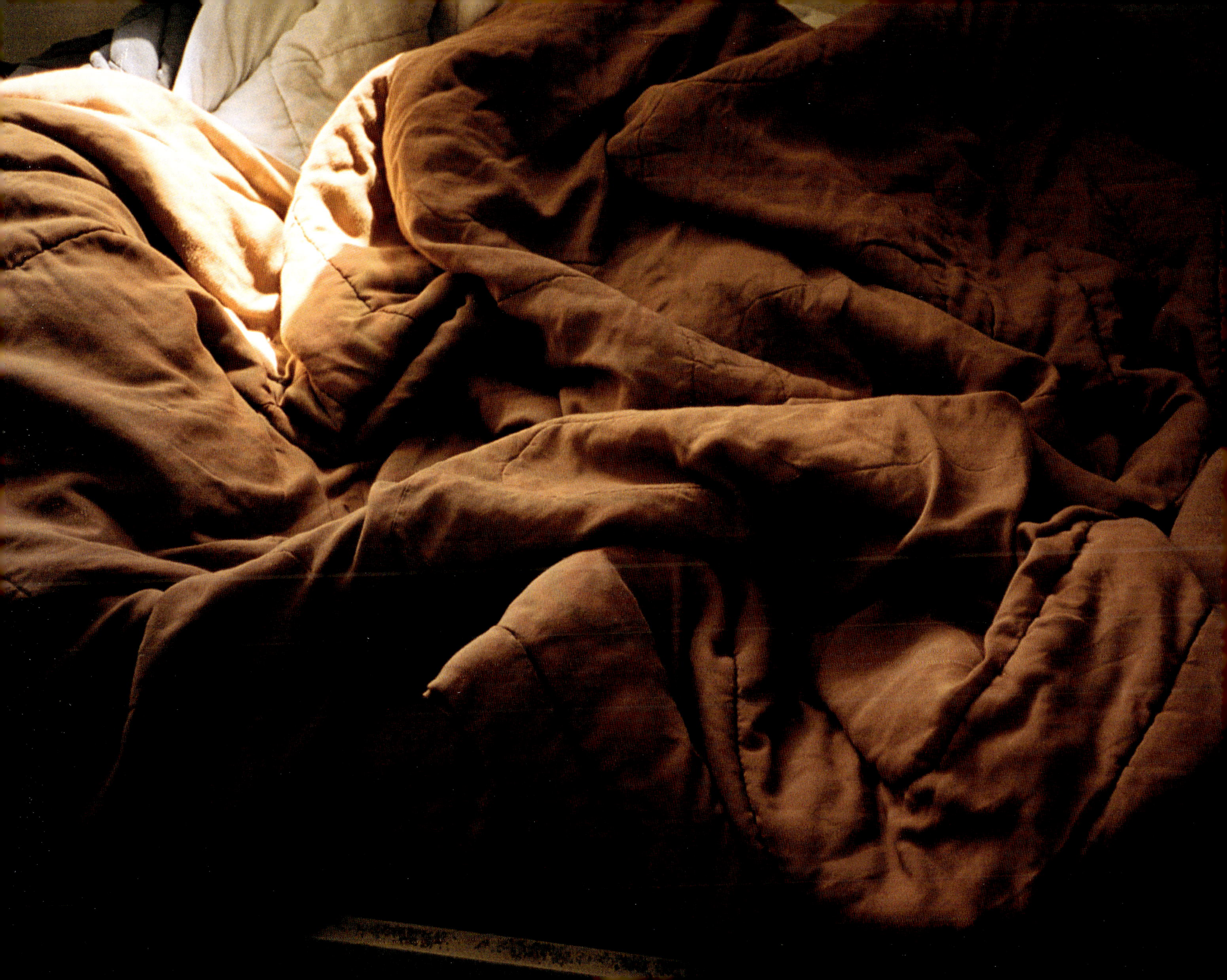

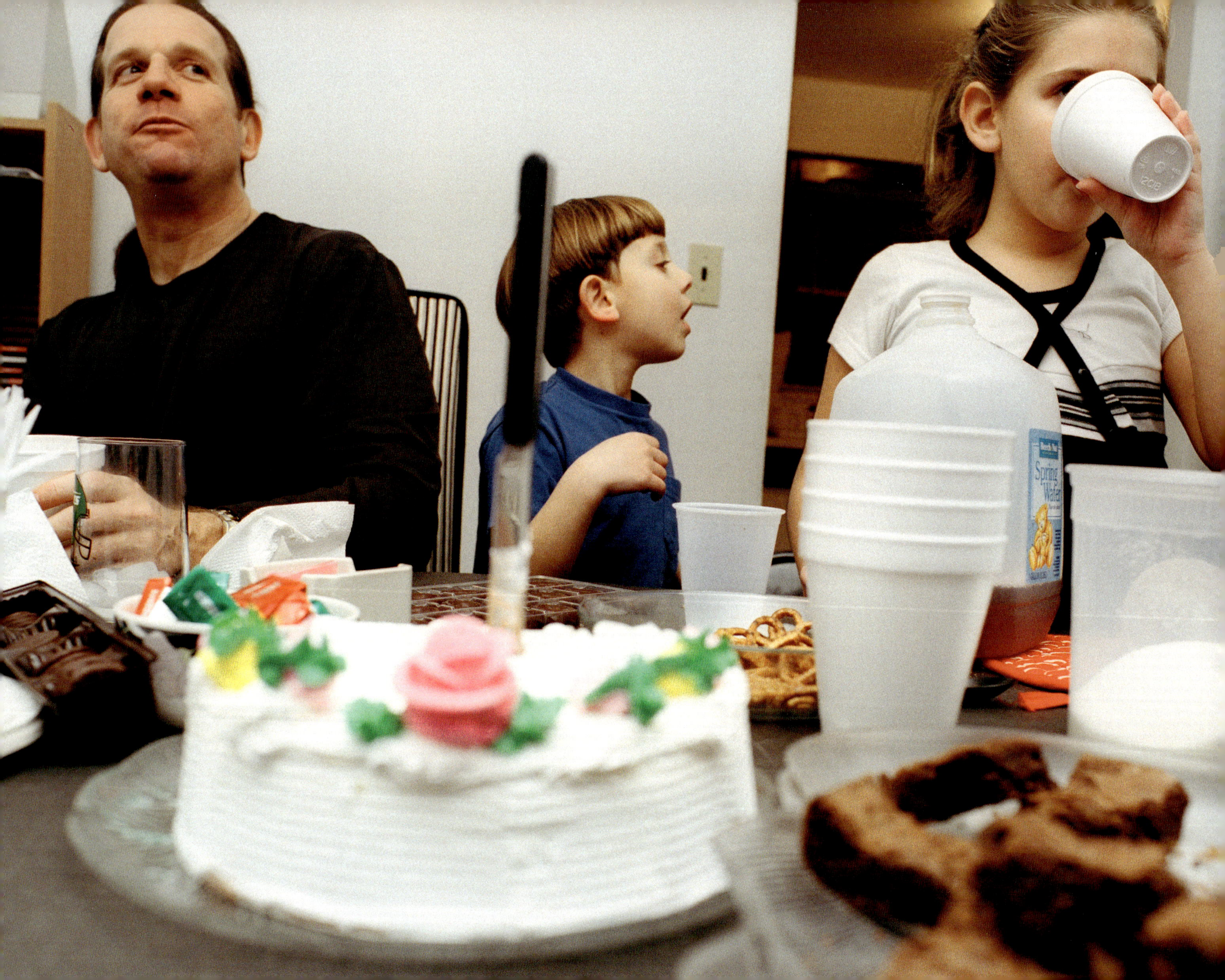

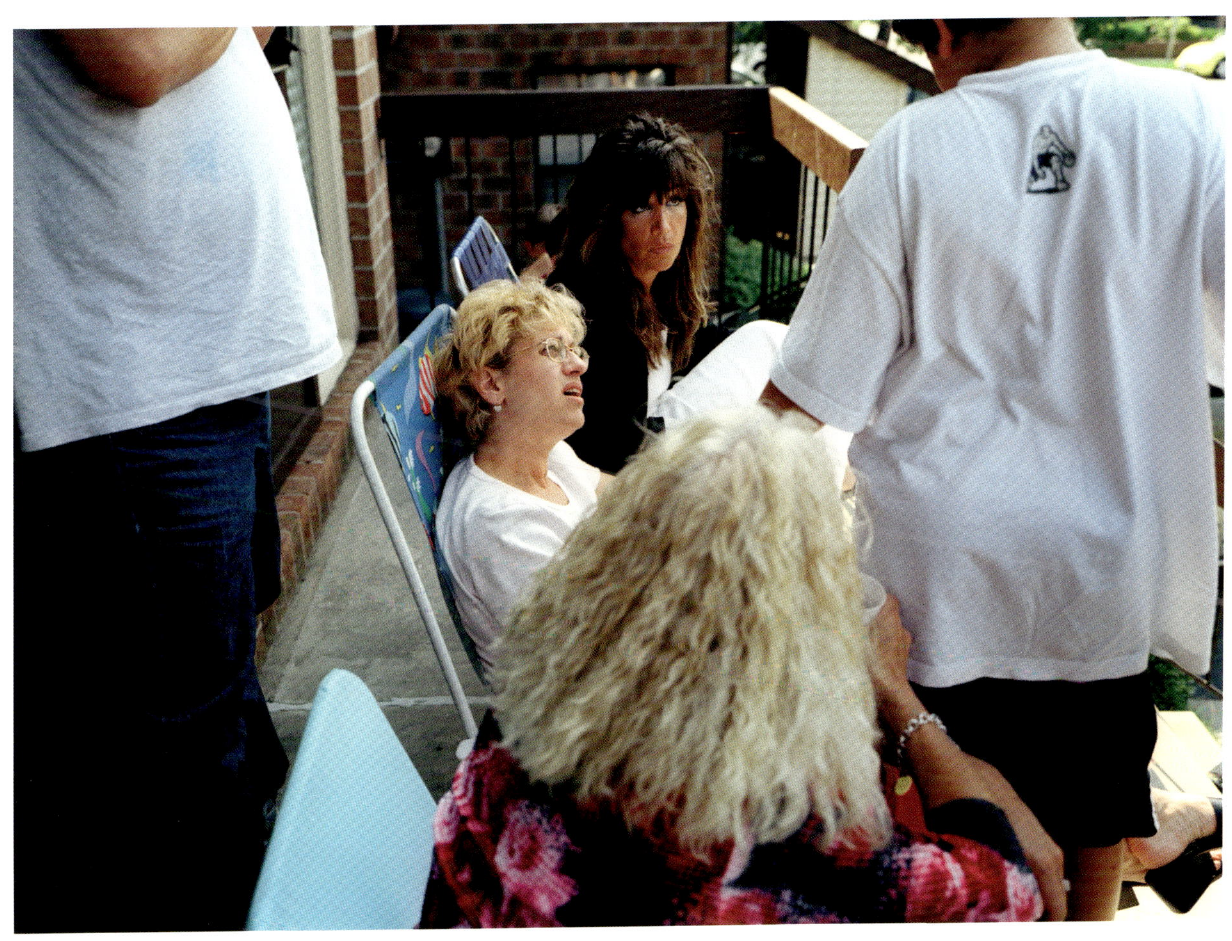

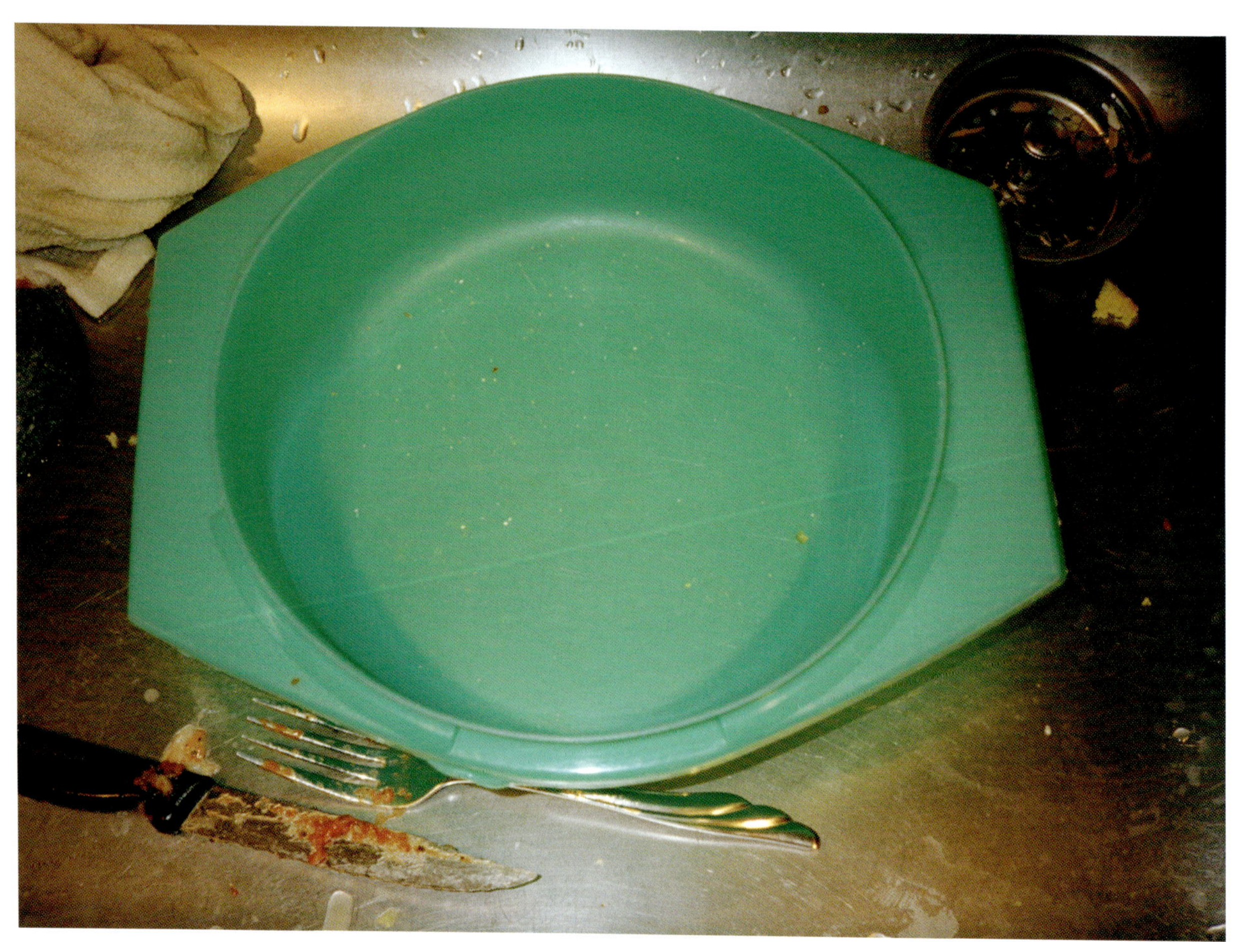

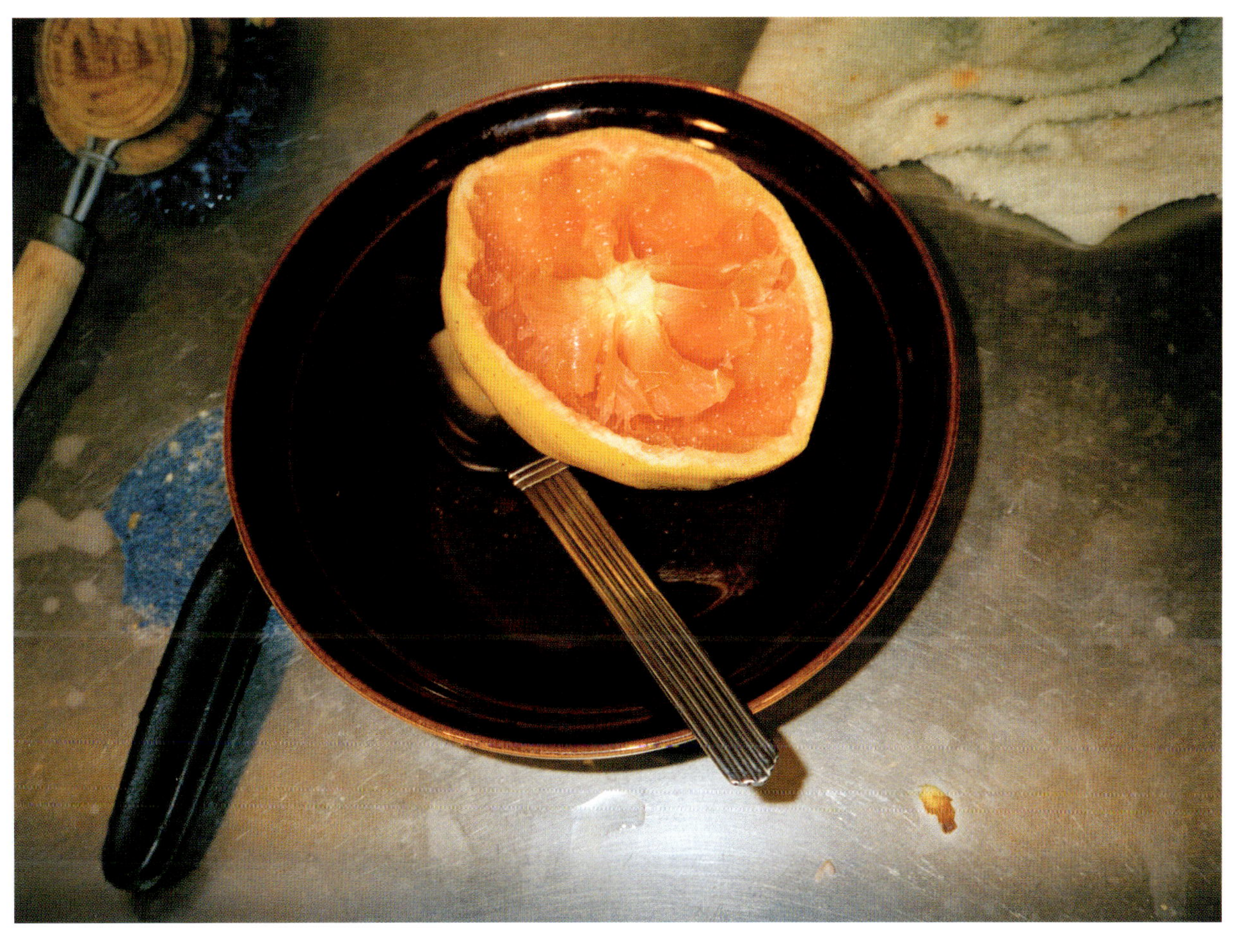

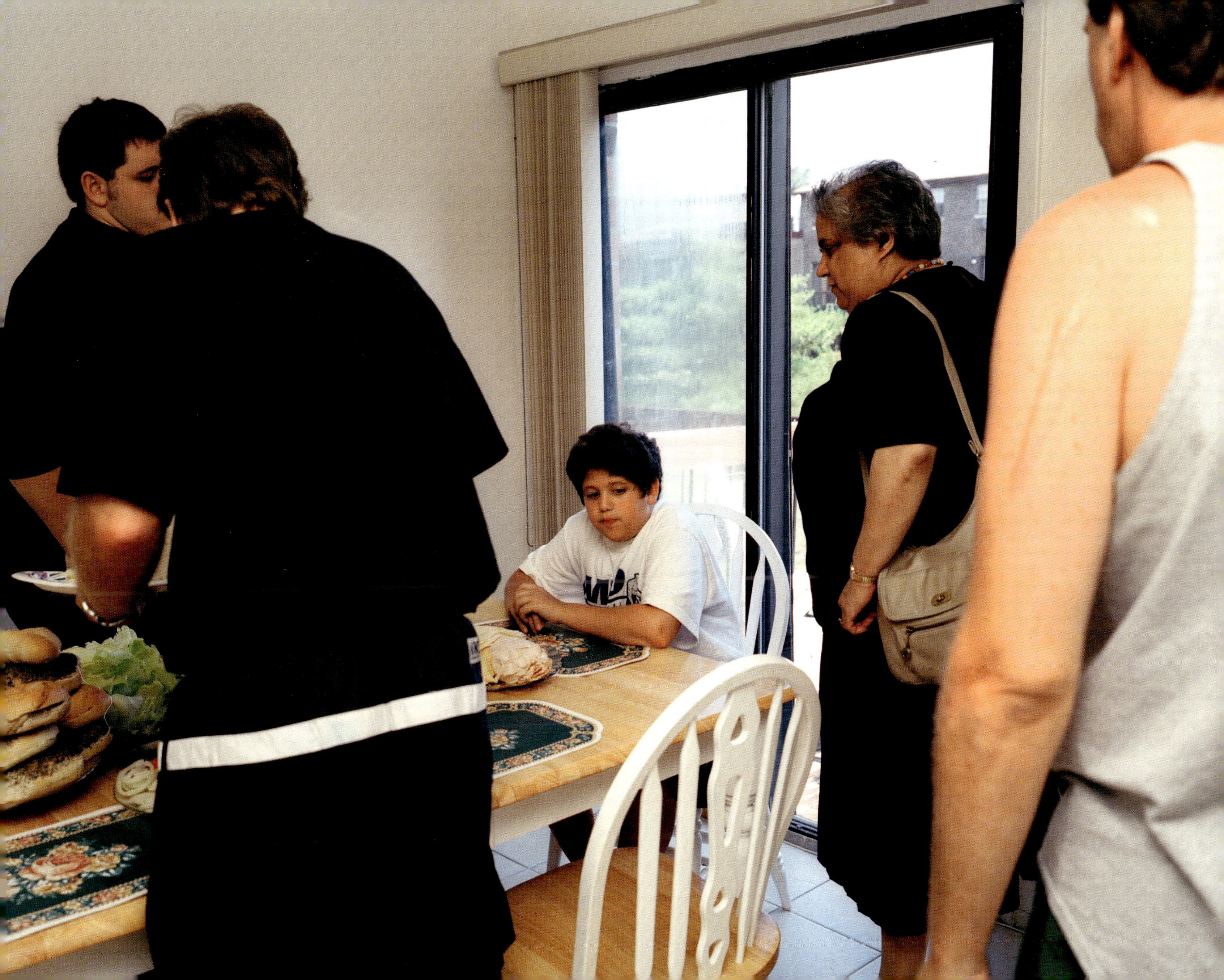

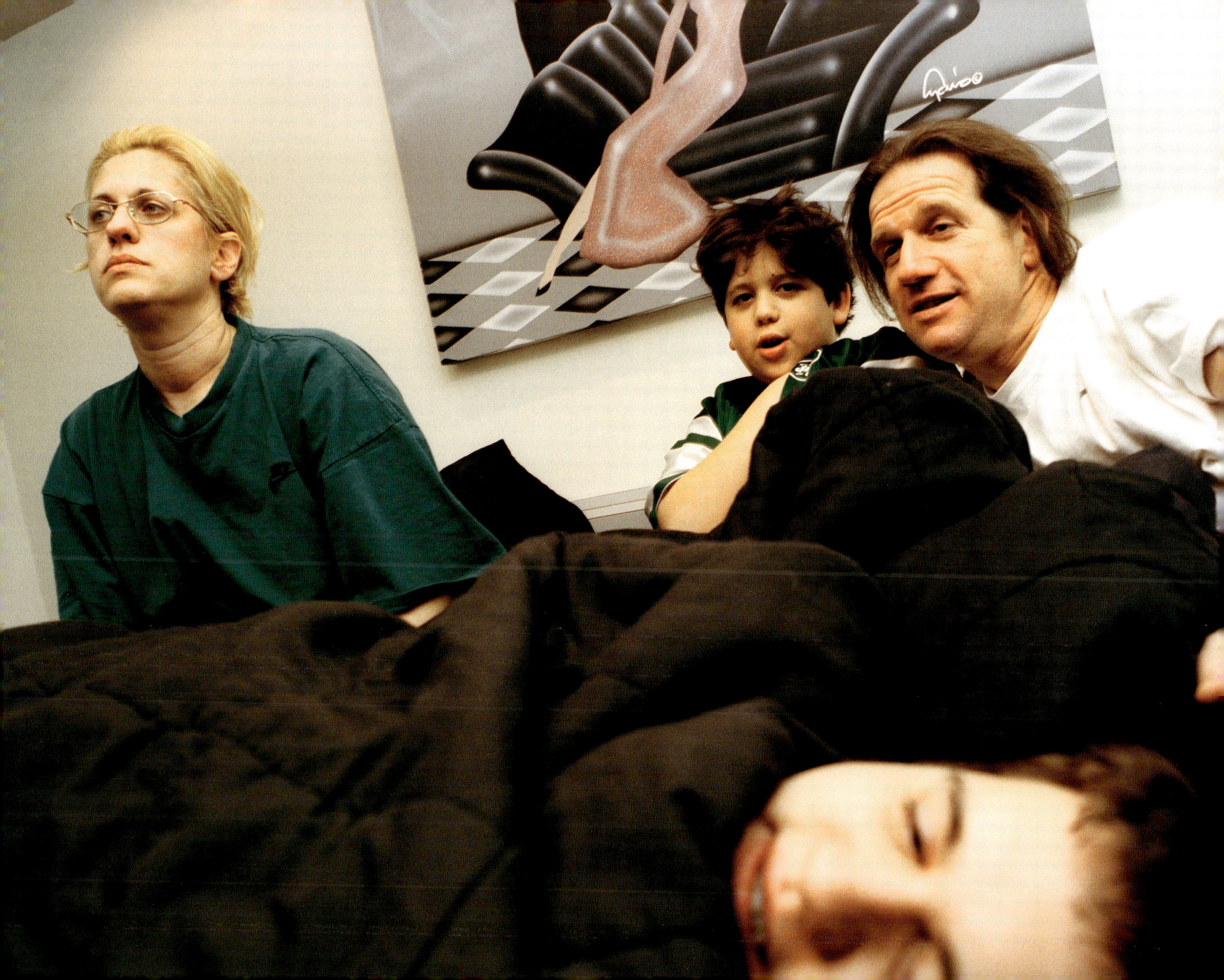

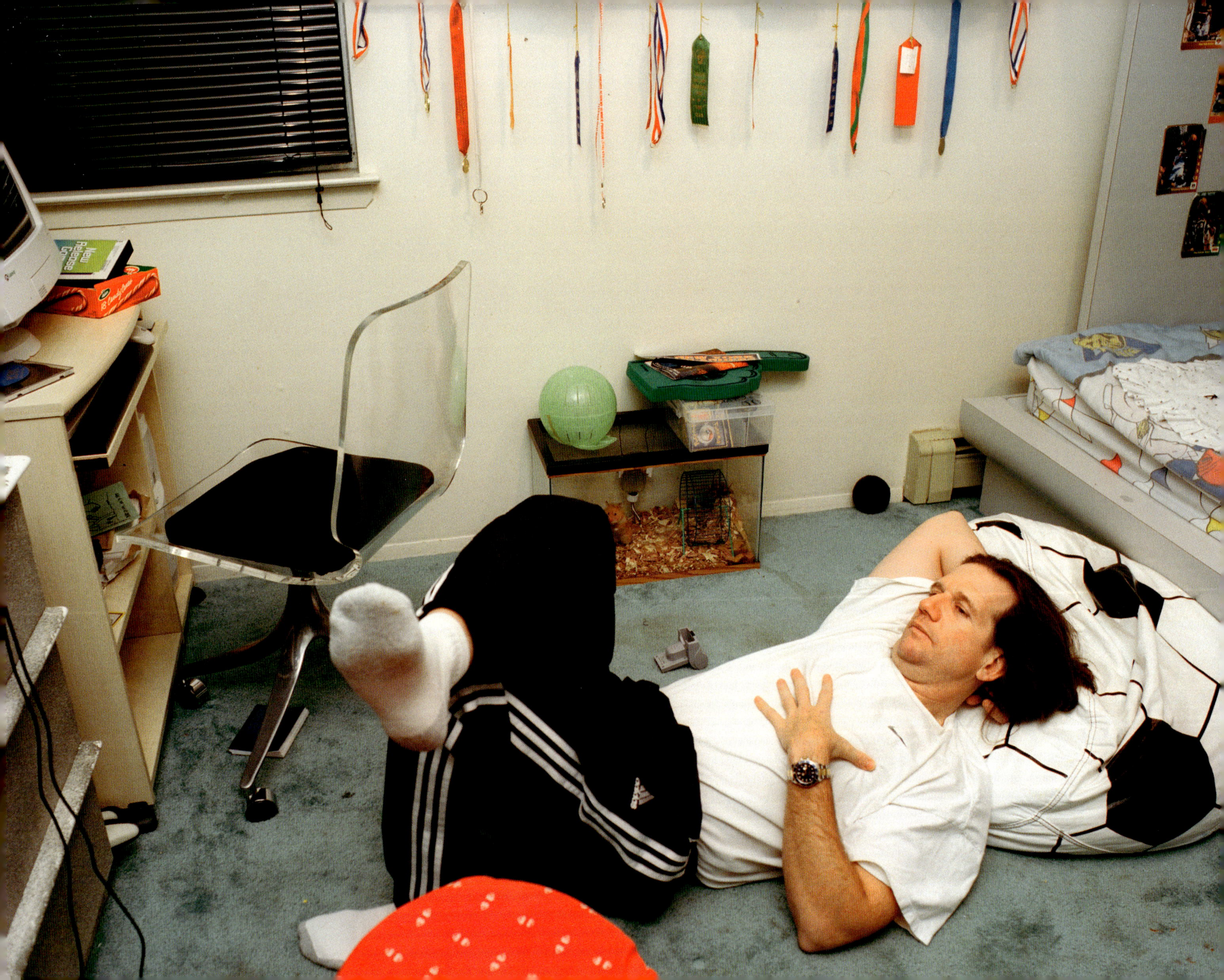

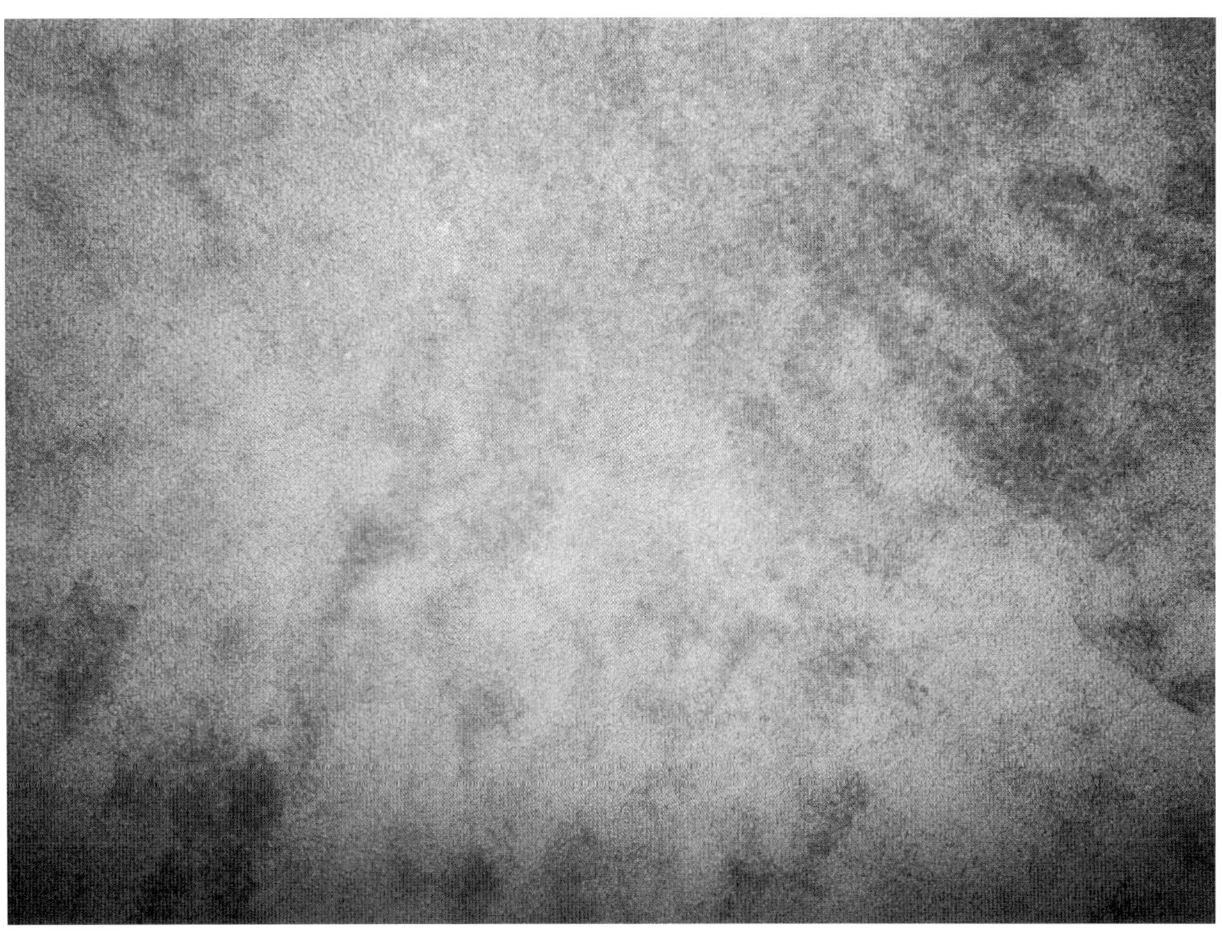

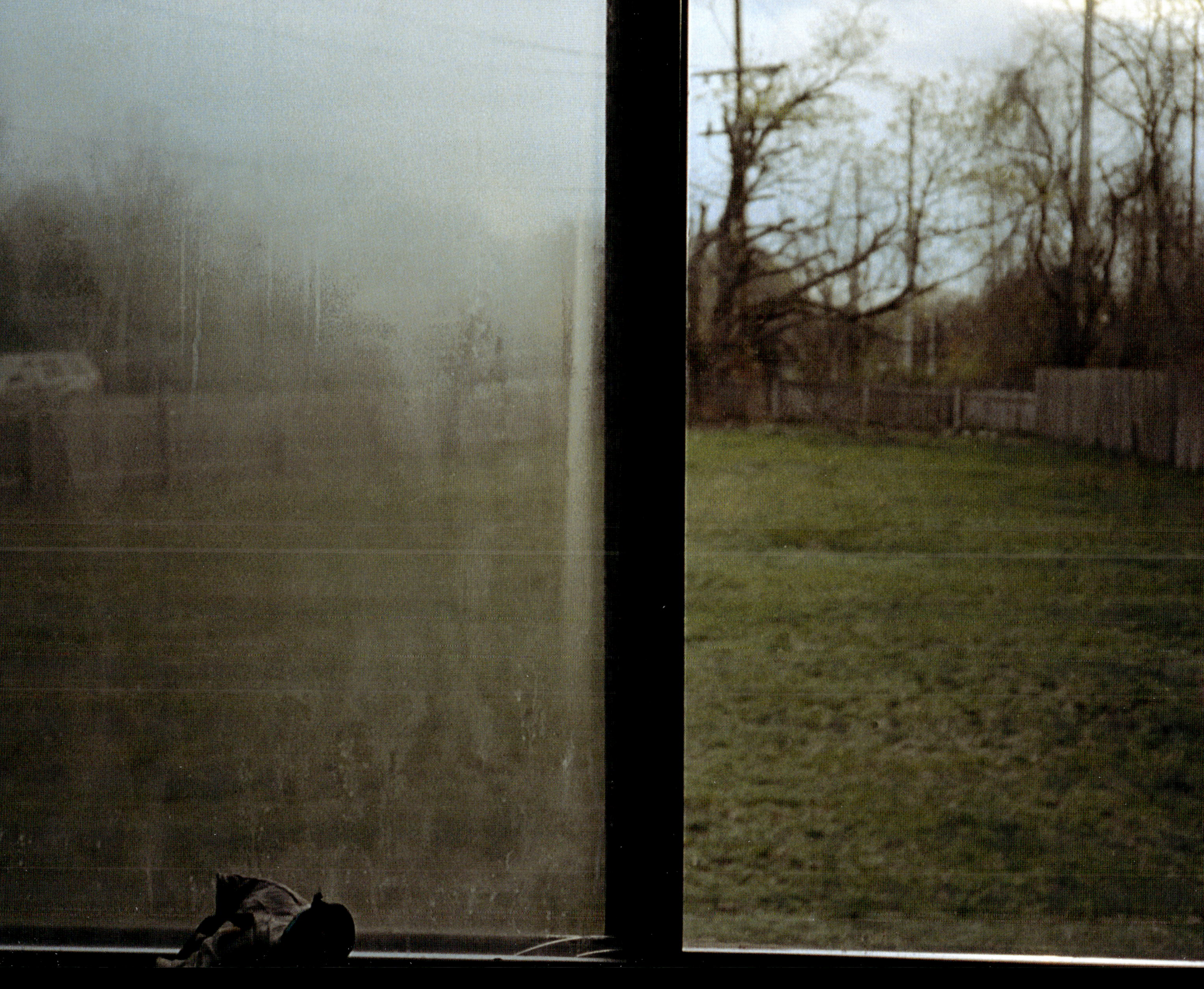

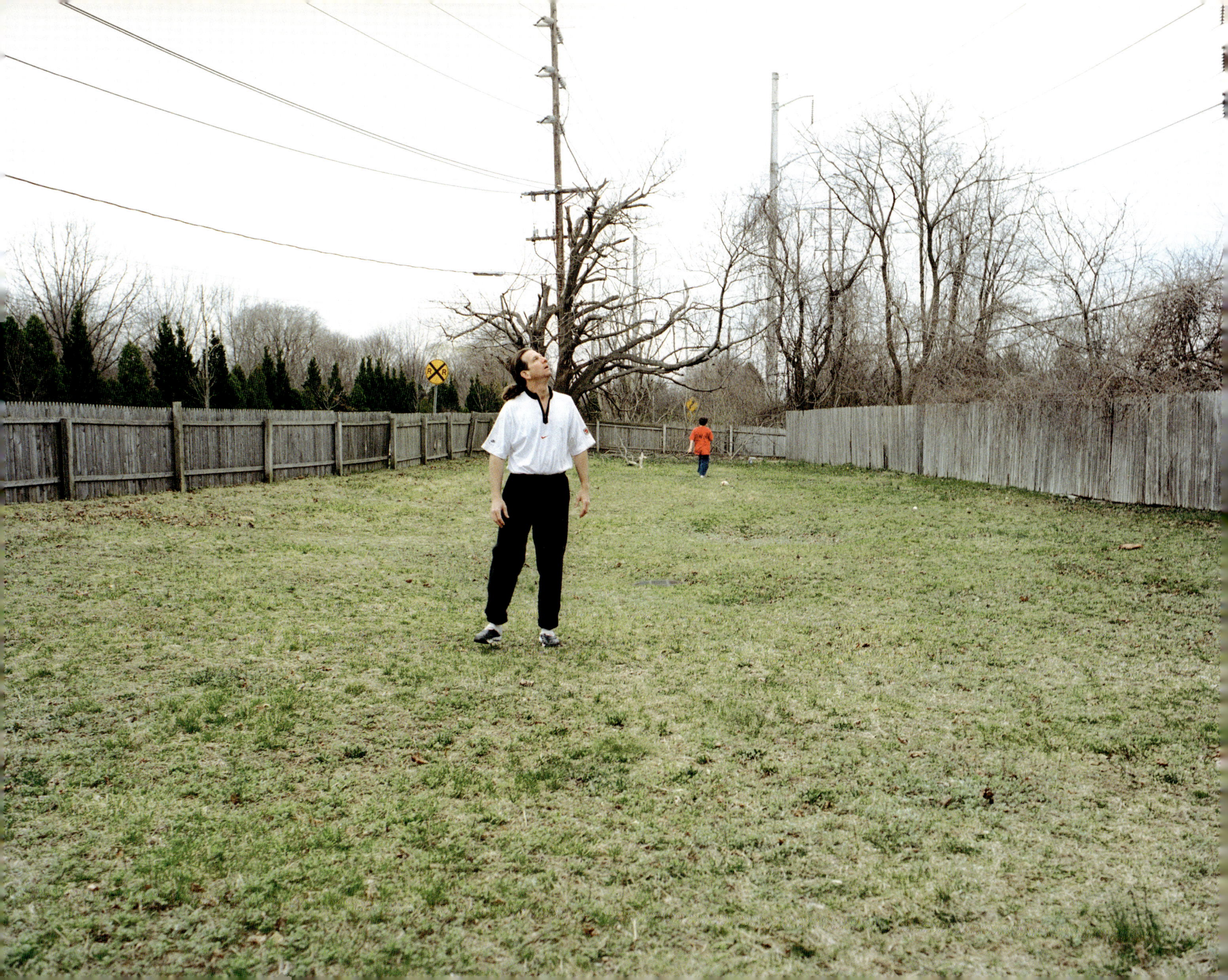

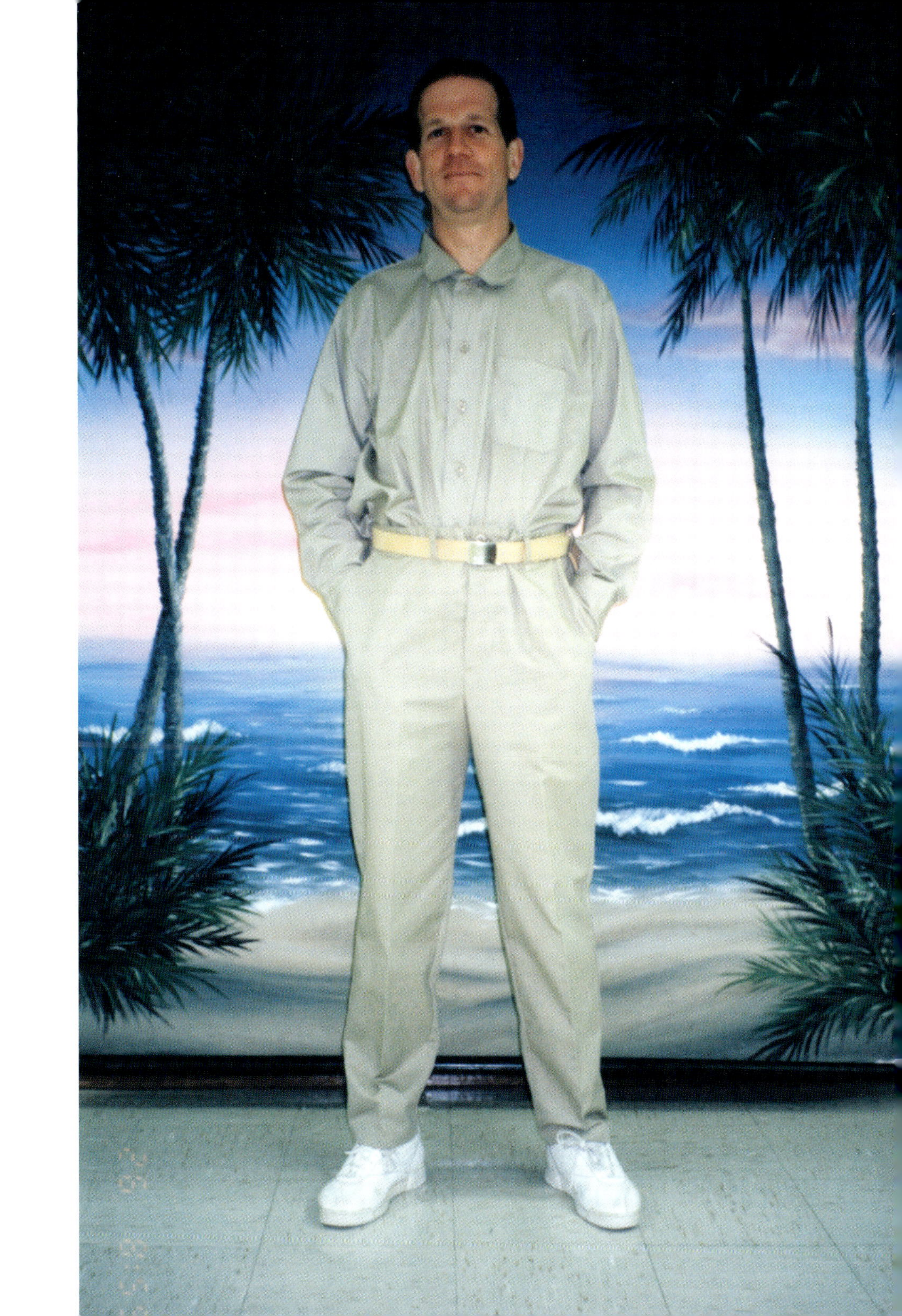

When I was found guilty of my crime I never could have realized where my life would go. It was like a bad dream, a black abyss. All of my life I worked hard to build a successful business. I loved my family and my work, but perhaps not in the right order. I was guilty of my actions, but I think the judge was harsh with his sentence. Instead of a possible twelve month sentence, I received five years. I was handcuffed and escorted out of the courtroom by an officer and it was at this moment I realized my life was no longer my own. The officer began the most inhumane search, as he inspected every part of my body. I was in shock. When they placed me into a holding cell I realized I was not going home. While waiting to be escorted from my cell to the bus outside, I recall pacing, allowing my feet to touch only the white tiles and never the black lines. I did this in the hospital awaiting the birth of both my sons.

I could not believe what I saw when the bus pulled up to the prison. The gun towers, razor wire fences, and the noises. Awful noises. The sound of the metal doors closing behind you, cutting you off from the rest of the world, this is the sound that I will never forget. At that moment, you must leave personal matters and your lifestyle behind you and readjust to prison. Up until this point of my life I was always in complete control, but once inside you must become a B.O.P. [Bureau of Prisons] robot. They tell you when to eat, when to sleep, and when you can move. You quickly learn that you must divorce yourself from the outside world and concentrate on surviving.

I will not talk about the events that I saw and encountered during my incarceration. Good people should not be exposed to the horrors of prison life. Yet, I will say that the emptiness can kill you if you let it. The first thing you learn in prison is to keep to yourself. I went four months without speaking to another inmate. I began talking to myself just to ease the pain and loneliness. I also began to count everything, years, days, hours, minutes, laps, and reps. I ran 10-20 miles every day. Rain, snow, and subzero weather, I ran and ran just to keep my head clear. You try to do the time and not let the time do you. You pray for your loved ones, but try not to think about them. That was the hardest thing to do. I felt absolutely helpless. I love my family and was paralyzed that I was unable to help them.

At the end of 51 months, my belongings fit in one average cardboard box. I returned to my family, but to a strange house. I had lost everything while incarcerated. We could no longer afford to live in the beautiful homes we once lived in together. I was skinny and weak, and hoped to regain the success I once enjoyed.

When I walked through the door, I remember the warmth I felt when my youngest son and I hugged. His acceptance was invigorating. Over the years I felt he missed and suffered the most. I could feel the distance between me and my oldest son and I hoped to regain his respect. Carrie was attached to her camera. I did not want her to take any pictures, but I didn't want to refuse her. These photographs are one half of my apology to my daughter.

Looking over these images, I recall how awkward it was to lie next to my wife and not worry about an insane inmate. The photos make me remember what it felt like to eat a meal in my own kitchen without prison rules and wear clothing that was my own. Most of all they remind me of how the freedom felt good.

Throughout these photographs I found it obvious that I wear my feelings on my face and that I felt enormous pain and disappointment. While away, I decided not to cut my hair to serve as a reminder of the mistakes I had made. To this day, I have not yet cut my hair. God only knows that I will never go back and that each day since I wish my family never had to experience my imprisonment.

Glenn Levy, 2005.

WITH THANKS TO:

My family.

Gigi Giannuzzi at Trolley for his support and courage, with Charlie Devereux, Kyna Gourly, Thomas Rees, Ruby Russell, Oliver Wood, Valentina Petrelli, and Anna Lopriore.

Sarah Harbutt.

Thank you to Newsweek, notably Simon Barnett, my boss, Lisa Miller, Nicki Gostin, Patty Alvarez, Jamie Wellford, Brona Hatchette, Paul Moakley, Bruce Jaffe, Myra Kreiman, Michelle Molloy, and Jeff Giles.

Jayne Costanzo, Jerry Vezzuso, Stephen Frailey.

Daniel Cooney, Mary Ellen Mark, Richard B. Woodward and Robert Dannin.

The Lerner family, Carrie, Faith, Les, Michelle, and Matthew, without whose generosity this book would not have been possible.

The Burrell Family, for giving me a home in England. Thank you all, Rebecca, Kevin, Jake, Joe, Alice, Orlando and Froggy.

Elsa.

My friends : Shira, Rena and Amy Diem, Alicia Ackerman, Monica Bradley, Ethan Hill, Christopher Perez, Larry Hess and Clare Ryan, Sarah Elkashef, Leah Seligman, Bernadette Purcell, Daniel Fodera, Amy Steiner, Eric Weeks, Mark Blum, Jill Diamond, Keith Ehrlich, Cameron Baity, Julien Jourdes, Joseph Sywenkyj, Katherine Kiviat, Dominik Rothbard, Jesse Sparhawk Eisenberg, Jay and Joanne Eisenberg, Mark Roussel, Sarah Pickering, Steffi Klenz, Jan Naraine, Paulina Egle Pukyte, Margarita Bofiliou, Greg Parmley, Toby Gorman, Gemma and James Caterer, Stuart Mogridge and Kerrie Lofthouse.

CREDITS

Published in Great Britain in 2005 by Trolley Ltd
www.trolleybooks.com

Photographs, texts © Carrie Levy, 2005
Design by M+W @ Fruitmachine

10 9 8 7 6 5 4 3 2 1

ISBN 1-904563-21-X

Printed in Italy by Soso Industrie Grafiche Spa